Parenting / Family Life

Nurturing Spirituality

Special Needs

M000315265

Theory, Research, and Practical Guidelines for Family Life Coaching

Kimberly Allen

Theory, Research, and Practical Guidelines for Family Life Coaching

 Springer

Kimberly Allen
North Carolina State University
Raleigh, NC, USA

ISBN 978-3-319-29329-5   ISBN 978-3-319-29331-8   (eBook)
DOI 10.1007/978-3-319-29331-8

Library of Congress Control Number: 2016937421

Printed on acid-free paper

This Springer imprint is published by Springer Nature
The registered company is Springer International Publishing AG Switzerland

This book is dedicated to my family. To my husband, Chris, for constantly suggesting I can do things I would otherwise never dream, let along attempt to do. To my beautiful children, Fiona and Sofia, who give me so much opportunity to practice what I teach. To my parents and my niece Catrina, for the support and love they give. And to my sister, whom I miss terribly. I love you all so much.

To my students, my colleagues, and the families I have served over the years-thank you. This journey is a result of all your generosity, kindness, and wisdom.

You are the ones that give me the passion and interest to learn more and share that information in an effort to improve the lives of all children and families.

Contents

Part I
Theoretical Underpinnings

Chapter 1
Introduction: Why a Book on Family Life Coaching?

You may wonder, why another book on coaching? While the field of coaching and science of coaching is growing (Grant, 2011), there is a gap of literature and books designed to educate life coaches dealing with families. This book, Coaching Families: Theory to Practice is a first of its kind, a specific how-to guide for family life coach training.

This book will provide an overview of the theory and practice of family life coaching, the process of helping clients sustain emotional or behavioral changes that help them reach their goals in the realm of family life. This is a new field in the literature on coaching, however the practice of coaching families is not brand new. In fact, family practitioners were writing about coaching well over a decade ago (Hanft, Rush, & Sheldon, 2004). There is a deficit of training materials for teaching coaching practices specifically on family life topics such as parenting, relationships, youth, families with special needs, and so many more. The time has come to offer a how-to guide for those wishing to become family life coaches.

This chapter includes the purpose, audience, organization of the book, chapter outlines, and an article delving into the frameworks of family life coaching. This chapter covers the origins of family life coaching, explains efforts made to promote the fields, and concludes with an original article, A Framework on Family Life Coaching.

Coaching, Where Are You?

If you have turned on the television lately, there is a chance you have seen life coaches featured as specials guest for segments of make-overs and fresh starts, how to make a better life, even on how to clean your home. There is also a growing number of television shows and movies that feature a life coach as the premise or a component of a show's main idea. This is especially seen in reality television shows, where life coaches often come to help ordinary people or celebrities reach

© Springer International Publishing Switzerland 2016
K. Allen, *Theory, Research, and Practical Guidelines for Family Life Coaching*,
DOI 10.1007/978-3-319-29331-8_1

their goals (see Starting Over, A Life Coach Less Ordinary, Home Rules, just to name a few). Pregnant women hire maternity coaches to help them prepare for the baby (Pregnant in Heels, Bravo TV).

It is not only on television. Coaching is now ubiquitous in our society. Students have success coaches help them in their schools, people with chronic diseases receive access to health coaches, and many health insurance companies now employ preventative health coaches. It seems as if everywhere we look, we see coaches helping with family life issues. The increased attention that has been placed on coaching is undeniable (Garman, Whiston, & Zlatoper, 2000).

Coaching has entered popular culture and is omnipresent. Coaching has been given the golden stamp of approval by the general public and is creeping into our vernacular and everyday experiences. Yet, there is a vast deficit of research, resources, training, or credentials regarding family life coaching.

This book bridges that gap by offering theoretical and practical insights to the field and practice of family life coaching. In addition, this book presents information to help prospective family coaches better understand what family coaching is, what it is not, and how it fits within the fields of family science and coaching psychology.

In my own circle of colleagues and acquaintances, coaching is being used to bring out one's potential. The leaders in my university talk of their coaching experiences as part of their leadership development. In the past year, I've had two leaders of my organization share their experiences of working with an executive coach to help them reach their full leadership potential. When asked, both said they were pleasantly surprised at how effective the coaching process has been for them. My immediate supervisor says, "Having a coach to help you process difficult decisions or organizational change is invaluable. They can help you best see situations from multiple angles and help you avoid blind spots. My experience is that a coach challenges you in a way that makes you a better leader" – Carolyn Dunn, Department Head, Youth, Family, and Community Sciences, NCSU.

Executive coaching has been the driver of the coaching industry movement. While coaching has been found in the psychological literature since the 1930s, its growth in popularity rose during the 1990s as part of the executive coaching movement. The top executive coaches are earning upwards of $3500 per hour for their executive coaching sessions (Coutu & Kauffman, 2009). However, before you get too excited about your high-paying prospects of coaching, I'd like to state for the record that the rate of pay for family life coaches is significantly lower. The average pay for family life coaching is closer to $100/hour (Allen & Baker, 2016). The good news is that families are interested in hiring coaches for family services, and they see it as an investment (Baker, Allen, & Huff, 2015). Many family science practitioners do not consider ourselves business people and most haven't had training in business practices. There is a need for a shift, and this is addressed in the final chapter of this book.

Life coaching is another area of the coaching field familiar to the general public. Life coaches work with individuals that have specific goals or ideas of how they want to improve their lives. Life coaches work with their clients to help them achieve goals that have been identified by the client. I once hired a life coach to focus on my goal of writing.

Before taking on the task of writing this book, I knew I was a writer. I have imaged myself as a writer since, well. . .always. I have fond childhood memories of setting under a big oak tree writing short stories in my journal. When I was a young adult studying to be a therapist, I took a course that taught visualization techniques. One technique was designed for us to find a place in our mind's eye where all is right with the world. The professor said that if we have this image in our mind, we can retreat there when things are emotionally turbulent in order to help us calm down and refocus. I found my peaceful place in my mind back in 1997 and I have found myself returning to that place when I need to refocus. What is this place in my mind? It is a one-room glass house writer's retreat nestled between a white sandy beach and beautiful field covered in wild flowers.

While I believe I am a writer, I was stuck in not writing anything but academic papers. I was not moving in the direction I wanted or needed. I knew it was time to write a book, so I hired a life coach. I worked with my life coach for about 3 months and during that time, we explored my lack of movement in creative writing, and she helped me envision what it would look like to be a writer. We looked at the anxiety I felt when I thought about writing a book, we planned and created action steps together, and although movement was not expeditious, I'm now writing a book. It is an academic book, but it is a book. And if you are reading this, it means actually I wrote it, partly thanks to my work with my coach.

When it came time to hiring a coach, credentials were important to me. I wanted a coach with a high education, a solid coaching credential, and experience. The coach I hired had a PhD in psychology, and had been a practicing as a health coach. She taught health coaching at Duke University and was a scholar and practitioner. She used a standard coaching process where I visualized where I wanted to be, identified action steps to get there, and she helped me with accountability and pointed me towards resources I needed to reach my goals. My hope is that this book, in a small way, will be a catalyst for change and resource for you, much like the coaching process was for me.

This book is designed as a step to help the profession of family life coaching move forward. Credentials, training, expertise, and experience are all important factors when finding a coach, and to date, there is not a systematic approach to family life coaching. This book highlights the movement thus far in the field of family life coaching, and identifies steps that need to be taken to grow this field. This book also offers a theoretical backbone and practical steps for individual's looking to become family life coaches.

The Title of Family Life Coaching: Deciding What to Call the Profession

The term *family life coach* is a new term to both the fields of family science and coaching psychology. The first mention of the term in the academic literature was in a paper I wrote called *A framework for Family Life Coaching* published in 2013 by

International Coaching Psychology Review. The article simply presented the idea of family life coaching as the merge of family life education and coaching psychology and can be read in its entirety at the conclusion of this chapter. There is a distinction between coaching psychology and family life coach. Coaching psychology is a discipline – a broader framework whereas family life coaching is an area within this discipline that also draws heavily from family science.

I came up with the concept and title of family life coaching somewhat by accident. When I first started in my role as Assistant Professor at North Carolina State University, I was tasked with creating a training program as part of our graduate degree that would train professional coaches to work with youth and families. While I came to the role with a strong background in marriage and family therapy and family life education, the concept of *Coaching* was somewhat new to me. I spent the first 3 years training to be a professional coach, and building our academic program. When I did my coach training, the majority of people in my class were master's level family practitioners, most of who were licensed therapists and worked with families or individuals on family life issues. There was a general consensus that coaching families was an up-and-coming approach, and the thrill was that coaching was strengths based and carried less stigma than therapy.

After my training, I continued with our program development, and due to the deficit of literature on coaching families also started researching family life coaches. As my teaching and research agenda's began to take direction, I found myself quite alone. I knew from my training there were other coaches working with families, but I never saw them in academia or among my professional associations of NCFR (National Council on Family Relations) NPEN (National Parenting Education Network), or NASAP (North American Society of Adlerian Psychology). I decided to reach out to those professional organizations, as well as marriage and family therapy (although I didn't get a response from them) and ask for an interest in collaboration to look at the future of family coaching.

To my great surprise, 47 people responded with an interest to be a part of a group to explore the future of family life coaching. We decided to meet monthly, with anywhere from 5 to 15 people joining the calls and the rest requesting email updates. We met monthly over most of 2014, with the end result a plan that identifies current patterns of family life coach training programs and future standards for family life coaches. As a result of those conversations, the Family Life Coaching Association was created.

While in our infancy, the Family Life Coaching Association (FLCA) has a mission to create research-based, globally recognized credentials, training standards, and networking opportunities for family life coaches through five immediate goals.

1. Clearly define family life coaching.
2. Create global FLC standards.
3. Create a nationally recognized FLC credential.
4. Create networking opportunities for FLCA members.
5. Organize the association for structure and sustainability.

Our vision is to elevate and lend credibility to the practice of family life coaching by serving as the collaborative center for the field.

Why do we call ourselves family life coaches? One thing that was apparent from the first meeting and in every correspondence and data collection point since was an issue with what to call ourselves. Some members of the group consider themselves family coaches or family life coaches while others consider themselves parent coaches, relationship coaches, or life coaches. Some members did coaching, but did not even call themselves a coach. The distinction is significant to the group of practitioners engaged in the conversations. The major contention appears to be around the issue of serving individuals vs. families, and serving adults vs serving youth. Parent coaches are clear that they only coach adults, and they do not coach the whole family system. Youth coaches might coach the youth in a school setting, but do not necessarily work with the whole family. There are a wide variety of audiences and topics covered under the umbrella of family life coaching.

The fields of marriage and family therapy and family systems both focus on helping the full family system (Nichols & Schwartz, 1998). To many, the term "family coach" connotes congruence with the term "family therapist". Family therapists often serve a whole family and even when they serve one member of a family, they do so with a family systems perspective. They think about how the work they do with an individual impacts all members of the family system.

The field of family life education focuses primarily on serving adults, although youth programs are considered a part of family life education (Duncan & Goddard, 2011). Unlike therapy, which typically happens with an individual or family system, family life education if often associated with groups (Powell & Cassidy, 2007). Family coaching might include similar content, but the family life education connotes congruence with group work.

McGoldrick and Carter (2001) were among the first researchers to address the process of coaching in the family science literature. In their article, *Advances in Coaching: Family Therapy With One Person*, the authors describe a process much like what is shared throughout this book. Coaching is a way of addressing individual or familial behaviors in the context of the family system. To me, that is the identity of **family life coaching–working with an individual, couple, parents, youth, or a family to address family-life issues through the coaching process.** By this identity, a parent coach would be a family life coach, even if they only serve parents. A relationship coach would also be a family life coach; an ADHD coach that serves youth would be a family life coach. Family life coach is an umbrella term that identifies professionals that serve clients in family related issues through the coaching process. The identity of family life coaching is in working with a familial entity (individual, couple, or family) on a family life related issue. This is not unique to family life coaching; one of the theoretical underpinnings of coaching psychology and the coaching industry is systems theory (McLean, 2012). Coaches understand that by changing one part of the system, the entire system is impacted.

Family coaching includes working with an individual, couple, or family to address family-life issues through the coaching process.

The strength of this identity is that together, we can begin to form and professionalize the field of family life coaching. If we want to look for a model in multidisciplinary approaches to professionalism, we can look at both the family life education (FLE) model and the coaching psychology (CP) model. Both groups have multi-disciplinary approaches to what they do. FLE professionals have 10 content areas (NCFR, ND) and Coaching Psychology is for professionals that coach in the business or personal realms (Stober & Grant, 2006).

Still, many ask, what does coaching look like? Members of FLCA have taken the work of Dr. Sara Meghan Walter (2015) to put together a graphic model of family life coaching. Dr. Walter's model began with three core areas: consulting, education, and counseling. The model shows a continuum where coaching practices are represented on one side and the continuum moves away from coaching towards a more didactic and prescribed process of helping families.

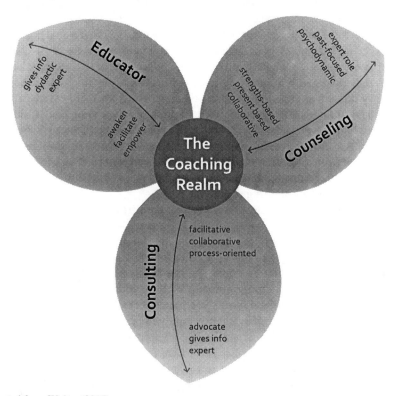

Adapted from Walter (2015)

This model helps to visually explain how family life coaching works, but still leaves questions about the coaching process. So when deciding what to call this book, I went back and forth between family coach, parent coach, and family life coach. While the field is still working to have an identity for coaches that serve youth and families, I believe the term family life coach is most inclusive and accurate to the work we do. I want this book to be inclusive of all the coaches that work with families on family life issues, including parent coaches. Of course the ultimate decision will be determined as the field progresses and professional affiliations grapple with terminology and inclusion.

"With coaching, families are transformed. It is amazing. I want every parent to have access to this." **Sheryl Stoller, Parent Coach**

Outline of Chapters

This book is presented in three sections: Background and Theoretical Overview (Chaps. 2, 3, and 4); Application and Skill Development (Chaps. 5, 6, 7, and 8); and Types of Family Life Coaching (Chaps 9, 10, 11, 12, and 13).

Part I includes chapters on the background research and theoretical overviews of coaching psychology, family science, and family life coaching.

- Chapter 2 focuses on coaching psychology and provides a historical background of the field of coaching, identifies theoretical underpinnings of coaching psychology with emphasis on the theories most related to FLC as well as current evidence-based practices of coaching psychology.
- Chapter 3 focuses on the field of family science, specifically the field of family life education (FLE). The chapter begins with a historical overview of FLE, its relevance to family science, and a theoretical overview again focusing on theories most relevant to FLC.
- Chapter 4 is the essence of family life coaching theory. This chapter provides the theoretical underpinnings of family life coaching, with suggested evidence-based family life coaching practices. Chapter 4 also provides an overview of the first grounded theory study on the practice of family life coaching (Allen & Baker, 2016) as well as other research helping to form a theoretical foundation for family life coaching.

The focus of Part II moves away from theory and towards the how-to of family life coaching.

- Chapter 5 begins with a clear description and definition of family life coaching and then describes the how-to of coaching families based on the current research of evidence-based coaching psychology and family life coaching. This chapter offers a clear description of the process of coaching families and presents a full transcript of a family life coaching session.
- Chapter 6 focuses specifically on the process leading up to a coaching session, including the paperwork for intakes, and the process of the first meeting. This chapter covers the ethics involved with coaching and provides a case study of the first session.

- Chapter 7 looks at specific coaching models and assessments for use in the coaching process including a case study on the use of assessments.
- Chapter 8 focuses on communication theory and the process of using powerful questions when working with families.

Part III focus on the specific subfields of family coaching, with chapters 9, 10, and 11 focusing on relationship, parenting, and special needs families, respectively. These three populations are the fastest growing fields of family life coaching and each of these chapters includes a case study.

- Chapter 9 covers relationship theory and provides tips on how to apply theory in the work of relationship coaching.
- Chapter 10 covers parent education and parenting theory and provides tips on using evidence-based parent education practices with parent coaching.
- Chapter 11 provides an overview of the literature on working with families that have children that have special needs. The focus of the chapter is on children with ADHD, but covers general approaches to serving families.
- Chapter 12 covers a variety of other fields of coaching, including health, maternity, youth, and life coaching. While those in the field of family science might already be familiar with these concepts, I attempt to connect the information as it pertains to coaching.
- Chapter 13 focuses on the professionalism of the field of coaching, what steps family life coaches need to take to establish credentials and training, and the mechanics and processes of building a coaching business. Trends, including education, training, and credentialing of family life coaches is covered first, followed by the how-to of building a coaching business.

Family Life Coaching Framework

In 2013, I submitted a framework to describe what I considered to be a foundation for family life coaching. This article was meant to be a discussion starter, and boy has it been! I have enjoyed correspondences with so many coaches serving parents and families. Thanks to the generosity of the editors of the International Coaching Psychology Review, I am happy to reprint the article below.

The following article is reprinted with permission from the International Coaching Psychology Review. It first appeared in the March edition of the journal. Allen (2013)

A Framework for Family Life Coaching

Kimberly I. Allen, Ph.D., BCC

The fields of Family Life Education (FLE) and Coaching Psychology (CP) are destined to unite. Historically, the field of family life education has been the primary mode for educating families. Ironically families were never a big part of the conversation in the field of coaching psychology. The field, however, is changing and family practitioners are utilizing the technique of coaching in their work with families. Likewise, the field of coaching psychology has historically catered to individuals, but there is a growing need for coaches to help families. Relationship coaching, youth coaching, and couples coaching are all growing areas of coaching psychology. Although work is happening in the area of family life coaching, there is a vast deficit of information for family practitioners about the practice of and theory of coaching families.

In order to establish a theoretical foundation and evidence-based approach to coaching families, there must first be a conceptualization and discussion of family life coaching. Coaching families has long been an informal methodology used in family practice, illustrating the need for family life coaching to be a part of the national conversation of family life and coaching psychology. This paper aims to present a framework to begin the conceptualization of family life coaching and to generate interests and debate on the role of family life coaching in the arenas of family life and coaching psychology.

Family Life Education

Family life education (FLE) is a field of study and application that involves qualified educators delivering family science principles designed to strengthen familial relationships and foster positive development of individual, couple, and family development (Duncan & Goddard, 2011). In its broadest definition, Family Life Education is a process where a professional provides skills and knowledge that helps families' function at their optimal level (National Council on National Council on Family Relations, 2009). The educational delivery may happen in a variety of settings, but typically occurs in settings outside of the formal education system. Information is delivered to individuals, couples, parents, and on occasion, to whole families. The theoretical foundation of FLE is diverse, having drawn from home economics, social work, family sociology, marriage and family therapy, education, and developmental psychology (Lewis_Rowley, Brasher, Moss, Duncan, & Stiles, 1993).

Although the scholarship of family life education is relatively new, application of family life education by professionals dates back over a century. The turn of the Twentieth century brought a great many changes to families, therefore creating a need for education for women and children (Allen, Dunn, & Zaslow, 2011). Family life education was formed as a response to those changes with the goal of helping families improve their wellbeing (Arcus, 1995) and continues to provide family science scholarship in applied settings.

Most often, family life educators aim to help parents and couples improve their relationships and gain skills to make their family life successful. Duncan and Goddard (2011) highlight seven principles of FLE: relevancy across the lifespan, based on needs of clients served, multi-disciplinary, varied content delivery platforms, focuses on education, honors diversity, and requires educated professionals to deliver education. In fact, to receive the credential of certified family life educator (CFLE), professionals must show competence in 10 content areas specific to family life (NCFR, 2009) (Table1.1).

Most often, family life education is considered to be a top-down process where a credentialed educator shares information with participants (Doherty, 2000). FLE does acknowledge that the family brings wisdom and experiences to the table, but the emphasis is generally on the expert sharing knowledge with participants, and participants using that knowledge for positive change. This approach has its strengths and weakness. Having an expert that can clearly articulate the evidence-based approaches can provide families with much needed credible information. On the flip side, however, families have little ownership in the process of change. There are varied approaches to family life education, some of which put less emphasis on the expert-model. For example, Duncan and Goddard (2011), identify six approaches to FLE, including the "critical inquirer approach" (p. 17) which bears resemblance to coaching. In this approach, educators utilize questions to help participants move forward and the approach acknowledges that participants have responsibility in their own life (Czaplewski & Jorgensen, 1993).

Although very little is written on using a coach approach to serving families in the family life education literature base, there is some information about the varying domains of practice. Doherty (1995) proposes that there are five levels of family involvement ranging from simple FLE lessons to full on family therapy. He identified differences between FLE and a licensed therapist working with families, and stated that FLE should contain components of imparting knowledge and skills while keeping a focus on the feelings, attitudes, and goals of the families served. Myers-Walls, Ballard, Darling, & Myers-Bowman, (2011) expanded Doherty's conceptualization of family life education by suggesting family case management as a third professional role in family life work. Because of the personal and emotional focus in working with families, family life education involves a relationship, making it unique and separate from other academic subjects or courses

Table 1.1 Family life education content expertise areas

Families and individuals in social contexts	Internal dynamics of families
Human growth and development across the life span	Human sexuality
Interpersonal relationships	Family resource management
Parenting education and guidance	Family law and public policy
Professional ethics and practice	Family life education methodology

one might study. While these one-on-one and group interactions may appear to resemble therapy and often contain elements of relational theory, Doherty stresses the importance of family educators to remain objective and refer the family, when necessary, for additional counseling and therapy (1995).

Though there are variations among service offerings and styles of services in FLE, the primary foci is on factors such as improving the relationship between parent and child in the specific context of the family, reduction in externalized child behaviors, and increasing the family's skills and resources (Gockel, Russel, & Harris, 2008). Family life education can take place across levels of intensity and settings, from basic workshops to more intensive interactions involving in-home services and coaching. Some might even argue that coaching is a natural fit with family life education. Very little, however, is written about the use of coaching with families.

Coaching Psychology

Like Family Life Education, the literature field of Coaching Psychology, or coaching, has experienced rapid growth over the past few decades (Grant, 2011). The roots of coaching psychology come from humanistic psychology (Grant, 2011). As the field grew, so did the theoretical framework of practicing coaching psychologists. Coaching frameworks now include Cognitive/Behavioral, Solution Focused, Psychodynamic, Rational Emotive, and Transactional among others (Whybrow & Palmer, 2006). The field of coaching is grounded in psychological theory, but consists of a variety sub categories. The focus of coaching practices includes executive, personal life, business, performance, leadership, career, team, mentoring, health, and sports. All coaches are not psychologists; in fact, 95 % of coaches are non-psychologists (Grant & Zackon, 2004).

The field of coaching psychology is young, although the practice of using coaching in work with individuals and groups is not new (Grant, 2011). The technique of coaching in psychological practice was written decades ago (see Filippi, 1968), but until recently, there was scarcely any literature about the filed of coaching psychology (Grant, 2003). There is now a theoretical foundation and major serge in research that is truly shaping the filed into a science-based approach to helping others.

The definition of coaching psychology is to enhance the "well-being and performance in personal life and work domains underpinned by models of coaching grounded in established adult learning or psychological approaches" (adapted from Grant & Palmer, 2002). This is done through a partnership with the client. Unlike FLE, coaching psychology leads with the premise that the client is an equal partner in the process and comes to the table with expertise, knowledge, and abilities to create the change they seek. Coaches work with their clients to create change; there is no hierarchy.

Some view coaching as similar or the same as therapy. Although there are similarities, there are also distinct differences (Hart, Blattner, & Leipsic, 2001).

Therapy or counseling is often used with clients that have significant mental issues while coaching clients tend to be more goal directed and mentally healthy (Hart et al., 2001). Coaching works to "enhance the life experience, work performance and well-being for individuals, groups and organizations who do not have clinically significant mental health issues" (Grant, 2006, p. 16). This approach tends to be for people that are the doing well, and express a desire to do even better. Over the past decade, the field of coaching has shifted somewhat to become more than problem solving or remediation; it now has a focus of preparing people and organizations to deal with emerging needs.

Although coaching practices have long been used in therapeutic settings (McGoldrick & Carter, 2001), coaching is, in many instances, a separate profession that utilizes different techniques than therapy. Unlike therapy, coaching deals with the present and future, and views emotions a natural (Williams & Menendez, 2007). Although some professional coaches do utilize a variety of techniques such as mentoring and consulting simultaneously, many consider coaching is separate from consulting and mentoring. Like therapy, both mentoring and consulting identifies an expert model whereas coaching is co-creative and both members form a part-nership. Williams and Menendez created a matrix that highlights the differences between therapy, mentoring, consulting, and coaching (see Table 1.2). These differences demonstrate the uniqueness of coaching in relationship to other helping professions.

One major disadvantage of the coaching profession is the lack of unified quality credentialing. Although there are some efforts underway to form a unified accred-itation or qualification process such as those with the International Coaching Federation, a rigorous, standard accreditation does not currently exist (Grant, 2006). As such, anyone can call themselves a coach, regardless of qualifications. Of the training programs that do exist, many are "credentialing mills"; that offer a short, expensive training that scarcely provides needed information and skills practice to be a professional coach (Grant, 2006, p. 14). Furthermore, there is a deficit of literature specifically regarding content necessary for quality education in professional coaching (Grant, 2011), as well as a deficit in integrating evidence-based coaching techniques (Moore & Highstein, 2004a, 2004b).

The good news is the literature of coaching psychology is growing, and there is an openness to new ideas, frameworks, and techniques to move the field forward. The world is getting more complex, and models of professional practice are emerging to help people positively respond to change (Cavanagh & Lane, 2012). Coaching psychology is a prime example of a professional rising to meet a unique need. Slowly and methodically, the bar is being raised for professional standards, the literature base is growing, and evidence-based techniques of coaching psychol-ogy are being documented. People like coaching and they want to be coached. In fact, the majority of individuals that have been coached say it positively impacts their lives (Fillery-Travis & Lane, 2006).

Table 1.2 Professional distinctions of coaching and other fields

Therapy	Mentoring	Consulting	Coaching
Deals mostly with a person's past and trauma, and seeks healing	Deals mostly with succession training and seeks to help someone do what you do	Deals mostly with problems and seeks to provide information (expertise, strategy, structures, methodologies) to solve them	Deals mostly with a person's present and seeks to guide them into a more desirable future
Doctor-patient relationship (therapist has the answers)	Older/wise-younger/less-experienced relationship (mentor has the answers)	Expert-person with problem relationship (consultant has the answers)	Co-creative, equal partnership (coach helps clients discover their own answers)
Assumes many emotions are a symptom of something wrong	Limited to emotional response of the mentoring parameters (succession, etc.)	Does not normally address or deal with emotions (informational only)	Assumes emotions are natural and normalizes them
The therapist diagnoses, then provides professional expertise and guidelines to give clients a path to healing	The mentor allows you to observe his/her behavior and expertise, will answer questions, and provide guidance and wisdom for the stated purpose of the mentoring	The consultant stands back, evaluates a situation, then tells you the problem and how to fix it	The coach stands with you, and helps you identify the challenges, then works with you to turn challenges into victories and holds you accountable to reach your desired goals

Williams and Menendez (2007)

Family Life Coaching Model

Clearly, family life education and coaching psychology are two strong fields of study that have much in common. The gap, however, is the use of coaching with families as a field of study. The time is right to introduce a theory of family life coaching. Family life education and coaching psychology both have unique qualities and offer a profound impact on the practice of serving families, yet little to no discussion and research has been conducted on the field of using coaching in family life. In a search for the words "Family Life Coaching" conducted by the author of this manuscript on Summon database in May, 2012 only 3 results were found. A similar search of "Family Coaching" yielded only 44 journal articles and of those, none addressed the field of coaching families from a theoretical or applied point of view.

The literature field is bare, yet the work is being done. Although it has never been labeled "family life coaching", there is evidence that family life educators have been using coaching techniques as an approach to helping families for many years, primarily in the field of social work and home-visitation programs. In the past 10 years, coaching has become an integral part of family interventions ranging from health and family education to professional and managerial work (Heimendinger et al., 2007). Often used as a parent education intervention, coaching is a process-driven relationship between a learner and a coach designed to foster achievement of agreed-upon goals to include growth, change, and fulfillment in life or work (Heimendinger et al., 2007). Specific to families, coaching provides a structured means by which knowledge can be imparted, skills can be shared in a reciprocal process and further honed, and nurturing feedback can be given to family members (Rush, Shelden, & Hanft, 2003).

It is time to consider family life coaching as a unique field of study and practice that is influenced by the theoretical foundations of coaching psychology and family life education. Combining tenants from both family life education and coaching psychology should be the first step towards identifying a new theory of practice. The theoretical foundation of family life coaching must come from the roots of coaching psychology and family practice. Based on humanistic psychology, FLC should be strengths based and optimistic, with the focus on a family's potential. FLC must also approach the family from a systems perspective, both the ecological system and the family systems theories, as no family moves through life in a vacuum.

The purpose of family life coaching will combine components of FLE and CP to help families reach their goals and achieve wellbeing. In order for families to achieve success, they will engage in a process with a certified family life coach that will partner with them to gain insight, acquire knowledge and skills, and build strengths–personally and as a family unit. Family life coaches will work with a family when the family seeks them out or shows an interest in the coaching process; the family or individual member of a family will guide the process based on their goals for change while the coach serves as a partner and appreciative inquirer. Once the family identifies the goal or issue to be explored, the family life coach will utilize a series of powerful questions to guide the process, and will offer educational nuggets as agreed upon by the family. Family Life Coaching is about creating positive change, enhancing familial well-being and fostering development of family life through models of coaching and family life education. The similarities and differences of FLC, FLE and CP are proposed in Table 1.3. This is presented as a first attempt to generate a global conversation on the field of coaching families, and is in no way conclusive or set in stone.

Limitations of FLC Model

Anytime there is a new concept introduced, there are possible limitations and this article is no exception. Although there is some evidence that family life educators are implementing coaching strategies with the families they serve (Heimendinger et al., 2007), the movement toward a collaboration of FLE and CP may not easily achieved. As mentioned earlier, FLE has a primary focus of teaching family relations content to families via an expert/recipient model. Family Life Educators would have to sustain a major shift to incorporate FLC model. Most dramatically, the focus would move away from the expert/recipient model towards a co-expert model; it is right to question whether this is a direction the field of FLE would consider.

Table 1.3 Comparison of FLE, CP and FLC

Family Life Education	Coaching Psychology	Family Life Coaching (Proposed)
Education focused; educator as expert	Collaborative partnership; client as expert; partnership with two equals representatives	Collaborative partnership with education as secondary approach; partnership with two equal representatives. Coach has expert credentials and shares family process information
Focus on family dynamics and relationships	Focus on individual, group or organizational relationships	Focus on family relationships, personal and familial well-being and goal setting
Primarily adult focus	Primarily adult focus	One-to-one, couple or full family support with focus on one or all members of the family unit
Foundational knowledge in family studies and lifespan development; pedagogical or anagogical	Foundational knowledge in psychology, strengths based methodology	Foundational knowledge in family studies and psychology, strengths based with emphasis on family studies and lifespan development
Unified credentialing process and standardized accredited education programs to prepare practitioners	Unstructured credentialing process and gap in quality accredited educational programs to prepare practitioners	No current: unified credentialing process and standardized accredited education programs to prepare practitioners expected
Non-formal public education (face-to-face trainings, publications, media)	Individual or family focused sessions or small group interactions often through distance technology	Individual or family focused sessions or small group interactions in face-to-face and/or distance technology

Furthermore, although family life education is somewhat broad in the scope of work done with families, there are additional family-related fields that merit consideration in a model of coaching families. Fields such as special education, occupational therapy, public and community education, sports, family resource management, K-12 education, health education all merit inclusion in a discussion on coaching families. There is room for collaboration in any field that serves families in such a way that a coaching approach could be implemented to help with familial growth. Although this article focuses on FLE, it is important to keep the conversation open to all family related fields.

Conclusion

Given what is known about the amount of work occurring in family life coaching and the promising results from coaching work with caregivers and their families, it is clear that the time is right to introduce a theory of family life coaching that will lead to evidence-based practice. It is time to expand the work of family life educators and connect the work of coaching psychology to build a model of family life coaching. This does not come lightly; there is a need for further discussion on what the theory should entail and further research is needed on the topic of coaching in family life. In fact, so little is written on this topic that first steps must include identifying theoretical foundations, understanding current practices, and creating a national dialogue to create this field of study.

Coaching is a practice being utilized in work with families. Those practitioners need a theoretical foundation and education to guide their work. Because there is currently no governing body determining who can serve as a coach, the idea that coaching is being offered for issues that typically fall under the jurisdiction of mental health practitioners is of concern (Capsi, 2005). The field of family life coaching needs to have a more defined role with family life practitioners and there needs to be an approach to make sure that the individuals involved with coaching families are the ones that are most prepared to take on the profession.

Chapter Summary

Family life coaching is a growing field that needs to be further developed in the realms of research, training, and practice. The goal of this book is to help bridge the gap between what is known and what needs to be known to create a viable field for supporting families through coaching. Throughout the remaining chapters of the book, current practitioners or budding family life coaches will find information on the background and theoretical foundations of coaching families, the how-to of family life coaching, and specific information about the most common subfields of family life coaching including relationship coaching, parent coaching, and working with families that have special needs children.

References

Allen, K. (2013). A framework for family life coaching. *International Coaching Psychology Review, 8*(1), 72–79.

Allen, K., & Baker, T. (2016). *Family life coaching: A grounded theory*. Manuscript in preparation.

Allen, K. I., Dunn, C., & Zaslow, S. (2011). Ozzie and Harriet never were: A century review of family and consumer sciences and the changing American family. *Journal of Extension* [On-Line], *49*(3), Article 3COM1. Available at: http://www.joe.org/joe/2011june/comm1.php

Arcus, M. E. (1995). Advances in family life education: Past, present, and future. *Family Relations, 44*, 336–344. doi:10.2307/584988. http://www.jstor.org/stable/584988?seq=1#page_scan_tab_contents.

Baker, T. Allen, K., & Huff, N. (2015). *Family life coaching: An exploratory study of parental perceptions*. Manuscript in preparation.

Capsi, J. (2005). Coaching and social work: Challenges and concerns. *Social Work, 50*(4), 359–362.

Cavanagh, M., & Lane, D. (2012). Coaching psychology coming of age: The challenges we face in the messy world of complexity. *International Coaching Psychology Review., 7*(1), 75–90.

Coutu, D., & Kauffman, C. (2009, January). What can coaches do for you? *Harvard Business Review Magazine* [online]. Retrieved from http://hbr.org/2009/01/what-can-coaches-do-for-you; https://hbr.org/archive-toc/BR0901

Czaplewski, M. J., & Jorgensen, S. R. (1993). The professionalization of family life education. In M. E. Arcus, J. D. Schvaneveldt, & J. J. Moss (Eds.), *Handbook of family life education* (Vol. 1, pp. 51–75). Newbury Park, CA: Sage.

Doherty, W. J. (1995). Boundaries between parent and family education and family therapy: The levels of family involvement model. *Family Relations, 44*(4), 353–358.

Doherty, W. J. (2000). Family science and family citizenship: Toward a model of community partnership with families. *Family Relations, 49*, 319–325.

Duncan, S. F., & Goddard, H. W. (2011). *Family life education: Principles and practices for effective outreach.* Thousand Oaks, CA: Sage.

Filippi, R. (1968). Coaching: A therapy for people who do not seek help. *Zeitschrift Fuer Psychotherapie und Medizinische Psychologie, 18*(6), 225–229.

Fillery-Travis, A., & Lane, D. (2006). Does coaching work or are we asking the wrong question? *International Coaching Psychology Review, 1*(1), 23–36.

Garman, A. N., Whiston, D. L., & Zlatoper, K. W. (2000). Media perceptions of executive coaching and the formal preparation of coaches. *Consulting Psychology Journal: Practice & Research, 52*, 203–205.

Gockel, A., Russel, M., & Harris, B. (2008). Recreating family: Parents identify worker-client relationships as paramount in family preservation programs. *Child Welfare, 87*(6), 91–113.

Grant, A. (2003). The impact of life coaching on goal attainment, metacognition and mental health. *Social Behavior and Personality, 31*(3), 253–263.

Grant, A. M. (2006). A personal perspective on professional coaching and the development of coaching psychology. *International Coaching Psychology Review, 1*(1), 12–22.

Grant, A. M. (2011). Developing an agenda for teaching coaching psychology. *International Coaching Psychology Review, 6*(1), 84–99.

Grant, A. M., & Palmer, S. (2002). *Coaching psychology.* Workshop and meeting held at the annual conference of the division of counselling psychology. Torquay, UK: British Psychological Society.

Grant, A. M., & Zackon, R. (2004). Executive, work-place and life-coaching: Findings from a large-scale survey of International Coach Federation members. *International Journal of Evidence-Based Coaching and Mentoring, 2*(2), 1–15.

Hanft, B. E., Rush, D. D., & Shelden, M. L. (2004). *Coaching families and colleagues in early childhood.* Baltimore: Paul H. Brookes Publishing Company.

Hart, V., Blattner, J., & Leipsic, S. (2001). Coaching versus therapy: A perspective. *Consulting Psychology Journal: Practive and Research, 53*(4), 229–237.

Heimendinger, J., Uyeki, T., Andhara, A., Marshall, J. A., Scarbro, S., Belansky, E., et al. (2007). Coaching process outcomes of a family visit nutrition and physical activity intervention. *Health Education & Behavior: The Official Publication of the Society for Public Health Education, 34*(1), 71–89. doi:10.1177/1090198105285620.

Lewis_Rowley, M., Brasher, R. E., Moss, J. J., Duncan, S. F., & Stiles, R. J. (1993). The evolution of education for family life. In M. E. Arcus, J. D. Schvaneveldt, & J. J. Moss (Eds.), *Handbook of family life education.* Newbury Park, CA: Sage.

McGoldrick, M., & Carter, B. (2001). Advances in coaching: Family therapy with one person. *Journal of Marital and Family Therapy, 27*(3), 281. doi:10.1111/j.1752-0606.2001.tb00325.x.

McLean, P. (2012). *The completely revised handbook of coaching: A developmental approach.* San Francisco: Wiley.

Moore, M., & Highstein, G. (2004a). Principles of behavioral wellness in coaching. *Paper presented at the international coaching federation.* Retrieved from http://www. healthandwellnessmatters.com/images/Behavioral_psychology.pdf

Moore, M., & Highstein, G. (2004b). Principles of behavioral psychology in wellness coaching. Paper presented at the International Coach Federation's coaching research symposium.

Myers-Walls, J. A., Ballard, S., Darling, C. A., & Myers-Bowman, K. S. (2011). Reconceptualizing the domain and boundaries of family life education. *Family Relations, 60,* 357–372.

National Council on Family Relations. (2009). *Family life education content areas: Content and practice guidelines.* Retrieved from www.ncfr.org

Nichols, M. P., & Schwartz, R. C. (1998). *Family therapy: Concepts and methods* (xix, 586 pages). Needham Height, MA: Allyn & Bacon.

Powell, L., & Cassidy, D. (2007). *Family life education: Working with families across the life span.* Long Grove, IL: Waveland Press.

Rush, D., Shelden, M., & Hanft, B. (2003). Coaching families and colleagues: A process for collaboration in natural settings. *Infants & Young Children: An Interdisciplinary Journal of Special Care Practices, 16*(1), 33–47. Retrieved from EBSCOhost.

Stober, D. R., & Grant, A. M. (2006). *Evidence based coaching handbook: Putting best practices to work for your clients.* Hoboken, NJ: Wiley.

Walter, M. S. (2015). *Conceptualizing family life coaching.* In preparation at UNC-Chapel Hill, North Carolina.

Whybrow, A., & Palmer, S. (2006). The coaching psychology movement and it development within the British Psychological Society. *International Coaching Psychology Review, 1*(1), 5–11.

Williams, P., & Menendez, D. (2007). *Becoming a professional life coach: Lessons from the Institute for Life Coach Training.* New York: Norton & Company.

Chapter 2
Roots of Coaching Psychology

I recently attended a talk by Anthony Grant, one of the leading researchers of coaching psychology. His slides began with images of the pioneers in the field of psychology—Freud, Rogers, Maslow, Skinner, Beck, Ellis, and Bandura. He also talked about the big names in the coaching industry—Thomas Leonard, Oprah, and Tony Robinson. While we all had a chuckle, his point was well taken. Combining the theories and rich scientific background of psychology and bringing that together with the industry of coaching is a great way to grow the fields of coaching and coaching psychology. Today the fields of psychology and the practice of coaching are convening, even though there has been resistance from both fields in the past (Grant, 2012, 2015).

To put it bluntly, Grant suggested, coaching is about helping clients reach their goals, and find solutions. Coaching is about collaborating with clients in a solution-focused, results-oriented process. Coaches facilitate the enhancement of performance, but it is the client that guides the process (Grant, 2015). Bringing together the fields of coaching and coaching psychology has provided a unique opportunity to increase the science and rigor of coaching, and grow the applied science of psychology. It is quite exciting to be in the field of coaching psychology right now, a young field on the cusp of greatness.

This chapter covers the theoretical roots of coaching psychology including adult learning theory, humanistic psychology, person-centered approach, positive psychology, and solution-focused theory. Because coaching psychology is considered a new and growing field, this chapter covers the history of coaching and reviews the current literature on the efficacy of coaching in personal change.

© Springer International Publishing Switzerland 2016
K. Allen, *Theory, Research, and Practical Guidelines for Family Life Coaching*,
DOI 10.1007/978-3-319-29331-8_2

History of Coaching

"Put me in coach, I'm ready to play!" Many think of sports coaching when they think of coaching, and for good reason. Coaching has its roots in the area of sports, dating back to ancient Greece when the top athletes were coached by well-paid coaching professionals (Carpenter, 2004). Some might argue that workplace coaching goes back centuries to the times of apprenticeships. However, the earliest forms of coaching as evidenced in the scientific literature come from the field of business. From the 1940–1970s, businesses hired psychologists and organizational development professionals trained to come into an organization to help increase overall productivity. This often occurred through the use of informal conversations (Kampa-Kokesch & Anderson, 2001). In the early years, coaching was used as a managerial technique, where the focus was on the employee and his/her abilities, rather than their faults (Burdett, 1998).

While coaching psychology is a relatively new approach to the psychological service field, coaching literature dates back to Coleman Griffith, a sports psychologist that made observations about the psychology of the athletes back in 1918 (Palmer & Whybrow, 2008). Griffith (1926) suggested that coaching is more than instructing; coaches are teachers. While the field of sports coaching has long been the field most associated with coaching, the field of business coaching was not far behind. Gorby (1937) wrote one of the first articles in the field; an article that detailed how coaching techniques could be used to increase productivity and profit in business. The literature on coaching in the business industry was the prominent focus of the coaching literature for most of the Twentieth century. Recently, that has begun to change as the literature on coaching and coaching psychology is rapidly increasing (Palmer & Whybrow, 2008).

While the literature on coaching continues to grow, so has the industry of coaching. From 1980 to 1994, the field of coaching expanded to a variety of fields far beyond athletics and business, and began finding success in life, health, and family arenas (Hudson, 1999). The number of publications on coaching in each of these fields also continues to grow every year. Today, The International Coach Federation estimates over 30,000 professional coaches are currently practicing (ICF, 2007). Today's coaches come from a wide variety of backgrounds and since there is not one unifying credential, it is hard to say exactly how many coaches there are in total or from what profession they come (Harris, 1999). The nature of coaching, both executive and life coaching, is enact and sustains change at the emotional, cognitive, and behavioral levels, leading to goal attainment and increased performance in personal or professional life (Stober & Grant, 2006a). In that respect, the fields of coaching and coaching psychology will likely continue on the path of growth.

Coaching and Coaching Psychology. Is There a Difference?

The origins of the coaching industry can be traced back to the 1950s in the humanistic approach to change. Humanists are optimistic in their perception of human behavior and work on interpersonal relationship improvement (McLean, 2012). This optimistic process takes place in a client/coach relationship. Cognitive Behavioral approach was also being used at this time, often through the work of industrial psychologists that worked for major industrial companies (Stober & Grant, 2006a, b). These psychologists used psychological methodology as the preferred approach to human growth.

The humanistic approach is open; it does not have barriers on who can or cannot practice, nor does it have limitations such as education or credentials. However, the development of credentialed training institutions created requirements to become certified in coaching. The CBT training institutions required that students be trained in health professions (Palmer & Whybrow, 2008). Therein lies the root of the difference between the coaching industry and coaching psychology. With few exceptions, the coaching industry accepts varying educational backgrounds and often uses the Humanistic approach to change, as in the GROW model or similar coach-specific models. The coaching psychology profession requires training in psychology and uses a variety of psychological theoretical approaches, all having gone through evidence-based evaluation. The academic and training requirements for coaches and coaching psychologists vary greatly.

There is a growing body of research that suggests significant research and training credibility is needed to grow the coaching profession (Grant, 2011). The need for rigor, training standards, and standardized competencies will help legitimize the field amongst other professionals. Additionally, there is still a question about the definitions of coaching and coaching psychology, and there is still a need for clarity of what coaching actually is (Stober & Grant, 2006a). There is lacking an established, clear delineation between the fields of coaching and coaching psychology. Palmer and Whybrow (2008) highlight the differences between the two in their book, The Handbook of Coach Psychology. First, they identify three definitions in the fields of coaching as told by Whitmore (1992), Downey(1999), and Parsloe (1995).

> Coaching is unlocking a person's potential to maximize their own performance. It is helping them to learn rather than teaching them—a facilitation approach. Whitmore (1992).

> Coaching is the art of facilitating the performance, learning and development of another Downey (1999).

> Coaching is directly concerned with the immediate improvement of performance and development of skills by a form of tutoring or instruction. Parsloe (1995).

Yet another definition of coaching includes more specific information on the process of coaching.

A coach is a person who facilitates experiential learning that results in future-oriented abilities." He goes onto say a "coach is someone trained and devoted to guiding others into increase competence, commitment, and confidence (Hudson, 1999, p. 6).

The International Coach Federation (n.d.) defines coaching this way:

Professional Coaching is an ongoing professional relationship that helps people produce extraordinary results in their lives, careers, businesses or organizations. Through the process of coaching, clients deepen their learning, improve their performance, and enhance their quality of life.

These definitions have much in common in that they all refer to coaching as a process with an ultimate goal of increasing a person's performance. Brennan and Prior (2005) identified common themes of coaching definitions. The themes included an egalitarian relationship, solution and goal attainment focus, and a need for abilities to facilitate learning and growth. Effective coaching is about asking the right questions and facilitating growth rather than telling a client what to do (Stober & Grant, 2006a).

What is absent in the themes of the previous coaching definitions is a specific need for developing a mastery in learning a theoretical underpinning. Coaching psychology, a newer distinction in the coaching industry, is considered an applied positive psychology. As with coaching, many definitions of coaching psychology include an increased performance element, but also include an expectation of professional training and a psychological theoretical underpinning (Stober & Grant, 2006a).

Coaching psychology is for enhancing well-being and performance in personal life and work domains, underpinned by models of coaching grounded in established learning theories and psychological approaches (Adapted from Grant and Palmer, 2002 as cited in Palmer & Whybrow, 2008).

This definition captures the importance of theory and evidence as an essential element of coaching psychology. While the coaching industry is working on improving rigor and more research is providing evidence of the efficacy of coaching, there is still a considerable difference of the two fields. Namely, it comes down to theoretical differences and qualifications of the practitioner.

Another working definition of coaching psychology was presented at the 2015 International Congress on Coaching by Vandaveer, Pearlman, Lowman, and Brannick (2015). The team reported on research and development currently under-way to develop a coaching competency model. Their research looked at the working definitions and practices of coaches in the US in order to create a working definition of coaching psychology, among other objectives. While the formal definition is still under development, the working definition includes the following components:

- Area of professional practice and research within broader discipline of psychology
- Individualized process of professional development in which a coaching psychologist works with individuals one-on-one and/or sometimes in a broader

context, to enhance their effectiveness in their organizational roles and environments.

- Designed to benefit both the individual and the organization
- Grounded in scientifically established psychological theories, principles, and methods.
- Practiced by qualified psychologists who, among other requirements, have a graduate degree in a psychology discipline accredited university + relevant post-graduate qualifications

So while the field of coaching psychology is growing, and the industry of coaching is beginning to merge with the field of coaching psychology, it is clear that we are on the cusp of an emerging field that will likely have staying power. In fact, in 2011, Division 13 of the American Psychological Association, Society for Consulting Psychology, which represents practitioners in the coaching industry, developed a memorandum of understanding with the International Society of Coaching Psychology (ISCP), a professional association of coaching psychologist. This created the first steps towards a merger of the coaching industry and field of coaching psychology. The questions the field still must answer are does it work, how does it work, and how do we ensure professionalism.

Coaching or Coaching Psychology: Does It Work?

Does coaching work, that is the million-dollar question.

Evidence of the effectiveness of coaching psychology is growing rapidly (Grant, 2012). If coaching practitioners want to truly be able to say that coaching is an effective method of personal change, then we must speak in a common language and evaluate a common method. To date, most research shows that clients improve having received coaching. Of course there could be flaws with some of the evidence, but overall the research shows that coaching psychology is effective (Theeboom, Beersma, and Van Vianen (2013). In other words, coaching has a positive impact on the overall quality of life for participants. People that receive coaching are more resilient, have increased well-being, have increased insight, and are more likely to reach their goals (Grant, 2015)

Evidence-based coaching is yet another distinction of coaching industry and coaching psychology. Evidence-base is a term long found in science and academia to describe practices that have scientifically supported results. While the field of science includes a hierarchy of methodological significance, with ideas, editorials, and case studies at the bottom and randomly controlled trials and systematic reviews at the top, it is easy to say that coaching psychology research has far to go. However, Theeboom et al. (2013), recently completed a meta-analysis of coaching outcomes. Specifically, the authors investigated the effectiveness of five individual-level outcome categories: performance, well-being, coping, work attitudes, and self-regulation. Results of this study indicated that coaching does, in fact, have significant positives effects on all five outcomes.

Lai and McDowall (2014) completed a systematic review of coaching psychology to better understand the knowledge, attitudes, and behaviors associated with the quality of coaching relationships and the outcome of coaching. Their research found that the quality of the coaching relationship is critical to the success of the coaching goal, and significant professional training is necessary to regulate and manage the client's emotional reactions. From this, we can begin to understand not only that coaching works, but that the relationship and qualifications of the coach are both paramount to the success.

Theeboom et al.'s and Lai & McDowall's work is a great start, but more work is needed to show evidence of efficacy. Stober and Grant (2006a, b) argue that coaching psychology is moving toward a model of professional coaching that includes informed-practitioners that have an understanding of methodologies for research and evaluation of their practice. While informed practitioners may not be expected to be producers of research, they are expected to be critical consumers of research, thus selecting practices that have evidence of efficacy and might improve their practice. The informed practitioner model has been evident and extensively used in behavioral sciences (Shapiro, 2002). Coaching psychology training programs that include this model will help students address the theory, methods, and critical thinking needed to provide effective, evidence-based coaching (Stober & Grant, 2006a, b).

The research on coaching psychology is young, and we have evidence that it works. However we still have far to go to truly understand how and why it works, and how effectively coaching interventions work. Future research that will help us understand the how and why will include closely investigating the coaching relationship, and the micro and macro factors of the coaching process.

All evidence indicates that coaching psychology is here to stay. Stephen Palmer (2015) outlined a few trends of coaching in his ISCP talk. He explained that there are currently an estimated 4000 coaches registered in national professional development groups right now, and more than 20,000 are showing an interest in the field. To date, nine countries, including the US, have formed a memorandum of understanding to bring together coaching psychology groups and the coaching industry. There has been a dramatic increase in the number of publications on coaching, and perhaps most importantly, professional qualifications, professional registers, and supervision of coaching psychologist are on the rise.

Theoretical Roots of Coaching Psychology

Humanistic, Person-Centered Approach

Open most any coaching book, and the theoretical foundation first identified as the underpinning for coaching psychology will almost always be the Humanistic approach. Perhaps that is because coaching is all about personal growth; it is about helping a person move forward. Carl Roger's, person-centered approach is only one of several Humanistic approaches. Other approaches that fit under this label include Gestalt, experiential and existential therapies. However, Person-Centered Humanistic approach is the one most often identified as a foundation for coaching psychology. A connection was found between the two in a review between Roger's approach and the literature on executive coaching (Hedman, 2001).

Roger's person-centered approach places great emphasis on the quality of the relationship between the client and the practitioner (Rogers 1961). First identified as an approach to psychotherapy, Roger's Humanistic approach fits ideally with the role of the coach and coachee. In fact, nearly all of the definitions reviewed for coaching and coaching psychology refer to performance increase, which can directly relate to Roger's idea of self-actualization. Roger's stated that the goal is for a client to move towards self-actualization as we all have "a tendency to actualize [our]selves" (Rogers 1961, p. 351).

While self-actualization might be a rather lofty goal for most, the movement towards a goal through a supportive process is the essence of coaching psychology. Like Humanistic psychology, coaching psychology focuses intently on positive movement toward growth. A coach's job is to work collaboratively with the client to help them move towards their goal, and as such, belief in the potential of the client to make that movement is critical for the success of the process.

Roger's theory suggests that the process by which change is most notably accomplished is through the quality of the relationship which is fostered through an optimal climate. Rogers (1980) stated the climate for change is best accomplished with unconditional positive regard, empathy, and genuineness. Unconditional positive regard, or the acceptance of the client through the building of a supportive relationship, helps the client move forward by valuing the client for who they are. Empathy allows the coach to best understand a person's experience from an emotional standpoint. While the coach works to best understand and support the client, the coach must also be authentic. Genuineness is best achieved when the coach takes stalk of his or her own experiences, reactions, and feelings, or being completely present in the moment.

In the Humanistic approach, as is true in coaching psychology, the client is seen as the expert in their own life (Rogers 1961). Identifying the client as the expert in their lives provides a framework for acknowledgement of an individual's strength, and allows for the facilitation of growth by the coach. It also builds upon the key concept of a trusting relationship that is based on empathy. Stober (2006) has identified other key concepts of Humanistic approaches considered foundational to coaching.

Growth-Oriented View of the Person This optimistic view of people does not deny that dysfunction exists, but rather it places the focus of the change process on an individual's capacity to move forward. Coaches must approach the relationship with optimism, and work with the clients in a supportive, mutually beneficial relationship.

Self-Actualization Rogers (1959) suggested that people have a natural tendency or possibility for forward development and that people strive to reach their full capacity. The coach that develops a supportive environment for the coaching process helps client's move towards self-actualization.

Holistic View of the Person In the Gestalt tradition, the sum of its parts is not as great as the whole. In coaching, we must see the connection of all facets of a client's experience. This means understanding their human experience, their uniqueness's, and how their systems influence their perceptions and reality.

Human Potential Movement Following in the work of Kurt Lewin, Human Potential movement emphasized the ability of the individual to fix themselves without having to be sick or have a diagnosis. It is the notion that self-improvement does not need to focus on the weakness of the individual.

Positive Psychology

In 1998, then APA president Martin Seligman stood at the podium to deliver his presidential address. That address, many argue, changed the face of psychology. Seligman presented a science of human strengths, and encouraged the field of psychology to move past the deficit-based approach so commonly presented in studies. In his speech, Seligman (1998) stated,

> Ideally, psychology should be able to help document what kind of families result in the healthiest children, what work environments support the greatest satisfaction among workers, and what policies result in the strongest civic commitment.
> Yet we have scant knowledge of what makes life worth living. For although psychology has come to understand quite a bit about how people survive and endure under conditions of adversity, we know very little about how normal people flourish under more benign conditions.

Positive psychology is the study of how people prosper in the face of adversity (Seligman & Csikszentmihalyi, 2000). While this seems an appropriate or even common area of study for psychology, the norm of psychology has historically been a medical model, meaning that people come to see a psychologist, become diagnosed with a mental health issue, then receive treatment for that issue to be fixed. The medical model has been the norm for decades, and is the primary way practitioners receive payment from insurance.

While Seligman has become the spokesperson for positive psychology, the roots of positive psychology can be traced back to the Humanist movement and work of Rogers, Maslow, and even to the earliest works of William James (Froh, 2004). While the theory of positive psychology is gaining much traction, the practice of positive psychology can be found in coaching psychology (Palmer, 2008, 2015). Coaching psychology puts the focus on where people want to go; how to move from here to there. Put another way, the heart of positive psychology is a movement away from pathology and dysfunction and towards a focus on strength and positive development.

Coaching psychology has been identified as the applied practice of positive psychology (Kauffman, 2006). The numbers of positive psychology interventions (PPIs) are increasing, and are showing promising results (Sin & Lyubomirsky, 2009). In a meta-analysis of 51 positive psychology interventions aimed at increasing positive feelings, behaviors, or thoughts, Sin and Lyubormirsky found that such interventions enhance wellbeing and decrease depressive symptoms. There is also growing literature on the efficacy of specific positive psychology coaching interventions that increase wellbeing (Madden, Green, & Grant, 2011).

Based on the concepts of positive psychology, the Authentic Happiness Coaching model was created to provide coaching approaches that were grounded in theory and supported empirically (Kauffman, 2006). The model includes a set of techniques to foster happiness and was designed to help a broad range of clients, from CEOs to parents (Seligman, Steen, Park, & Peterson, 2005). It is for people who are mentally healthy but want to find more joy in their lives. The process includes an educational component where the coach explains Seligman's pathways to happiness through emotions, connections, activity, and through personal meaning. Seligman calls these three areas the pleasant life, engaged life, and the meaningful life. The coach then works with the client(s) to help them identify steps to improve one of the three areas. For more information on this process, see Chap. 7.

Adult Learning Theory

While there is a growing literature on coaching youth, the bulk of all coaching research deals with coaching adults. Unlike traditional, younger learners, adults come to the coaching process with varied life experiences and often with formal and informal education. Adult Learning Theory tends to focus on andragogy, or the study of helping adults learn (Knowles, 1978). According to Knowles, Holton, and Swanson (1998), adults are self-directed, goal-oriented, and come with life experiences that provides important insights and direction. Coaches will benefit from focusing on real-life issues and keeping the session relevant to the individual's specific needs and goals. Knowles et al. suggest adults have intrinsic motivation, and as such coaching should focus on the internal process or internal goals of the client being served.

Experiential learning principles (Kolb, 1984) focus on the idea of learning through action. Kolb directly connects his perspective on the works of Dewey, Lewin, and Piaget. He emphasized the importance that experiences play in the learning process. Rather than distinguish experiential learning as a separate or alternative to behavior and cognitive theories, Kolb considers experiential learning theory as a holistic approach that integrates experience, perception, cognition, and behavior.

While the experiential learning model has been an important component of adult learning theory, the model is also a staple in youth development, and in particular, for use with 4-H learning activities. The experiential learning model has five components in three sections (Pfeiffer & Jones, 1983).

DO:

1. Experience the activity.

REFLECT:

2. Share reactions and observations
3. Process the experience; analyze what happened.

APPLY:

4. Generalize to connect the experience to real-world examples
5. Apply what was learned to other situations

This is relevant to coaching because most clients come to sessions with a goal of immediately implementing change strategies in their life. Adult learning theory tends to focus on the present and future (Berg & Karlsen, 2007). Experiential learning has been used successfully in coaching, perhaps most notably with the GROW model, which was created by Alexander and made common by Whitmore 1992 (Cox, 2006). In GROW, G = goal setting, which equates to concrete experience. R = reality, or the observation. O = options, or generalization. W = will, or what will you do, is the application.

Cox (2006) identifies additional theories that are considered staples of adult learning theory, and necessary to consider when coaching adults. In addition to andragogy and experiential learning, reflective practice, learning styles, life course development, values/motivation, and self-efficacy are all aspects of adult learning theory that are relevant to coaching.

Cognitive Behavioral

Aaron Beck is considered to be the pioneer of cognitive behavioral therapy, a therapeutic process that seeks to identify the faulty thinking that can lead to emotional turmoil and dysfunction. The CB model describes how a person's thinking or perceptions of an issue influences emotional and behavioral reactions (Beck, 1976). Beck describes how psychological problems often come from faulty learning, incorrect inferences, or simply failing to distinguish between imagination and reality.

A contemporary of Aaron Beck, Albert Ellis, developed the ABC rational-emotive therapy (RET), an approach that also identified faulty thinking as a contribution of mental well-being. Ellis (1979) explained that faulty beliefs, also called cognitive distortions, are what influences how we feel.

A: **A**ctivating experience
B: irrational **B**elief about the experience
C: emotional **C**onsequences

For example, it is common for people in a relationship to have faulty perceptions of their relational experience. I have worked with several clients that have a suspicion or feeling that something is wrong when their partner identifies no such issue. This typically happens early in the relationship, when moving from the beginning stage, romantic love, onto the stage of accommodation or reality.

Many times I have heard couples say that things in their relationship are not what they used to be. One particular couple came to work with me after they had been in a relationship for about 6 months. She was concerned that he was no longer interested in the relationship because he stopped many of the behaviors of court-ship; sending flowers, multiple daily calls, and going out on romantic dates. While these concerns had merit, her message to herself was that he was just like her last boyfriend. In her former relationship, the boyfriend had lost interest and stopped showing affection right before he left her. Although her current partner repeatedly told her he was invested in the relationship, she had a faulty belief that he was leaving. Through a coaching process, she was able to identify other reasons that his behavior had changed, such as that sending flowers and going on fancy dates can become expensive. Her irrational beliefs about the experience were actually caus-ing her great frustration and were creating difficulty in the relationship. Through the coaching process, we were able to identify faulty thinking, and perhaps even more important, we were able to identify new behaviors that provided cognitive evidence that the boyfriend was invested in the relationship. This new way of thinking helped her change her thoughts, which changed her actions.

As a coach using cognitive behavioral techniques, we can help challenge the thinking of the client to help them identify their irrational belief system. David Burns (1980) identified "cognitive distortions" and Auerbach (2006) has translated those distortions for coaching.

1. *All or nothing thinking.* Black and white; no room for possibly alternative explanations.
2. *Overgeneralization.* Seeing a pattern from isolated incidents.
3. *Mental filter.* When someone sees only a negative detail when there are many positives that could be viewed.
4. *Disqualifying the positive.* Actively rejecting positive experiences by thinking they are not important.
5. *Mind reading.* Concluding that people have negative thoughts about you despite lack of evidence supporting this thought.

6. *The fortune teller error*. The belief that things will turn out badly before there is any evidence to support that belief.
7. *Catastrophizing*. Exaggerating the importance of a minor event.
8. *Emotional reasoning*. Belief that negative emotions are facts.
9. *Should statements*. The idea that things should be done in a certain way, the following negative self-talk.
10. *Labeling*. A form of overgeneralization of lumping all negative into one label rather than looking at specific events.

Burns (1980) describes the triple-column technique as a way of identifying cognitive distortions. These often begin with automatic thoughts, which can be categorized as one of the ten cognitive distortions above. The coaching goal, then, would be to help the coaching client identify the irrational thought and replace it with a rational response. If we think about the case above where the woman is concerned that her partner is losing interest in the relationship, we could coach her into identified rational responses.

Example of multi-column technique in family life coaching

Automatic thoughts (self-criticism)	Cognitive distortions (faulty belief)	Rational responses	Possible power questions
1. He never brings me flowers anymore.	*Overgeneralization. Mental Filler*	Flowers are not the only way of expressing interest in a relationship.	What other ways has he shown interest in you or the relationship?
2. He has no reason to stay with me. Men always leave me anyway.	*The fortuneteller error.*	Of course there are many reasons for him to stay in this relationship!	What positives do you bring to the relationship?
3. I'm just a fool to think this relationship will work	*Labeling*	I'm not always a fool; in fact, I'm smart in many areas of my life.	How have other relations in your life been successful?

Goal-Focused Approach

With so much emphasis in the field of coaching placed on goal setting, it is important to draw on the literature from goal-setting, self-determination, and personality. Anthony Grant (2012) lays out an approach to integrating goal-focused coaching work, with much emphasis on self-regulation. According to Grant (2006, p. 153)

> the core constructs of goal-directed self-regulation are a series of processes in which the individual sets a goal, develops a plan of action, begins action, monitors their performance, evaluates their performance by comparison to a standard, and based on this evaluation, changes their actions to further enhance their performance and better reach their goals. In relation to coaching, the coach's role is to facilitate the coachee's movement through the self-regulatory cycle

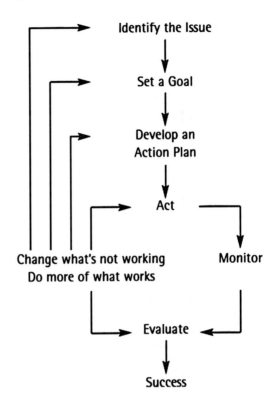

Fig. 2.1 Generic model of goal-directed self-regulation (Grant 2012, Reprinted with permission)

This process can be seen in Grant's model (2012) of goal-directed self-regulation figure (Fig. 2.1).

Solution-focused approaches have been used in coaching both for organizational change (Bloor & Pearson, 2004) and in life coaching (Grant, 2003). Solution focused interventions were described by Berg and Dolan as "the pragmatics of hope and respect" (p. 1). Like positive psychology, solution focused approaches focus on what can be, and the client's view is considered a valuable resource and necessary to create change (Berg & Dolan, 2001). In solution focused coaching, it is the role of the coach to help the client turn toward solutions.

Grant (2006) identifies two key factors in the process:

1. Changing the viewing.
2. Changing the doing.

In essence, solution focused coaching is about helping the client create and negotiate the future (Berg & Dolan, 2001). One of the most popular approaches to changing the viewing comes in the form of a "magic question", which is this:

> ... in the middle of the night, a miracle happens and the problem that prompted you to talk to me today is solved! But because this happened while you are sleeping, you have no way of knowing that there was an overnight miracle that solved the problems. So, when you wake up tomorrow morning, what might be the small change that will make you say to yourself, 'wow, something must have happened. The problem is gone! (p. 7).

This miracle question, which is one of many powerful questions often used by coaches (see Chap. 8) helps the client become familiar with a solution. It helps them change the viewing, and see what they are looking for. The second step, or changing the doing, occurs with goal setting and action steps.

Smart Goals
S: Specific
M: Measurable
A: Attainable
R: Realistic
T: Timely

Goal setting is the groundwork of good coaching. Goal-focused coaching is proving to be an evidence-based framework for practice and teaching (Grant, 2007). Goals are what lay the foundation for action steps, or the changing of the doing. Many coaches focus on setting outcome goals, a statement of a desired outcome (Hudson, 1999). Most coaching professionals have a list of goal types. SMART goals, (originally delineated by Raia, 1965) are Specific, Measurable, Attainable, Realistic and Timely and are often found in the coaching literature as are performance and avoidance goals. Helping a client set goals, and plan the action for accomplishing those goals are critical steps in the coaching process. Solution-focused approaches have been identified and implemented into models of coaching (Palmer, 2008).

Understanding that goals are an essential process of coaching psychology is critical to coaching success. While building a relationship and focusing on solutions are critical components of successful coaching, facilitating goal alignment can help clients gain insight and behavioral changes (Grant, 2012). As Grant states, goal identification and attainment "is surely the overarching goal of the coaching enterprise itself" (p. 161).

A Meta-Model of Coaching

To summarize this chapter, coaching psychology is a new field that brings together a rich and varied theoretical background to offer a vibrant and evidence-based approach to help people lead meaningful and fulfilling lives. While this chapter is a summary and only touches on the intricacies of the field of coaching psychology, my hope is that you have enough information to want more information. I have included a list of recommended readings for more information.

While there are many models of coaching, most with varied theoretical under-pinnings and practice suggestions, there are themes that ring true for most coaching models (see Chap. 7 for more coaching models and assessments). I want to leave you with Stober and Grant's (2006a, b) concept of a meta-model of coaching.

They suggest seven thematic factors of coaching that together identify most themes and principles of coaching psychology.

1. *Goals.* The coaching process has an explicit outcome. Goals are an essential element of the coaching process, and as such, coach and client can work together to identify the needs to be addressed.
2. *Rationale.* Clients need understanding and coaches will do better with an explanation of how the process of coaching will help meet the needs of the client.
3. *Procedure.* The coach will follow set up steps that will include participation from both the coach and the client.
4. *Relationship.* As was discussed in most all theoretical underpinnings of coaching psychology, building a meaning relationship whereby the client feels supported is essential.
5. *Alliance.* Coaches will play the role of helping to expand the client's skills and performance. This is more than building a relationship; it is challenging while supporting the client.
6. *Client's Change.* Coaching is about change, and specifically about the client's ability and readiness to change.
7. *Coach's Role in Client Change.* The coach must have the abilities and skills to assist in the client's change process.

These steps, or the meta-model of coaching, can be boiled down to the "how" of coaching psychology. Stober and Grant (2006a, b) identify these steps as the common themes of coaching. While there are plenty of specific models that must continue to be evaluated and new models that will be developed, it is important to understand the common themes of the coaching psychology process and recognize the contextual model.

Chapter Summary

The fields of coaching psychology and the coaching industry are in the process of merging. The field of coaching is growing, and many efforts are underway to help ensure professionalism and efficacy. Professional associations are an important element of professionalism. The International Society of Coaching Psychology (ISCP) is an international professional membership organization working to grow the professionalism of coaching. Facilitated primarily by the work of coaching psychologists Stephen Palmer in the UK and Anthony Grant in Australia, the process of creating global professionalism is underway (Palmer & Whybrow, 2006). To date, over 18 counties have joined efforts of inclusion in the International Society of Coaching Psychology in an effort to bridge the work being done in individual countries with international collaborations.

Since the field is new, there are questions being researched such as how effective is the coaching process, why is the coaching process effective, and how should coaching psychologists be trained and managed (Cavanagh & Lane, 2012). I would add the question, how do we move past the terminology of "coaching psychologist," which implies the exclusion of other helping scientists, such as family life coaches, social workers, and marriage and family therapists. Family life coaching is a sub section of the broader field of coaching psychology, and an understanding of how family science and coaching psychology can co-exist is the essence of family life coaching. Clearly the field is coming of age, and psychology is at the foreground of the movement (Palmer & Cavanagh, 2006), but I suggest there is room for family science in the field. The remaining chapters will focus highly on the theory, research, and practice of family science, helping to close the gap between coaching psychology and family science.

References

Auerbach, J. E. (2006). Cognitive coaching. In D. R. Stober, & A. M. Grant (Eds.), *Evidence based coaching handbook: Putting best practices to work for your clients* (pp. 17–50). Hoboken, NJ: Wiley.

Beck, A. (1976). *Cognitive therapy and emotional disorders.* New York: New America Library.

Berg, I. K., & Dolan, Y. (2001). *Tales of solutions: A collection of hope-inspiring stories.* New York: W. W. Norton & Co.

Berg, M. E., & Karlsen, J. T. (2007). Mental models in project management coaching. *Engineering Management Journal, 19*(3), 3–14.

Bloor, R., & Pearson, D. (2004). Brief solution-focused organizational redesign. A model for international mental health consultancy. *International Journal of Mental Health, 33*(2), 44–53.

Brennan, D., & Prior, D. M. (2005). *The future of coaching as a profession: The next five years 2005–2010.* Lexington, KY: International Coach Federation.

Burdett, J. (1998). Forty things every manager should know about coaching. *Journal of Management Development, 17*(2), 142–152. doi:10.1108/02621719810206050.

Burns, D. D. (1980). *Feel good: The new mood therapy.* New York: Williams Morrow.

Carpenter, B. (2004).*The first Olympics: The early Greek games were not as pristine as we like to imagine* (U.S. news & world report). Retrieved from http://www.usnews.com/

Cavanagh, M., & Lane, D. (2012). Coaching psychology coming of age: The challenges we face in the messy world of complexity. *International Coaching Psychology Review, 7*(1), 75–90.

Cox, E. (2006). An adult learning approach to coaching. In D. R. Stober, & A. M. Grant (Eds.), *Evidence based coaching handbook: Putting best practices to work for your clients* (pp. 17–50). Hoboken, NJ: Wiley.

Downey, M. (1999). *Effective coaching.* London: Orion.

Ellis, A. (1979). The practice of rational-emotive therapy. In A. Ellis & J. Whitely (Eds.), *Theoretical and empirical foundations of rational-emotive therapy.* Monterey, CA: Brooks/Cole.

Froh, J. J. (2004). The history of positive psychology: Truth be told. *NYS Psychologist,* 18–20. Retrieved from http://mina.education.ucsb.edu/janeconoley/ed197/documents/FrohTheHistoryofPosPsych.pdf

Gorby, C. B. (1937). Everyone gets a share of the profits. *Factory Management & Maintenance, 95,* 82–83.

Grant, A. (2003). The impact of life coaching on goal attainment, metacognition and mental health. *Social Behavior and Personality, 31*(3), 253–263.

Grant, A. (2011). Developing an agenda for teaching coaching psychology. *International Coaching Psychology Review, 6*(1), 84–99.

Grant, A. (2012). An integrated model of goal-focused coaching: An evidence-based framework for teaching and practice. *International Coaching Psychology Review, 7*(2), 146–165.

Grant, A. (2015, February). *Putting the psychology into coaching, and the coaching into psychology: Lessons from the road (less traveled)*. Presented at the 5th international congress of coaching psychology, San Diego, CA.

Grant, A. M. (2006). An integrative goal-focused approach to executive coaching. In D. R. Stober, & A. M. Grant (Eds.), *Evidence based coaching handbook: Putting best practices to work for your clients* (pp. 153–192). Hoboken, NJ: Wiley.

Grant, A. M. (2007). Past, present, and the future: The evolution of professional coaching and coaching psychology. In *Handbook of coaching psychology: A Guide for practitioners* (pp. 23–39). London: Routledge.

Grant, A. M., & Palmer, S. (2002). *Coaching psychology*. Workshop and meeting held at the Annual Conference of the Division of Counselling Psychology. Torquay, UK: British Psychological Society.

Griffith, C. R. (1926). *Psychology of coaching: A study of coaching methods from the point of view of psychology*. New York: Charles Scribner's Sons.

Harris, M. (1999). Look, it's an I-O psychologist. . .no, it's a trainer. . .no, it's an executive coach. *TIP, 36*(3), 1–5.

Hedman, A. (2001). The person-centered approach. In B. Peltier (Ed.), *The psychology of executive coaching: Theory and application* (pp. 66–80). New York: Taylor & Francis.

Hudson, F. M. (1999). *The handbook of coaching*. San Francisco: Jossey-Bass Publishing.

International Coach Federation. (2007). *Global coaching study*. Retrieved from: http://coachfederation.org/about/landing.cfm?ItemNumber=831

International Coach Federation. (n.d.). *ICF ethical guidelines*. Retrieved from: www.icfphoenix.com/wp-content/. . ./icf_ethical_guidelines.pdf

Kampa-Kokesch, S., & Anderson, M. (2001). Executive coaching: A comprehensive review of the literature. *Consulting Psychology Journal: Practice and Research, 53*(4), 205–228.

Kauffman, C. (2006). Positive psychology: The science at the heart of coaching. In D. R. Stober & A. M. Grant (Eds.), *Evidence based coaching handbook: Putting best practices to work for your clients* (pp. 17–50). Hoboken, NJ: Wiley.

Knowles, M. (1978). *The adult learner: A neglected species*. Houston, TX: Gulf Publishing.

Knowles, M., Holton, E. I. I. I., & Swanson, R. (1998). *The adult learner* (5th ed.). Houston, TX: Gulf Publishing.

Kolb, D. A. (1984). *Experiential learning: Experience as the source of learning and development*. Englewood Cliffs, NJ: Prentice Hall.

Lai, Y., & McDowall, A. (2014). A systematic review (SR) of coaching psychology: Focusing on the attributes of effective coaching psychologists. *International Coaching Psychology Review, 9*(2), 118–134.

Madden, W., Green, S., & Grant, A. M. (2011). A pilot study evaluating strengths-based coaching for primary school students: Enhancing engagement and hope. *International Coaching Psychology Review, 6*(1), 71–83.

McLean, P. (2012). *The completely revised handbook of coaching: A developmental approach*. San Francisco, CA: Wiley.

Palmer, S. (2008). The PRACTICE model of coaching: Towards a solution-focused approach. *Coaching Psychology International, 1*(1), 4–8.

Palmer, S. (2015). *ICCP welcome*. Presentation at the 5th international congress of coaching psychology, San Diego, CA.

Palmer, S., & Cavanagh, M. (2006). Editorial-Coaching psychology: Its time has finally come. *International Coaching Psychology Review, 1*(1), 1–3.

Palmer, S., & Whybrow, A. (2006). The coaching psychology movement and its development within the British Psychology Society. *International Coaching Psychology Review, 1*(1), 5–11.

Palmer, S., & Whybrow, A. (2008). *Handbook of coaching psychology: A guide for practitioners.* New York: Routledge.

Parsloe, E. (1995). *Coaching, mentoring, and assessing: A practical guide to developing competence.* New York: Kogan Page.

Pfeiffer, J. W., & Jones, J. E. (1983). *Reference guide to handbooks and annuals.* New York: Wiley.

Raia, A. P. (1965). Goal setting and self-control: An empirical study. *Journal of Management Studies, 2*(1), 34–53.

Rogers, C. R. (1959). A theory of therapy, personality, and interpersonal relationships. In S. Kock (Ed.), *Psychology: A study of science* (pp. 184–256). New York: McGraw-Hill.

Rogers, C. (1961). *On becoming a person.* Boston: Houghton Mifflin Company.

Rogers, C. R. (1980). *A way of being.* Boston: Houghton Mifflin.

Seligman, M. E. P. (1998). Building human strength: Psychology's forgotten mission. *APA Monitor, 29*(1), 1.

Seligman, M. E. P., & Csikszentmihalyi, M. (2000). Positive psychology. An introduction. *American Psychologist, 55*(1), 5–14.

Seligman, M., Steen, T., Park, N., & Peterson, C. (2005). Positive psychology process: Empirical validation of interventions. *American Psychologist, 60*(5), 410–421.

Shapiro, D. (2002). Renewing the scientist-practitioner model. *The Psychologist, 15*(5), 232–233.

Sin, N. L., & Lyubomirsky, S. (2009). Enhancing well-being and alleviating depressive symptoms with positive psychology interventions: A practice-friendly meta-analysis. *Journal of Clinical Psychology, 65*(5), 467–487. doi:10.1002/jclp.20593.

Stober, D. R. (2006). Coaching from the humanist perspective. In D. R. Stober & A. M. Grant (Eds.), *Evidence based coaching handbook: Putting best practices to work for your clients* (pp. 17–50). Hoboken, NJ: Wiley.

Stober, D. R., & Grant, A. M. (2006a). *Evidence based coaching handbook: Putting best practices to work for your clients.* Hoboken, NJ: Wiley.

Stober, D. R., & Grant, A. M. (2006b). Toward a contextual approach to coaching models. In D. R. Stober & A. M. Grant (Eds.), *Evidence based coaching handbook: Putting best practices to work for your clients* (pp. 17–50). Hoboken, NJ: Wiley.

Theeboom, T., Beersma, B., & Van Vianen, A. E. M. (2013). Does coaching work? A meta-analysis on the effects of coaching in individual level outcomes in an organizational context. *The Journal of Positive Psychology, 9,* 1–18. doi:10.1080/17439760.2013.837499.

Vandeveer, V., Pearlman, K., Lowman, R., & Brannick, J. (2015, February). *Coaching competency model for psychologists: Research and development.* Presentation at the 5th international congress of coaching psychology, San Diego, CA.

Whitmore, J. (1992). *Coaching for performance.* London: Nicholas Brealey.

Chapter 3
Roots of Family: Family Life Education

Coaching families requires more than an understanding of coaching psychology. Family and parent coaches do best with an understanding of family science to ground their work in helping families change. This chapter covers family science theory and how those theories can be applied to family life coaching. The primary focus on this chapter, however, is that of Family Life Education (FLE). FLE is one professional area of family science, and family life coaching draws heavily from the theoretical and practical applications of family life education. Theories reviewed include family systems, human growth and development, parent education, and interpersonal relationships.

The goal of this chapter is to help illustrate the importance of understanding family science while working with families by including insights from industry professionals, as well as a recap of recent research on the opinions of use of family coaching in family life. Readers will complete this chapter with a firm understanding of family science theories, evidence based practices of FLE, the ten content areas of FLE, and how those concepts apply to coaching families.

History of Family Life Education

Family Life Education (FLE) is a multidisciplinary practice that seeks to help families gain skills and knowledge necessary to lead a happy, functioning life. While it is likely that families have forever helped each other with family life issues, professional FLE efforts can be traced to just before 1800s, around the onset of self-help books and mother study groups (Duncan & Goddard, 2011). The education of home and family life has evolved around the issues of necessity: food, shelter, and clothes, which was often considered "women's work" (Arcus, Schvaneveldt, & Moss, 1993, p. 28). As the literature of the early days of FLE shows, women would help other women better understand and complete the tasks of family life. During the latter part of the 1800s, formal education and publications

© Springer International Publishing Switzerland 2016
K. Allen, *Theory, Research, and Practical Guidelines for Family Life Coaching*, DOI 10.1007/978-3-319-29331-8_3

were found to help with the education of family life (Arcus et al., 1993). In 1840, Catherine Beecher became an educator, writer, and leader on the issues of family life, particularly on issues of interest to women and the family, and is consider a founder of the field in family science (Levitt, 2002).

From then on, the field continued to grow, in both formal and informal settings. Around the turn of the last century, Cooperative Extension, and more specifically, Family and Consumer Sciences Extension, became a leading organization offering programs to help the family system (Allen, Dunn, & Zaslow, 2011). During the beginning of the first half of the twentieth century, women in agrarian settings worked long hours conducting a variety of tasks such as gardening, caring for the house and children, and helping with the crop production (Jones, 2002). The need for education of rural farmwomen became evident. Research of the time revealed that farm life was isolating, and women and children needed education on the practices of family life (Comer, Campbell, Edwards, & Hillison, 2006). The government set up funding through the Smith-Lever Act of 1914 for Home Demonstration Extension Agents to help educate women and children, and build supportive communities (Jones, 2002). These agents understood that in order to help families, they needed to understand the complexity of the changing family system in America. This became one of the first groups to offer family life education, although then it was called demonstration clubs (Allen et al., 2011). It was through these clubs that women and children learned about farming and economic practices, but equally important, these clubs were social outlets that fostered education of family-life issues (Jones, 2002).

While Extension agents still compromise a large number of family life educators, FLE practice extends far beyond Cooperative Extension. Family Science emerged as a field to help address the needs families were having in dealing with the social problems of the nineteenth century (Doherty, Boss, LaRossa, Schumm, & Steinmetz, 1993). Throughout the past century, concern for limited resource families, particularly those in urban areas, have been the emphasis of many government programs funded to help increase the wellbeing of children and their families. Many of these grant funded programs employed and continue to employ FLE practitioners. In fact, the precursor for Parents as Teachers was established before the turn of the last century (Duncan & Goddard, 2011). Parent education was particularly of interest to the general public. In the 1950s, the Adlerian focus on parenting education was strong as many parents and families came to family demonstrations, or sessions where an Adlerian psychologist would give demonstrations to help parents gain interpersonal insight and parenting skills (Croake, 1983).

While the field of family science, and family life education specifically has grown steadily, with that growth has come many names (i.e. home economics, human ecology) and areas of foci. Arcus et al. (1993) identified two distinct areas of family science; home economics and societal problems relating to family life. To help professionals along the spectrum of family life education and family science, the National Council of Family Relations was formed in 1938 (NCFR, n.d.). While there are other professional organizations that are prominent in the family science field (American Association of Marriage and Family Therapists- AAMFT, American Psychological Association (APA), American Association of Family and Consumer Science-AAFCS, National Extension Association of Family & Consumer

Sciences-NEAFCS to name a few), NCFR holds the certification for family life educators and is a premier multidisciplinary association that is the professional home to 3200 members. NCFR publishes three top scholarly journals of family science, holds a national annual conference, and provides numerous resources to family life educators and family scientists.

Defining Family Life Education

For over 50 years, sizable effort has been expended into the definition of FLE (Arcus, Schvaneveldt, & Moss, 1993), yet there is still no unified definition for family life education (Duncan & Goddard, 2011). One of the earliest definitions of FLE came from Avery & Lee, (1964, p. 27)

> Family life education involves any and all school experiences deliberately and consciously used by teachers in helping to develop the personalities of students to their fullest capacities as present and future family members—those capacities which equip the individual to solve most constructively the problems unique to his family role.

This definition was well received, but some felt the definition too broad. As such, professionals set on the quest to develop a universal definition. From 1964 to 1989, 17 iterations of the definition were highlighted in the FLE literature (Arcus, Schvaneveldt, & Moss, 1993). Today, working definitions can be found in popular FLE texts, such as Duncan and Goddard (2011, p. 4), which define FLE as:

> any educational activity occurring outside a traditional school classroom setting, usually involving adults, that is designed to strengthen relationships in the home and foster positive individual, couple, and family development

Perhaps the most common definition is that of The National Council on Family Relations. On their website, they define FLE as:

> Family life education focuses on healthy family functioning within a family systems perspective and provides a primarily preventive approach. The skills and knowledge needed for healthy functioning are widely known: strong communication skills, knowledge of typical human development, good decision-making skills, positive self-esteem, and healthy interpersonal relationships. The goal of family life education is to teach and foster this knowledge and these skills to enable individuals and families to function optimally.

In addition to the debate on the definition of family life education, there is a continued discussion in the field of the principles and theories guiding FLE work. Thomas and Arcus (1991) state that rather than debating the definition, time would be better spent conducting an analysis of FLE concepts through analytical inquiry. What features must be present in order to be called FLE was the question they explored. Kerchoff (1964) states that FLE had originally been designed to help families prevent and deal with social problems. The development of FLE had three overarching goals: dealing with problems, preventing problems, and developing potential (Arcus, Schvaneveldt, & Moss, 1993). As a result of the decades of discussion on the definition and purpose, Arcus (Arcus et al., 1993) identified operational principles of FLE that were adapted by Duncan and Goddard (2011) as follows:

- Is to be relevant to individuals, couples, and families, across the lifespan;
- Is based on the felt needs of individuals, couples, families, and communities;
- Draws on material from many fields and multi professionals in its practice;
- Is offered in many venues, including community workshops, videos, and print media, publications, the Internet, and other settings;
- Is educational rather than therapeutic;
- Is respectful of diverse values;
- Requires qualified family life educators to realize its goals

The purpose of Family Life Education, then, is to help students better understand relationships. The focus of FLE is on family relationships, both couple relationships, and other familial relationships such as parent-child, sibling, or nontraditional families and through that understanding, build strengths in individuals and families (Arcus, Schvaneveldt, & Moss, 1993). The National Council on Family Relations (1970) went on to say the purposes of family life education was to aid individuals in developing a fulfilling life, guiding them and their families in improving interpersonal relations, and furthering their maximum potential to improve the quality of their life (Arcus et al., 1993). For those having studied coaching psychology, the fit of coaching appears evident in that the goals of coaching are also to build strengths of individuals and help them further potential (Stober & Grant, 2006). It is easy to see how the two fit so well to create family life coaching.

Ten Content Areas of FLE

The National Council of Family Relations offers a national certification to practitioners that have completed practice and education in family life. As part of that certification process, NCFR created ten Family Life Education content areas in which all Certified Family Life Educators (CFLE) must have completed study to be eligible for certification. Additional, academic programs with CFLE academic program approval for undergraduate or graduate programs must include coursework and practice in these ten domain areas:

1. Families and Individuals in Societal Context
2. Internal Dynamics of Families
3. Human Growth and Development Across the Lifespan
4. Human Sexuality
5. Interpersonal Relationships
6. Family Resource Management
7. Parent Education and Guidance
8. Family Law and Public Policy
9. Professional Ethics and Practice
10. Family Life Education Methodology

These ten content areas, described in more detail below, provide a useful content knowledge base for family life coaching. Allen (2013) proposed a framework for

FLC that included the theoretical and practical applications of both coaching psychology and family life education. These ten content areas serve as the primary content areas for the family life coaching framework. Reprinted with permission from the National Council of Family Relations:

FAMILY LIFE EDUCATION CONTENT AREAS

#1. **Families and Individuals in Societal Contexts** - An understanding of families and their relationships to other institutions, such as the educational, governmental, religious, and occupational institutions in society.

> e.g., Structures and Functions; Cultural Variations (family heritage, social class, geography, ethnicity, race & religion); Dating, Courtship, Marital Choice; Kinship; Cross-Cultural and Minority (understanding of lifestyles of minority families and the lifestyles of families in various societies around the world); Changing Gender Roles (role expectations & behaviors of courtship partners, marital partners, parents & children, siblings, and extended kin); Demographic Trends; Historical Issues; Work/Leisure & Family Relationships; Societal Relations (reciprocal influence of the major social institutions and families, i.e., governmental, religious, educational, and economic).

#2. **Internal Dynamics of Families** - An understanding of family strengths and weaknesses and how family members relate to each other.

> e.g., Internal Social Processes (including cooperation & conflict); Communication (patterns & problems in husband-wife relationships and in parent-child relationships, including stress & conflict management); Conflict Management; Decision-making and Goal-setting; Normal Family Stresses (transition periods in the family life cycle, three-generation households, caring for the elderly, & dual careers); Family Stress & Crises (divorce, remarriage, death, economic uncertainty and hardship, violence, substance abuse); Special Needs in Families (including adoptive, foster, migrant, low income, military, and blended families as well as those with disabled members).

#3. **Human Growth and Development Across the Lifespan** - An understanding of the developmental changes of individuals in families throughout the lifespan. Based on knowledge of physical, emotional, cognitive, social, moral, and personality aspects.

> e.g., Prenatal; Infancy; Early and Middle Childhood; Adolescence; Adulthood; Aging.

#4. **Human Sexuality** - An understanding of the physiological, psychological, & social aspects of sexual development throughout the lifespan, so as to achieve healthy sexual adjustment.

> e.g., Reproductive Physiology; Biological Determinants; Emotional and Psychological Aspects of Sexual Involvement; Sexual Behaviors; Sexual Values and Decision-Making; Family Planning; Physiological and Psychological Aspects of Sexual Response; Influence of Sexual Involvement on Interpersonal Relationships.

#5. **Interpersonal Relationships** - An understanding of the development and maintenance of interpersonal relationships.

> e.g., Self and Others; Communication Skills (listening, empathy, self-disclosure, decision-

#6.   Family Resource Management - An understanding of the decisions individuals and families make about developing and allocating resources including time, money, material assets, energy, friends, neighbors, and space, to meet their goals.

> e.g., Goal Setting and Decision-Making; Development and Allocation of Resources; Social Environment Influences; Life Cycle and Family Structure Influences; Consumer Issues and Decisions.

#7.   Parent Education and Guidance - An understanding of how parents teach, guide and influence children and adolescents as well as the changing nature, dynamics and needs of the parent/child relationship across the lifespan.

> e.g., Parenting Rights and Responsibilities; Parenting Practices/Processes; Parent/Child Relationships; Variation in Parenting Solutions; Changing Parenting Roles across the Lifespan.

#8.   Family Law and Public Policy - An understanding of legal issues, policies, and laws influencing the well-being of families.

> e.g., Family and the Law (relating to marriage, divorce, family support, child custody, child protection & rights, & family planning); Family and Social Services; Family and Education; Family and the Economy; Family and Religion; Policy and the Family (public policy as it affects the family, including tax, civil rights, social security, economic support laws, & regulations.)

#9.   Professional Ethics and Practice - An understanding of the character and quality of human social conduct, and the ability to critically examine ethical questions and issues as they relate to professional practice

> e.g., Formation of Social Attitudes and Values; Recognizing and Respecting the Diversity of Values and the Complexity of Value Choice in a Pluralistic Society; Examining Value Systems and Ideologies systematically and objectively; Social Consequences of Value Choices; Recognizing the Ethical Implications of Social and Technological Changes, Ethics of Professional Practice.

#10.   Family Life Education Methodology - An understanding of the general philosophy and broad principles of family life education in conjunction with the ability to plan, implement, and evaluate such educational programs.

> e.g., Planning and Implementing; Evaluation (materials, student progress, & program effectiveness); Education Techniques; Sensitivity to Others (to enhance educational effectiveness); Sensitivity to Community Concerns and Values (understanding of the public relations process).

References

Bredehoft, D.J. & Cassidy, D. (Eds.) (1995). Family life education curriculum guidelines (2nd ed.). Minneapolis: National Council on Family Relations.

Bredehoft, D.J. & Walcheski, M.J. (Eds.). (2011). The family life education framework poster and PowerPoint. Minneapolis, MN: National Council on Family Relations.

National Council on Family Relations. (2014). Family life education content areas: Content and practice guidelines. Minneapolis, MN: Author. Retrieved from https://www.ncfr.org/sites/default/files/downloads/news/fle_content_and_practice_guidelines_2014.pdf

Family Life Education's Role in Family Science

Although family science incorporates a variety of practice and practitioners, there has recently been a debate amongst family scholars about the boundaries of practice. Bill Doherty (1995) established a hierarchal system with five levels of family practice designed to help professionals understand boundaries when serving families. His premise was that ethically speaking, educational efforts are quite different than therapeutic efforts and thus he felt it important to identify those differences in order to create boundaries to protect both the individual and the practitioner. Doherty said it this way: "here, then, is the conundrum: In order to accomplish its purpose, parent and family education must have more personal depth than other forms of education, but too much depth or intensity risks harming participants, or at least scaring them away" (1995, p. 353).

Doherty proposed these five levels:

1. **Minimal emphasis on family.** These programs are factually based and limited in scope. Example: parent-teacher conference.
2. **Information and advice.** Level two programs are collaborative and the presenter typically has specialized information to share. Example: one-time parenting workshop.
3. **Feeling and Support.** While similar in knowledge and skills of level two, level three includes emotion and shared experiences. Level three practitioners need training specific to working with families as they are engaged in a relationship that is more than the transfer of knowledge. Duncan and Goddard (2011) cite this stage as being where much of FLE takes place. Example: 8-week parent education program.
4. **Brief Focused Intervention.** At this level, FLE educators might work with families with higher needs such as high populations or special needs. This level is more personal in nature, and requires training above and beyond typical FLE training settings. Example: I would argue family coaching fits in this level, but could also be populations such a teen parents where the FLE educator works on systemic problems and solution.
5. **Family Therapy.** Level five is outside the boundaries of family life and parent education as it requires specific training in psychology and therapeutic interactions.

Doherty's levels became a staple in family life education, but many in the field expressed concerns about the boundaries. In response to Doherty's levels of family involvement model and other research on the roles of family life educators. Myers-Walls, Ballard, Darling, and Myers-Bowman (2011) introduced a reconceptualization of the domain and boundaries of Family Life Education. In their article, they stated that Doherty's levels do "not provide an accurate description of FLE, nor does it identify the boundaries and differentiation we seek" (p. 358). They worked to broaden the scope by introducing domains of practice for family life education, family case management, and family therapy. Their article generated a great deal of conversation and is helping to shape the direction of family life education for the twenty-first century.

The discussion on what family life education is and where it fits in family science demonstrates that the profession is still emerging and in flux. Family life educators must be relevant and must draw a clientele in order to remain viable. Family life coaching is perhaps the newest attempt in the literature on how to help FLE remain current. Allen and Huff (2014) suggested family life coaching be considered a 4th domain of family practice. There is more on that study in Chap. 4. What is clear is that there is a great amount of energy and attention being paid on how to best serve and improve the well-being of children and families, and much of that work happens with family life education.

Understanding boundaries and domains are not the only points of contention in FLE. Doherty (2000) described family life education as a "trickle down model of research and practice" (p. 319) where the university-level family life scholars create new knowledge and evidence-based programs, and then pass that information onto families in the community through family life practitioners. In essence, families get research-based, evidence-based information, and programs that are developed by PhD professionals, and that information is then disseminated by community practice experts such as parenting educators, family life educators, and other community-based programs. There are advantages of this model, according to Doherty, in that problems can be addressed scientifically. The down side, then, is limited contribution from families and communities. In the trickle down model, families are seen as consumers, and not collaborators.

While Doherty outlines the idea of a top-down approach to family life education, Duncan and Goddard (2011) point out that there are a variety of roles in family life education, which are designed to be inclusive of community and families more as partners than consumers. Although the expert role is widely used, the facilitator approach is also a common role for family life educators. The facilitator approach, which is also common in coaching, favors greater flexibility and promotes decision making by the participants. Other roles identified by Duncan and Goddard include: the critical inquirer, the collaborator, the interventionists, and eclectic approaches. For more information on these roles, see Duncan & Goddard, 2011, chapter one.

While there is some debate on the roles and best model for family life education, it is advised that practitioners have a clear idea about what they hope to accomplish with FLE (Powell & Cassidy, 2007). Program Development, which will be reviewed in more detail below, is a staple of family life education. With program development, practitioners must identify a need, plan and implement a program to meet that need, and then evaluate the effectiveness of the program regarding that need. Program development and family life education in general, focus on identifying program goals and objectives to suit the needs of the consumers. However, some will argue that family life education is much more than programming or knowledge transfer. Guerney and Guerney (1981) argue that family life education is an intervention, and thus should be labeled so. Although there is still debate in the field about who we are and how we fit in family science, there is no debate that the goal is to help families improve the quality of their lives.

The exciting part about introducing family and parent coaching into the realm of family science is that Doherty's concern is overtly addressed because coaches not only collaborate with families, but they see the family as the expert of their own lives. Coaching is not a top down approach; rather it is a partnership based on equality. Coaches work as partners with families, albeit partners with process and content expertise, working together on helping families reach their potential. Family life coaching utilizes a family systems perspective. Although family life coaches might work directly with only one member of a family (often a parent or partner), they coach under the systems framework noting that all members of a family will be impacted by the change of one member.

Theoretical Overview of FLE

Family science is a field rich in tradition and theories. While the gamut of family science theories is far too wide and complex to include them all in this chapter, I have created an outline of the theories most closely identified with family life education. In addition, I spend even greater attention on the theories that convene well with family life coaching. The outline below highlights six categories of family science most often associated with FLE and the primary theorists associated with each theory. This is by no means a theoretical overview nor is it a comprehensive representation, but rather an acknowledgement of the varying theories underpinning family life education.

- Psychoanalytical Theories

  - Psychosexual: Sigmund Freud
  - Psychosocial: Erik Erikson

- Behavioral & Social Learning Theories

  - Behaviorism: Classical Conditioning—John Watson & Operant Conditioning—B.F. Skinner
  - Social Learning: Albert Bandera

- Biological Theories

  - Maturationism: G. Stanley Hall & Arnold Gesell
  - Ethology: Konrad Lorenz
  - Attachment: John Bowlby

- Cognitive Theories

  - Cognitive Development: Jean Piaget
  - Socio-cultural: Lev Vygotsky
  - Learning: Montessori
  - Individual Psychology: Alfred Adler

- Systems Theories

  - Ecological Systems: Urie Bronfenbrenner
  - Family Systems: Murray Bowen, Virginia Satir
  - Lifespan

- Learning Theories

  - Adult: Malcolm Knowles
  - Gestalt: Wolfgang Kohler
  - Constructivism: Jean Piaget, Lev Vygotsky

- Communication & Interpersonal Relationship Theories

  - Relationship: John Gottman
  - Social Exchange Theory
  - Symbolic Interaction

- Diversity, Culture and Theories of Inclusion

While each theory deserves time and attention, this chapter will focus on Human Ecological, Family Systems, Life Cycle, Program Development, and Adult Learning Theories.

Human Ecological Theory

Urie Bronfenbrenner's ecological theory (1986) is the foundation for most applied family work, either directly or indirectly. Bronfenbrenner's theory provides a framework that describes how physical and social surroundings (social networks, neighborhood, school, workplace, community, government institutions, etc.) influence individuals and families. This also includes how individuals and families may influence their surroundings.

Considering human ecology in FLE is necessary because families function within systems and without understanding those systems, the work of family science is not possible. As Bronfenbrenner puts it, in order to better understand a system (i.e. individual, couple, or family, and their behaviors and decisions), it is critical to understand how the system influences those factors and is influenced by other systems (environment/surroundings). As individuals who will serve adults, children, youth and families, you can focus on how family, community, social, economic, and political factors affect situations of those being served. You can help facilitate change, even if you are not an expert about the system. Bronfenbrenner's (1986) systems include:

- The microsystem—activities and interactions in the child's immediate surroundings: parents, school, friends, etc.
- The mesosystem—relationships among the entities involved in the child's microsystem: parents' interactions with teachers, a school's interactions with the daycare provider

- The exosystem—social institutions which affect children indirectly: the parents' work settings and policies, extended family networks, mass media, community resources
- The macrosystem—broader cultural values, laws and governmental resources
- The chronosystem—changes which occur during a child's life, both personally, like the birth of a sibling and culturally, such as racial intolerance

These systems can feel abstract, so to illustrate a point, I want you to think about a child you know. First, think about that child's microsystem; their parents, friends, teachers—would you consider that child to be in a supportive microsystem? Now think about the mesosystem; does he or she have parents that engage with other adults in the microsystem? Do the child's parents, for example, meet with teachers? What institutions are supportive to this child? Are the parents able to easily take off work when the child is sick, for example? Now let's look at the broader culture; the macrosystem. Is this child Latino? Black? White? Living in a suburb or city? What laws or cultural values impact this child? Finally, think about the chronosystem, or the changes this child has had. Did she have a stable life?

If we think about helping families, we must remember to think about the fit between the individual and their environment. This is done by developing, maintaining, or strengthening supportive interventions and reducing, challenging, or replacing stressful systems. The Search Institute (2007) created a tool called the 40 developmental assets. Originally, the tool was used to help child development practitioners better understand the child's environment from a strengths-based approach. The tool helps the provider understand what assets are accessible to the child. Now, however, the Search Institute is a broad organization that helps professionals assess the strengths of families as well as youth and communities. For more information, see http://www.search-institute.org/research/developmental-assets.

Family Systems

Families are made of strange glue—they stretch, but never let go. (Nichols & Schwartz, 1998)

Although the individual's environment is considered in human ecology, the family system is identified as the most influential system in which family scientists can implement change. In fact, most family scientists agree that the familial system is the heart and soul of wellbeing for individuals and communities. Families are systems of interconnected and interdependent individuals, and this theory views the family as a collective organism that includes family roles, rules, expectations, boundaries, and equilibrium (Nichols & Schwartz, 1998). The family system impacts wellbeing from birth to death. Patterns and traditions, overtly or covertly are past down from generation to generation.

Virginia Satir (1972) is considered one of the pioneers of family systems theory. While we focus on family communication in Chap. 8, communication is, of course, a major component of family systems theory. Satir is considered to be a leading figure in the model of family communication theory and she believed the role of the family origin has a significant influence on a person's life and wellbeing. While individuals come to the table with past experiences that shape their interpersonal relationships, Satir also understood that people are doing the best they can at any given time. Satir believed dysfunction comes with poor communication in the family of origin, and when given skills, they do better. To Satir, communication was the core of happy, healthy families and she saw it as the practitioner's role to help the client become aware of and then access their inner resources (Miller & McLendon, 2010). With new skills, people can and will make healthier behaviors that benefit the whole family system.

Satir suggested that families are not only complex and influential, but also that family balance is contingent upon the individuals and their roles. She proposed the idea of role theory, the idea that roles provide regularity to complex social situations. The roles we play in our family are important in understanding individual motives. Changing a role isn't that easy; if one person changes, it impacts the whole system. For example, if the father leaves the family unit the stay at home mother is forced to go to work to financially support the family. All other members of the family must adjust their roles to account for the new role the mother must adopt. That is one reason that change is difficult.

Family rules is another family systems concept identified by Satir. Rules are the ideas and exceptions for how the family operates. Some rules are clearly stated while others are simply understood. The rules and the family roles contribute to the families' homeostasis and balance. Families with dysfunction, then often have difficulty with roles and rules and as result, have low self-esteem and defensive behaviors. It is the role of the therapist, then, to make contact with all family members and affirm their worth. Building a positive Rogerian-style relationship rapport helps create a readiness for change (Rogers, 1961). Once rapport has been established, the therapist disturbs the status quo by offering insights and helping the families see new understanding of each other's roles and rules. Finally, the therapist's role is helping the family integrate new skills and balance based on high functioning behaviors.

Murray Bowen's family systems theory (1993) is another top theory to come out of the family systems movement. Bowen focused a great deal of his theory on multi-generational issues. Like most family systems theorists, Bowen suggested that families bring with them family secrets and patterns from generations past. While generations were a big part of Bowen's work, he also focused greatly on siblings and parents, and the concepts of Triangulation—bringing in a third person (often from the family) during conflict. In this concept, one family member will bring in a third person to help win an argument. For example, a parent might bring in the child to help support their point of view "I'm not the only one that feels this way; our child thinks you are a bad parent too. Just ask her. Heck, I'll ask [engages child in the conversation]...Julia, tell dad how you really feel about his parenting."

Bowen believed that change was slow, and that the role of the therapist was to help families identify patterns, and then change those patterns. Like Satir, Bowen believed communication was key, and promoted the use of disclosure to help families understand patterns. Therapists might explain how triangulation works with their own family in order to demonstrate the point. One of the benefits of Bowen therapy is to help parents learn to keep their children out of the adult conflict patterns.

There are a myriad of family systems theorists that could be explored. For example, Salvador Minuchin's Structural Therapy, Albert Ellis' Rational Emotive Therapy, Bateson's Mental Research Institute (MRI), Madanes and Haley's Strategic and Solution Focused therapy (to be discussed on Chap. 8) are all significant contributors to family systems theory. The overarching concepts of family systems include effective communication, family structure and interactions, patterns of behaviors, boundaries, and feelings of connectedness. One important assumption is that family systems theory does not view families or individuals as pathological, but as dysfunctional.

Family life coaches can employ a significant amount of information from family systems theory to help their clients meet their goals. As coaches, understanding that the decisions of one individual directly impact all family members is critical for successful change. In fact, it is our responsibility to help family members understand as they move forward towards their desired goals, this will also affect other members in their family unit. A goal of family coaching then would be towards family, family of origin, and intergenerational connectedness. It is helpful when families can normalize their functioning, and create healthy patterns of engagement. In fact, we can assist a "derailed" family in getting back on their developmental track.

Family Life Cycle

The education of a family life educator must include information about the life cycle of the family. This developmental theory of the family often is identified in stages, but as the current family structures of our times suggest, family stages are certainly not linear in nature. So while some might consider the life cycle somewhat arbitrary (Winton, 1995), it is still of conceptual importance to both family life educators and family coaches. As with most theories, there are a variety of life cycle or family development models. Duvall (1977) identified an eight-stage cycle of family development.

1. Married couple
2. Childbearing
3. Preschool age
4. School age
5. Teenage
6. Launching center

7. Middle aged
8. Aging family members

The criticisms of Duvall's stages are that many families no longer (or may have never) fit into the stage cycles presented. In fact, new statistics on family structures show that there are more unmarried couples than couples and the rate of couples opting to remain childless is growing. Hill and Rogers (1964) developed a more general model that attempted to be more accepting of family structures and Mattessich and Hill (1987) focused more on the processes of change than the specific stages. Although much debate has littered the field of the family life cycle, there is some agreement about the common phases of the family life cycle. It can be helpful to conceptualize stages of families' life cycles, such as the stages below, even though not all individuals become a couple and not all couples have children.

1. Childhood
2. Becoming an adult
3. Becoming a couple
4. Becoming parents
5. Having adolescents
6. Launching phase
7. Later life

Clearly, a model of family life cycle is in need of flexibility and accommodation for the changing dynamics of family structure. However, as Powell and Cassidy (2007) point out, the process of analyzing roles and developmental tasks common in life cycle stages can help families prepare for what is next. Furthermore, having discussions about the nature and dynamics of family processes and structures can help family professionals better understand the realities of family life. Powell and Cassidy (2007) also note that family life educators would benefit from organizing family life programs around stages, as they tend to have better long-term effectiveness and address current trends and issues. The same is true of family life coaches. Having a clear understanding of the developmental process of families is useful in helping clients navigate changes. Transitions are difficult for many people, and parents typically seek out help during periods of transition (Baker, 2014). When working with families and the family life cycle, it is also important to recognize cultural and generational differences.

Program Development in Family Life Education

Program development is one on the ten contents of family life education, and virtually no student graduates from a CFLE approved program without receiving extensive training on programming. Arcus and Thomas (1993) present family life education as preventative education; in fact they call prevention a guiding principle of family life education. As such, the focus of most family life education programs is to create protective factors and resiliency in family life content areas while also understanding the risk factors (Duncan & Goddard, 2011). Based on risk and protective factors, many models of program development were created (see Hughes, 1994; Dumka, Roosa, Michaels, & Suh, 1995; Bogenschneider, 1996 for examples). The common thread in each of these models includes the steps of designing a program, creating content, and evaluation.

Further investigation of program development demonstrates that effective programs are theory driven, have enough sessions to influence progress, are compressive, engaging, developmentally appropriate, and are culturally competent (Small, Cooney, & O'Conner, 2009). Duncan and Goddard (2011) created a comprehensive model for program development that included the following stages:

1. *Problem analysis.* In this stage, the program developer researches the topic of interest to identify current literature and existing evidence of promising practices. This step includes identification of the theoretical underpinning and the creation of a stakeholder coalition that will work together to address the program.
2. *Program Design.* Once a review has been completed and the foundation analysis is finished, the program designer will begin to directly assess the needs of the target population and create learning objectives. Program evaluation is also under development in this second stage, which is where the instruments that measure the outcomes of the learning activities will be developed. Programmatic decisions, such as length of program, program activities, and logistics will be planned.
3. *Pilot testing.* In this stage, the program is delivered to a subgroup of the target population in order to be tested and evaluated before launching to a larger population. Evaluation is a major component of pilot testing, as results can inform needed changes.
4. *Advanced Testing.* Based on the outcome and process evaluation of the pilot test, changes are made and the program is refined. During this stage, the evaluation component is testing for evidence of efficacy. Many programs seek the highest levels of program evaluation, including randomized control trials or experiential design that includes pre/post/follow up evaluation with a control group design.
5. *Dissemination.* Once evaluation results are in, the program has been found effective, and changes have been made, it is time to share the program with the larger target audience with the goal being widespread adoption of the program.

Program design is critical to family life educators, as the best programs follow a modicum of adherence to this scientific process. However, this process is vastly different than coaching. Unlike Family Life Educators, coaches do not necessarily develop or implement programs as part of the practice. It is important, however, for those serving families and parents to understand the process of coaching will more than likely become a part of a holistic approach to serving families. I suspect families will have and utilize access to both family life programs (classes, for example) in conjunction with coaching. In fact, many programs are already combining the two areas to create more meaningful experiences for families.

An example of a combination of coaching and program development can be found through North Carolina State University's Very Important Parent program (VIP). The VIP program followed the five-stage process of program development to create a program designed to help teen parents and their children lead successful lives. VIP is a 12 week program that works with teen parents, their families, and their childcare providers to cultivate knowledge of child development, parenting, interpersonal relationship and life skills.

In an approach commonly found in Family Life Education program development, the literature was reviewed, researchers surveyed the needs of teen parents through focus groups and created a year-long face-to-face program that incorporated a great deal of technology. The program was piloted with four cohorts over the course of a year, and found that although the outcomes were being met, the teens wanted information presented in a different way. Based on their feedback, the program was tweaked so that it became a 12-week online program with engagements lasting a year. With limited research on online teen parenting training programs, it was discovered that an important element was missing; the building of the one-on-one relationship that allowed parents to learn and reach their personal goals.

Zach and his daughter Zailyn engaging in online coaching with their VIP coach, Christina

What makes VIP innovative and effective is that it also included family life coaching as a critical component of the parent education program. Teen parents now receive the educational information of a traditional program, while also receiving a minimum of six coaching sessions throughout the 12-week program.

Young parents attend weekly sessions that provide education on topics such as positive discipline, emotion coaching, and relationship education and that is coupled with six session of individualized family life coaching. In the coaching sessions, the parents work with the coach to identify specific goals, and then develop action steps for achieving those goals.

Evaluation of the program is underway, but preliminary evidence shows that this combined approach fosters knowledge and skill development with the online education, and enhances personal parenting performance and increased goal attainment. The one-on-one process paired with educational programming is proving to be highly effective and is a model being showcased in other family service fields including social work and development disabilities therapy.

Family life coaching is certainly part of the plan on the future for family science, and when our field does an even better job of promoting the warm, fruitful relationships of humanistic and coaching psychology with the tried and true methods of family life programming, families will benefit.

Adult Learning Styles

While few texts or articles talk specifically about adult learning styles, many references to how adults learn are explored in family life texts (see Powell & Cassidy, 2007; Duncan & Goddard, 2011; Arcus et al., 1993). Andragogy, or the art and science of helping adults learn (Knowles, 1998) is a useful knowledge base for family life educators and coaches. Adults that take part in unconventional education come with a motivation to learn. Understanding learning styles, delivery methods, and engagement experiences are helpful components of adult education. Information must be relevant, problem centered, activity based, and experiences crucial in order for adult learning to be effective.

It is common knowledge that we all learn differently. The field of education is continually growing as we are learning more and more about how children learn and how adults learn. Learning can be broken into how we receive information (perception) and how we use information (order) (Gregorc, 1982). Learning styles can often be broken into four styles:

Concrete Sequential (CS): GOLD
Abstract Sequential (AS): GREEN
Abstract Random (AR): BLUE
Concrete Random (CR): ORANGE

Concrete sequential learners are orderly, and prefer a clean plan that gets them from point A to B. Abstract sequential learners often are analytic in their thinking, and want a great deal of information and time to process their options. Abstract random learners are sensitive and often have keen perception. These learners tend to care deeply, and are often interested in how decisions will impact others. Concrete random learners are often curious, creative, and realistic. These learners are innovative, and might challenge the process, or even the teacher by thinking independently.

Color personality quizzes have become a fun and entertaining way to better understand oneself, and are sometimes used in professional development settings. The colors are most often Gold, Green, Blue, and Orange; these colors relate directly to the Gregorc learning styles. So someone that identifies as gold (CS) likes order, respects rules, and procedures. Greens (AS) are visionary; they are careful and systematic, and like to collect data before making a decision. Blues (AR) are the sensitive types that are caring and nurturing. Orange (CR) are the adventurous types; they are quick, fun, and often perform well under pressure.

Do you see yourself in a learning style? What about your client? It is important to consider your own learning style and to pay attention to how that style relates to that of your client. There are many non-scientific color personality tests available for free on the internet. Completing an online inventory can be a fun way to gain insight about yourself. It can be quite useful as well; our learning styles often impact how we interact with others, and specifically how we coach others. Knowing our own styles can be helpful in understanding what we need to do to motivate and support our clients, which could likely be from a different style. There is no right or wrong style; and some styles mesh better than others. It is also important to recognize that most of us are a combination of these styles, and so no one person will fit exactly into only one category.

Chapter Summary

The past two chapters have articulated the theoretical and practical backgrounds that create the underpinnings of family life coaching. The field of coaching families and parents exists, and has been in practice for more than a decade, yet there is scant literature on training competencies, professional certifications, or professional associations for family life coaches. Chapter 13 provides a rich discussion on the need for professionalism in family life coaching as it relates to family science and coaching psychology. In the mean time, the next several chapters work to clearly describe the process of coaching as well as the specific theories and evidence-based practices of family life coaching with targeted audiences of couples, parents, and families with disabilities.

"Imagination is more important than knowledge. For while knowledge defines all we currently know and understand, imagination points to all we might yet discover and create." **Albert Einstein**

References

40 Developmental Assets for Adolescents. (2007). Retrieved February 16, 2015, from http://www. search-institute.org/content/40-developmental-assets-adolescents-ages-12-18

Allen, K. (2013). A framework for family life coaching. *International Coaching Psychology Review, 8*(1), 72–79.

Allen, K., Dunn, C., & Zaslow, S. (2011). Ozzie and Harriet never were: A century review of family and consumer sciences and the changing American family. *Journal of Extension* [On-Line], *49*(3), Article 3COM1. Available at: http://www.joe.org/joe/2011june/comm1.php

Allen, K., & Huff, N. L. (2014). Family coaching: An emerging family science field. *Family Relations: An Interdisciplinary Journal of Applied Family Studies, 63*(5), 569–582. doi:10.1111/fare.12087.

Arcus, M. E., Schvaneveldt, J. D., & Moss, J. J. (Eds.) (1993). *Handbook of family life education: The practice of family life education* (Vol. 2). Newbury Park, CA: Sage.

Arcus, M. E., & Thomas, J. (1993). *The nature and practice of family life education*. In M. E. Arcus, J. D. Schvaneveldt, & J. J. Moss (Eds.), *Handbook of family life education: The practice of family life education* (Vol. 2). Newbury Park, CA: Sage.

Avery, C. E., & Lee, M. R. (1964). Family life education: Its philosophy and purpose. *The Family Life Coordinator, 13*(2), 27–37.

Baker, T. (2014). *Family coaching: An exploratory study of parental perceptions* (Master's thesis). Retrieved from http://repository.lib.ncsu.edu/ir/handle/1840.16/1/simple-search?query=family+coaching

Bogenschneider, K. (1996). An ecological risk/protective theory for building prevention programs, policies, and community capacity to support youth. *Family Relations, 45*, 127–138.

Bowen, M. (1993). *Family therapy in clinical practice*. Lanham, MD: Rowman & Littlefield.

Bronfenbrenner, U. (1986). Ecology of the family as a context for human development: Research perspectives. *Developmental Psychology, 22*(6), 723–742.

Comer, M., Campbell, T., Edwards, K., & Hillison, J. (2006). Cooperative extension and the 1890 land-grant institution: The real story. *Journal of Extension [On-line], 44*(3). Available at: http://www.joe.org/joe/2006june/a4.php

Croake, J. W. (1983). Adlerian parent education. *The Counseling Psychologist, 11*(3), 65–71.

Doherty, W. J. (1995). Boundaries between parent and family education and family therapy: The levels of family involvement model. *Family Relations, 44*(4), 353–358.

Doherty, W. J. (2000). Family science and family citizenship: Toward a model of community partnership with families. *Family Relations, 49*, 319–325.

Doherty, W. J., Boss, P. G., LaRossa, R., Schumm, W. R., & Steinmetz, S. K. (1993). Family theories and methods: A contextual approach. In P. G. Boss, W. J. Doherty, R. LaRossa, W. R. Schumm, & S. K. Steinmetz (Eds.), *Sourcebook of family theories and methods: A contextual approach* (pp. 3–30). New York: Plenum Press. doi:10.1007/978-0-387-85764-0_1.

Dumka, L. E., Roosa, M. W., Michaels, M. L., & Suh, K. W. (1995). Using research and theory to develop prevention programs for high-risk families. *Family Relations, 44*, 78–86.

Duncan, S. F., & Goddard, H. W. (2011). *Family life education principles and practices for effective outreach*. Los Angeles: Sage.

Duvall, E. M. (1977). *Marriage and family development* (5th ed.). New York: Lippincott.

Gregorc, A. F. (1982). *An adult's guide to style*. Columbia: CT: Learning Style United.

Guerney, B., & Guerney, I. F. (1981). Family life education as intervention. *Family Relations, 30*, 591–598.

Hill, R., & Rogers, R. H. (1964). The developmental approach. In H. Christensen (Ed.), *Handbook of marriage and the family*. Chicago: Rand McNally.

Hughes, R. J. (1994). A framework for developing family life education programs. *Family Relations, 43*, 74–80.

Jones, L. A. (2002). *Mama learned us to work: Farm women in the new south*. Chapel Hill: University of North Carolina Press.

Kerchoff, R. K. (1964). Family life education in America. In H. T. Christensen (Ed.), *Handbook of marriage and the family* (pp. 881–911). Chicago: Rand McNally.

Knowles, M. S. (1998). *The adult learner* (5th ed.). Houston: Gulf.

Levitt, S. A. (2002). *From Catherine Beecher to Martha Steward: A cultural history of domestic advice*. Chapel Hill, NC: University of NC Press.

Mattessich, P., & Hill, R. (1987). Life cycle and family development. In M. B. Susssman & S. K. Steinmetz (Eds.), *Handbook of marriage and the family*. New York: Plenum Press.

Miller, A., & McLendon, J. (2010). *Instructor's manual for Satir family therapy*. Retrieved from http://www.psychotherapy.net/data/uploads/5113e4b6b7d5d.pdf

Myers-Walls, J. A., Ballard, S. M., Darling, C. A., & Myers-Bowman, K. S. (2011). Reconceptualizing the domain and boundaries of family life education. *Family Relations, 60*(4), 357–372.

National Council on Family Relations. (1970). Position paper on family life education. *The Family Coordinator, 19*, 186.

National Council on Family Relations. (n.d.). *We are NCFR*. Retrieved from https://www.ncfr.org/sites/default/files/downloads/news/general_ncfr_powerpoint_2015_update.pdf

Nichols, M. P., & Schwartz, R. C. (1998). *Family therapy: Concepts and methods* (xix, 586 pages). Needman Heights, MA: Allyn & Bacon.

Powell, L., & Cassidy, D. (2007). *Family life education: Working with families across the life span Long Grove*. IL: Waveland Press.

Rogers, C. (1961). *On becoming a person*. Boston: Houghton Mifflin Company.

Satir, V. (1972). *Peoplemaking*. Palo Alto, CA: Science and Behavior Books.

Small, S. A., Cooney, S. M., & O'Conner, C. (2009). Evidence-informed program improvement: Using principles of effectiveness to enhance the quality and impact of family-based prevention programs. *Family Relations, 58*, 1–13.

Stober, R. D., & Grant, A. M. (2006). *Evidence based coaching handbook: Putting best practices to work for your clients*. Hoboken, NJ: Wiley.

Thomas, J., & Arcus, M. (1991 or 1992). *What's in a name? Home economics education or health education or family life education*. In Proceedings of a Canadian symposium: Issues and directions for home economics/family studies education (pp. 129–144). Winnipeg, Manitoba.

Winton, C. A. (1995). *Frameworks for studying families*. Guilford, CT: Dushkin.

Chapter 4
Theoretical Applications, Research, and Practice of Family Life Coaching

So far you have learned why there is a need for a book on coaching, including the logic of the term "family life coach." Theory and practice of both coaching psychology and family life education have been reviewed as they relate to family life coaching. This chapter explores the current research on family life coaching with emphasis on the results from a grounded theory study of family life coaches. Based on the results of that study, as well as other recent studies of family life coaching, a model of theory and practice of family life coaching is presented. I would like to note that while I categorize all coaches that work specifically on family life related content as FLC, many have alternative titles, including parent coach, family coach, and family educator (as discussed in Chap. 1).

The theoretical underpinnings of family life coaching come from three primary sources: family life education literature, coaching psychology literature, and literature on family life coaching. To be clear, family life coaching literature is new, and much of what is presented in this chapter comes from my own research. I will highlight the theories identified in a current grounded theory study (Allen & Baker, 2016) of family life coaches. Seventeen FLCs were interviewed and asked about their theoretical perspectives in coaching. However, there is a great deal of coaching literature related to family life issues (see Chap. 12 for family life coaching content literature review), and the theories listed here come from a combination of the three literature fields.

> What I love about coaching families is that it is encouraging, and it's supportive to the family. It's much a more respectful process. The role of the coach allows more enthusiasm with the family, while underlining the strengths and values of the family. **Susan Gasman, Trainer, Curriculum Developer**

© Springer International Publishing Switzerland 2016
K. Allen, *Theory, Research, and Practical Guidelines for Family Life Coaching*,
DOI 10.1007/978-3-319-29331-8_4

Theoretical Underpinnings of Family Life Coaching

It is the responsibility of every practicing coach to understand the theory directing his or her coaching practice. However, we must begin with a definition. While a formalized definition of Family Life Coaching is still under development, we can safely say that Family Life Coaching is a model of infusing coaching psychology and family life education as an approach to helping families create and reach their goals (Allen, 2013). Family life coaching involves engaging the family (individual, couple, parents, or family unit) as partners in the change process—working with families as they gain insight, knowledge, and skills to make meaningful changes in their lives. In its most basic form, family life coaching is a process where the coach helps the client reach self-identified goals.

> Therapy is about uncovering and recovering, while coaching is about discovering. Partick Williams

Like most areas of family science, the coaching process aims to help a client succeed in family-life related areas. Scholars suggest that coaching and other family science forms, such as therapy, come from the same roots of psychology and human development (Williams, 2003). Yet there are many fundamental differences that must be identified. In coaching, clients define their success and are viewed as an expert in their own lives. A FLC coach is a trained professional in both family science and coaching practices. The coaching process fosters personal and familial growth by offering encouragement, values clarification and accountability, primarily through powerful questions. Coaching is a development model rather than a medical model, and is future focused (Williams, 2003).

In preparation for this book, I conducted a study where I interviewed 17 coaches that currently coach on family life issues. Upon reflection on that data, the theoretical underpinnings identified included Ecological Theory, Positive Psychology, Adlerian Theory, Solution Focus Coaching, Adult Learning Theory, Humanistic Theory, Gottman's Emotion Coaching and Bandura's Social Learning Theory. Although this list is not fully inclusive of all theoretical underpinnings used in family life coaching, these are the theories most relevant to serving families, are congruent with family life education and coaching psychology, and were identified in the grounded theory as most relevant to coaching parents and families. Therefore they are the focus of this chapter.

One other observation made was that there were relatively few mentions of coaching ideology or coach-specific theory in this study. This reinforces, in my opinion, the importance of both the coaching psychology and family life education theoretical backgrounds. The work being done in family life coaching is congruent with both family life education and coaching psychology theories, which both have roots in family science and psychology. Although coaching models were not listed in this study, they are important and should be addressed, therefore a few of the most common coach models will be explored in Chap. 7.

Specific to families, coaching provides a structured means by which knowledge can be imparted and skills can be shared in a reciprocal process. These skills can be further honed and the reciprocity of nurturing feedback can be exchanged in the family to the key people in a child's life, their caregivers and/or parents (Rush, Shelden, & Hanft, 2003). Coaching can take place in the home, in office/clinic settings, or remotely, making it an easy and convenient resource for busy families. Broadly defined, coaching is a process-driven relationship between a learner and a coach designed to foster achievement of some set, agreed-upon goals to include growth, change, fulfillment, and so forth, in life or work (Heimendinger et al., 2007). This definition includes the broad family-life issues families encounter through the life course.

Humanistic Approach

Having the ability to establish a positive, supportive relationship with a client was one of the most common answers listed about what is important in the role of a family life coach. While Rogers, or the Humanistic perspective were not specifically named by a great number of the participants, nearly all spoke highly and often about the importance of building a relationship. In his book, On Becoming a Person, Carl Rogers (1961) talked about what the research of his time said about the quality of the therapeutic relationship and its impact on the therapy process. Although family life coaches are not therapists, the quality of the client/coach relationship continues to be highly important in the coach/client relationship (Grant, 2014). In the spirit of Carl Roger's person-centered approach to build quality relationships, coaches need to be trustworthy and dependable as well as authentic and genuine. Perhaps even more importantly, coaches must express "attitudes of warmth, caring, liking, interest, respect" and be able to separate their own experiences from their clients' experiences (Rogers, 1961, p. 52). Finally, Rogers stated to be an effective catalyst for change, a practitioner must always understand and accept that the client is in the process of becoming. Clients in the process means they have a journey; they will make mistakes and have limitations, but it is their journey and we, the coaches, must provide unconditional positive regard during that process.

Wildflower and Brennan (2011) outlined coaching applications from the Humanistic approach that are relevant to the work of coaches. They suggest coaches should:

- **Establish collaboration**: the relationship works best when the coach engages the client in a partnership.
- **Be empathetic**: attentively listening and reflecting on the client's experiences facilitates growth
- **Identify strengths**: communicate to the client a belief in their ability to make positive changes in their life

- **Focus on the relationship:** being respectful, encouraging, and supportive has shown to indicate client success
- **Be authentic:** although kindness and empathy are critical, the coach must also be genuine and provide open and honest feedback in a kind and supportive manner

Solution-Focus Coaching

The work of the Humanist theorists, such as Rogers, Maslow, and Perls, identified the role of the supportive therapist as a major factor in the process of growth. Their view was grounded in a strengths-based approach with the idea that clients did not need fixing, but rather their clients were resourceful and capable of change. Based on that ideology, Berg and de Shazer created the solution-focused model. Solution-focused therapy is present and future focused; it is brief in nature and focuses on the positives of a person's experiences and abilities (De Shazer & Berg, 1993). The process includes getting clients to identify solutions that have worked in the past, and then see how to utilize similar strategies for solutions in the present. Solution-focused coaching is gaining a great following in the coaching arena and is becoming the target of a great deal of research (Grant, 2015). Grant (2006) explains that while the suggestion of focusing on a solution may seem simplistic, it is actually the essence of great coaching. For a more detailed look at solution-focused theory, see Chap. 8.

Approaches to coaching based on solution-focused theory have been outlined by Wildflower and Brennan (2011). They suggest coaches:

- Assist clients in identifying a solution to the problem by use of the miracle question, or how would things look if the problem was gone.
- Ask questions of clients to help them see the possibilities of change.
- Use scale questions, such as on a scale of 1–10, how do you rate...
- Redirect or move away from absolute thinking
- Reinforce resiliency tendencies recognized in the client.

Positive Psychology

In his book Authentic Happiness, Seligman (2002) tells the story of the first longevity study on happiness. In the story, Seligman shares the writings of nuns as they complete college and are transitioning into their work life. Two nuns' writings are compared; the first nun, Cecilia O-Payne, talks about the past year having been a "very happy one" and explains that she looks with "eager joy" on the start of her new role. The second nun, Marguerite Donnelly, wrote a short description of life events and states that she planned to "do my best for our order." In the study, it showed nuns that were cheerful and used happy language lived longer. "It was discovered that 90 % of the most cheerful quarter in the study was alive at age eighty-five versus only 34 % of the least cheerful quarter" (p. 4). In this study, positive feelings related to living longer.

There is something about happiness that is important; and the field of positive psychology is working to better understand that phenomenon. Positive psychology is the study of well-being and happiness. While some good has come out of the decades of psychological inquiry of mental illness (i.e., there are now a variety of effective treatments for many mental illnesses), the science of positive psychology wants to better understand positive qualities and how people or groups flourish.

Seligman and Csikszentmihalyi (2000) identify three pillars of positive psychology: positive emotion, positive traits, and positive institutions. The authors mentioned the importance of having positive psychology not only in the good times, but also to combat or better deal with the bad time. Moreover, they suggested that happiness is derived from three sources-experiencing pleasure, finding meaning in one's life, and experiencing the phenomenon of flow. We often think of happiness as being connected to happy times, but Seligan (2002) shares a story of a mock experiment he conducted with his students. He had them go out and have a fun time, then complete a philanthropic activity. His students responded by explaining that although the fun times were fun, the time they spent helping others truly improved their life in a more meaning way. Seligman explained that gratification, although connected to happiness is separate, in that it "calls on your strengths to rise to an occasion and meet a challenge" (Seligman, 2002, p. 9).

Seligman's research is encouraging because it suggests that people can learn happiness. Of course there is a genetics component (50 %) and life circumstances component (10 %) to happiness, but research suggests we can control about 40 % of our happiness levels (Lyubomirsky, King, & Diener, 2005). Positive Psychology Interventions (PPI) are processes that focus on positive psychology, and they have been found to impact well-being (Seligman, Steen, Park, & Peterson, 2005).

When working with families in a coaching environment, using positive psychology interventions (PPIs) can help the client move forward. Wildflower and Brennen (2011) suggest the following tips for coaches:

- Increase feelings of wellbeing
- Use positive psychology assessments and tools (see Chap. 7)
- Help clients identify and focus on the positives in their lives
- Have clients identify activities that can enhance happiness

"I love Appreciative Inquiry and the importance of asking questions. I try to remember to ask questions rather than give statements. It is sometimes hard to keep asking questions, but I continue to be better and better." **Adrian Kalikow, Parent Coach**

Appreciative Inquiry

Appreciative Inquiry (AI) is a strengths-based approach to positive change based on the assumption that there is something good in every system (Cooperrider,

Whitney, & Stavros, 2008). Finding what works well is the starting point for creating positive change. Rather than focusing on solutions to a problem, the AI approach is life affirming and focuses on inquiry. Cooperrider et al. (2008), explains that Appreciative inquiry is a process that includes drawing out the best of what has happened in the past, identification of what one wants more of, and exploration of what is wanted for the future. The underlying propositions of AI are (p. 4):

1. Inquiry into the "art of the possible" in life should begin with appreciation.
2. Inquiry into what is possible should yield information that is applicable.
3. Inquiry into what is possible should be provocative.
4. Inquiry into the human potential of organizational life should be collaborative.

The underlying propositions of the AI approach make a distinct and obvious connection with coaching. In the coaching process, ideally all four of these propositions are occurring throughout the coaching sessions. The process for coaching in AI style is best seen through the 4-D Cycle of AI, which begins with an affirmative topic of choice, and includes Discovery, Dream, Design, and Destiny.

Discovery is the process of reflection on what has worked in the past. The strengths-based logic behind discovery is the assumption that every system, be it an individual, family or even an organization, has past successes. The first of the 4-D cycle is about finding those positive past experiences, or the exceptions to the problem a client may have already identified. Discovery is about exploring and finding value in the things from our experiences that helped us reach desired goals and it is also about exploring meaning and appreciation in the past with the intent of discovering how to move translate accomplishments into the future. When coaching clients, a family life coach could ask "what has worked in the past?" or "what is the exception to this problem" to help a client identify times of success. The follow up to this is to have the client identify how they might utilize past successes to inform their existing challenge.

Dream is the process of visualizing what is possible and what might be. Too often, families come to coaching with the understanding there is a problem that needs to be solved, but less often, families come with a clear picture of what change they would like to see. This is what the dream process is all about—helping a client visualize the new possibilities. We are much more likely to reach our dream if we have a clear, concise idea of what our dream is. A family coach could ask the miracle question, "if you woke up tomorrow and all of the sudden you realized the situation had improved, what would that look like?" or simply ask the client to describe in detail how they will know if they have reached their goal or achieved success.

Design is the process of taking steps to achieve your dream. Design is when the client creates a plan, but it is more than planning. Design is a statement of intention that includes the realities of past successes combined with new ideas of the future put together in a realistic plan for growth. Treated similarly to the action step development in traditional coaching models, it is here, in the steps, where a family life coach helps their client construct a future that incorporates past experiences and future goals. This is an action step in itself, and could include questions such as, "how would you take what worked in the past to create a plan for the future?" and then working with them to craft that design.

Destiny is the final step; the product of the discovery, dream, and design steps. In Destiny there is continued movement towards the ideal. It is the process of creating what will be. Destiny is the process that continues even after the coaching has stopped because it is the delivery of the dream. AI process creates momentum, and destiny is the manifestation of that momentum.

Steps of FLC	Appreciate inquiry
Establish a relationship	Discovery: Identify what has worked in the past
Problem or solution identification	Dream: What might be
Goals clarification	Design: What should be
Action steps	Destiny: What will be
Results/evaluation	

Adapted from Cooperrider et al. (2008)

When working with a client using the Appreciate Inquiry approach, a coach could:

- Use the process of discovery, dream, design and destiny in their approach.
- Accentuate the positives and ask the client to highlight past positive experiences.
- Help the client identify how past experiences could influence their design and destiny.
- Encourage them to envision a destiny, and identify the steps to continue toward that path.

Adlerian Theory

Although family life coaching is considered a relatively new field, a coaching approach to helping individuals and families is nothing new. Adlerian theory has been noted as a modern day antecedent to coaching (Williams, 2003) and Adlerian based coaching was first addressed in literature over a decade ago. The philosophy of coaching fits well with the Adlerian philosophy; both focus on improving lives and helping people succeed. In fact, Adler recognized the client as an essential part of the change process, and often included clients in the problem solving of therapy (Ansbacher & Ansbacher, 1956). Although he was talking about the role of the counselor (which was clearly separated from the role of a therapist), Dreikurs reports, "the technique I found most helpful is that of interpreting the patient to himself;" "It is possible to show the patient a picture of himself, and let him draw his own conclusions (1967 p. 252)." Again, a unique essence of the coaching approach is to reflect the client's language in a way that helps her better understand herself.

This happened to me during my first coaching session as a client. I was talking with my Adlerian coach about an issue I had at work where I felt a great deal of anxiety from having to work with an unpleasant co-worker. I had gone to my supervisor for help, and accidentally copied my co-worker on a private email to my boss. This caused me a great deal of anxiety. I told my coach I knew it was stupid to have anxiety over such a small issue, and she responded by saying, "so you think your feelings are stupid". She showed me a picture of myself, and I immediately got her point. I certainly do not think feelings are stupid. Her reciting my own words to me helped me better understand how hard I was being on myself, and I was eventually able to move towards owning and validating my feelings. This is the very thing I encourage clients to do in my coaching sessions now. It helped me to have experienced this interaction of using the client's words first hand.

Both coaching and Adlerian therapy hold optimistic and holistically views of individuals and have long held firm the notion of social interest and the importance of systems. Social interest, a key Adlerian concept, honors the importance of an individual's contribution to the society in addition to the societies' influence on the individual (Dreikurs, 1989). Concepts of family group systems, goals and priorities, encouragement, feedback and consequences, forward movement, insight, personal responsibility and freedom, growth, and reframing are all Adlerian constructs (Ansbacher & Ansbacher, 1956) that are highly relevant to coaching. Adlerian life tasks of work, love, and friendship fit within the realms of coaching psychology.

Adlerian parenting is such an important part of coaching parents that I have another section on Adler in Chap. 10, identifies Adlerian practices that are recommended for coaches:

- The client sets the agenda.
- The coach is a facilitator and the client is the expert on content.
- Trust the client.
- If you are not sure, ask.
- Encourage clients to identify solutions
- Resistance is viewed as a product of the coach/client relationship, not a quality or a deficit held by the client.

Adult Learning Theory

Andragogy, a concept and practice of adult learning theory made known by Knowles (Knowles, Holton, & Swanson, 2005), focuses on the process of learning in adults. Knowles identified six assumptions of the adult learner:

1. The information must be relevant.
2. Process should be self-directed or allow some amount of student control.

3. Include life experiences of the student.
4. Meet the need of the student.
5. Attach it to real-world issues or a practical application to real life.
6. Make it purposeful; help them to grow.

Each of the six assumptions fit well with family life coaching. Coaching logically follows the assumptions of andragogy. For example, coaching goals are identified by the client, and thus are relevant; coaching includes student control through the belief that the client is the expert and sets the agenda and goals. Coaching also facilitates a partnership and the process is designed to meet real life issues by sharing real life experiences. The goal is to be purposeful and help the client grow.

Learning styles are another component of adult learning theory (see Chap. 3) that are relevant to family life coaching. Kolb (1984) talked about the importance of understanding how people learn as an effective approach. As such, family coaches could:

- Help the client identify their learning style through assessments or inventories.
- Assist clients in identifying how their learning style is significant to the change process.
- Help clients understand how their learning style impacts the people around them.
- Keep their own style of learning in check, and use strategies designed to be useful for the style of learning exhibited by the client.

Gottman's Sound Relationship House

John Gottman and Nan Silver are two researchers paving the way to a clearer understanding of interpersonal relationships for family science practitioners. Their names were brought up several times in our study (Allen & Baker, 2016), both for their work with parents and their work with couples. Their work is expanded in great detail in Chaps. 9 and 10, but they are certainly worth mentioning here.

The sound marital house: a theory of marriage (Gottman, 1999) and the sound relationship house (Gottman, 2011) both showcase the components of a healthy relationship based on the research of John and Julie Gottman. Their research suggests in order for a relationship to last, couples must be friends, manage conflict, and support each other's goals and co-create a vision for the future. Although there is such great information about the sound relationship house, the concepts can be condensed into nine components:

1. **Build love maps.** This requires the deep understanding of a partner's inner psychology.
2. **Share fondness and admiration**. This requires expressing kindness and respect.
3. **Turn Towards.** This includes responding regularly to bids for connection.
4. **The positive perspective.** This is about being positive when solving problems.
5. **Mange conflict.** Finding positive ways to manage differences, recognizing that resolving difference might not be possible.

6. **Make life dreams come true**. This includes creating a warm environment so that individuals are safe and supported in their aspirations.
7. **Create shared meaning**. This happens when couples have positive narratives about their relationship.
8. **Trust**. This is built over time when individuals repeatedly show that that they have their partner's back.
9. **Commitment**. This is about believing that your partner will remain your partner for life.

It is fairly easy to see how this theory of interpersonal relationships can easily translate into coaching. The ideas expressed here are strengths-based and fit with the process of coaching. To incorporate Gottman's theory into coaching, coaches could:

- Help clients identify positives in their relationship, strive to support family members, and actively create shared experiences.
- Assist in language and emotional changes that support goals and dreams for the future and show trust for each other.
- Help clients identify behaviors and strategies for deeply understanding family members, and responding to those needs appropriately.

Bandura's Social Learning Theory

Albert Bandura's social learning theory suggests that belief in one's ability to carry out a behavior is essential to success. In family life coaching, one of the goals is to help clients not only identify the goals they wish to attain, but also increase the client's sense of self-efficacy. Self-efficacy refers to an individual's belief in his or her capacity to execute behaviors necessary to produce specific performance attainments (Bandura, 1986). Feelings of self-efficacy are often based on one's previous knowledge, skills, and achievements (or lack thereof). These past experiences are not always the most accurate predictors of success. Although past experiences tell an important story, people often get stuck by thinking they are not capable or believing they do not have the skills necessary to be successful. However, if that were the case, how would anyone ever overcome adversity and find success?

Family life coaching is grounded in Bandura's social learning theory in that the role of the coach is to challenge the thinking and belief process of the client, which helps them increase their belief in success. Although a client's knowledge, skill, and previous experiences will not always be accurate predictors of future success, they might not know that. According to Gist and Mitchell (1992), three types of assessment processes are involved with forming self-efficacy; task requirement analysis, analysis of the experience, and assessment of personal and situational resources or constrains (see table below).

Self-Efficacy—Performance Relationship

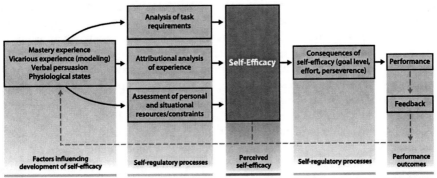

Adapted from model by Gist & Mitchell, 1992

If you think about a client that comes to you for a family life related issue, you can be assured they are thinking about the task at hand. They will also be cognizant of their past experiences, while assessing their own resources or constraints. Bandura's key ideas in regard to the role of self-efficacy beliefs in human functioning is that *"people's level of motivation, affective states, and actions are based more on what they believe than on what is objectively true"* (1997, p. 2). For this reason, how people behave can often be better predicted by the beliefs they hold about their capabilities than by what they are actually capable of accomplishing.

These self-efficacy perceptions help determine what individuals do with the knowl-edge and skills they have. This helps clarify why people's behaviors are sometimes disjoined from their actual capabilities and why their behavior may differ widely even when they have similar knowledge and skills. Understanding and believing in one's ability is a major element of reaching goals. Bandura (1986) suggests that self-efficacy measures need to be tailored to the domain of interest in order to maximize prediction.

I once had a client come to me with an issue of getting her child to stay in bed at night. The 3 year-old had a habit of getting out of bed a number of times throughout the evening and into the night. The mother had thought long and hard about the situation and knew the child was coming in to get attention and be connected with the parents. The parent had "tried everything" she could think of to get the child to stay in bed with no success. She was tired, frustrated, and needed a change. She was, in her opinion, a great mom with a lot of patience, but at the end of the night she found herself feeling furious with her child and wanted very much to make a change in the child's behavior. As we talked, it became clear that the parent did not believe there were any other options left to try, and had come to coaching to gain another perspective. Although it was her intention to remain calm and address the situation with an effective solution, her past experiences with volatile parents, her own inability to remain calm at night, and her thought that she had "read every-thing" about the topic left her feeling hopeless. In our session, it became clear that she couldn't see any other options.

It is actually a very encouraging theoretical perspective; individuals have the ability to influence their own behavior and the environment in a purposeful way. Bandura suggests that behavior is a product of "both self-generated and external sources of influence" (Bandura, 1986, p. 454). My client was looking at her past experiences of her parent's style of parenting as well as her own style at night (which looked dramatically different than her style during the day). It came down to her belief in her ability to make a change, and the resources available to her in terms of ideas for how to be successful. In fact, the issues were not even about her child getting out of bed. It was about her response. She wanted very much to remain calm, and not yell at her child. Once we were able to ease through her thinking and belief system, she was able to identify a new belief in her abilities to parent in a calm, nurturing way that supported her own idea of being a good parent.

As family life coaches, we will work with clients that may struggle with self-efficacy and will need to

- Inform our clients that knowledge, skill, and prior experiences are not necessar-ily good predictors of subsequent success. Rather, it the beliefs we hold about our abilities and the possibilities of success that matter most.
- Individuals possess self-beliefs that enable them to exercise a measure of control over their thoughts, feelings, and actions, therefore working with them to change their thoughts can lead to improved results.
- Bottom line is that we need to empower clients as to what people think, believe, and feel affects how they act and if they are successful (Bandura, 1986).

Coaching in Early Childhood

While this technically is not a theory, there are so few models specific to coaching families that I want to include the work of Hanft, Rush, and Sheldon (2004). Based on their experiences of working with children, families, and practitioners in the field of developmental disabilities, Hanft et al. identify coaching as an ideal approach to behavioral change. Coaching is ideal with special needs families for two reasons; the nature of creating a partnership and collaboration fosters continued buy in from the families, and the approach has been an effective strategy for change. The authors identify key descriptions of coaching that are essential in the coaching process:

1. Collaborative relationship between coach and learner;
2. Reflection and use of questioning;
3. Reciprocal observations and actions;
4. Focus on performance; and
5. Context-driven process determined by learner.

The process of coaching families of young children includes the use of nonjudgmental, supportive relationships that foster growth and development through observation, action, and reflection. These components are central to the coaching process. The steps taken by the coach are initiation, observation, actions, reflection, and evaluation. In the initiation phase, the coach and family identify specific outcomes and address any unforeseen issues. The process of observation happens when the coach observes the family either in person or through video technology. Next, actions or practice of interventions are practiced by the family. Reflection of the action step includes incorporating the coach's feedback questions, active listening, and questions, then the family is able to adjust and move toward their goal. Finally, the evaluation stage is when both partners review the process. To assist in the process of coaching in early childhood, Rush and Sheldon (2011) have created a series of tools for use by early childhood intervention specialists, such as a series of worksheets, logs, rating scales, and tips for coaching families.

While the process of coaching in early childhood mirrors many of the coaching specific strategies already given, this is the first model that identifies a process specifically for practitioners that serve families. Lessons derived from this model for family life coaching are directly tied to the five coaching descriptions mentioned above. Family life coaches should:

- Work to build a collaborative relationship with the family or client.
- Using powerful questions and empathetic listening, coaches can reflect on the coaching process with the families.
- Use reflection strategies to enhance the learner's perceptions and help guide growth.

Current Research on Family Life Coaching

Over the past 3 years, the literature on family life coaching has began to grow. This section will focus on a few of my current research projects happening at NCSU in partnership with my students and colleagues. The first study I review looks at research on the fit of FLC in FLE. I, along with my colleague Nichole Huff, recently conducted research on the opinions and experiences of family life professional on the topic of family life coaching (Allen & Huff, 2014).

In 2014, my graduate student, Tara Baker, and I interviewed 17 family life and parent coaching professionals to better understand the theoretical and practical aspects of family coaching practices. Since the literature to date on coaching and family science in limited, this is one of the first attempts at creating a grounded theory of family life coaching. In this research, we inquired about all facets of family life and parent coaching, including professional backgrounds, training experiences, processes of coaching, building of a business, and lessons learned along the way. The interviews, which lasted between 60 and 90 min each, provided a wealth of information on a topic that is devoid in the literature. Therefore in addition to the theoretical overview, this chapter identifies information on the lived experiences of those whom have become a family or parent coach.

Additionally, a group of family and parent coaches have recently convened to talk about the need for professionalism in family life coaching. As a result of that group, we have collected data on the current US training options for family and parent coaches. I have had two graduate students do research on parental attitudes of coaching and coaching in social work. Much of what is shared in this chapter is based on that research. My hope is that the readers of this chapter can learn from our experiences and be able to replicate effective strategies for helping others in family settings.

Family Life Coaching and the Fit Within Family Science

Although family practitioners are "coaching" families, there is a gap in literature with regard to theoretical and empirical research on family coaching. The fit of family coaching within family science is only just now being discussed. In a 2014 article by Allen and Huff in Family Relations, the topic of Family Coaching as it relates to family life education and family science was introduced for the first time. In the article, the authors argued that family coaching fits as a unique approach to family science, and suggested that coaching should be considered a fourth Domain of Family Practice.

It important to understand where coaching and parent education fall in the continuum of serving families. Doherty (1995) proposes that there are indeed differences between family life educators and a licensed therapist working with families. Parent education, according to Doherty, should contain components of imparting knowledge and skills while keeping a focus on the feelings, attitudes, and goals of the families served. Because of the personal and emotional focus in working with families, parent education involves a relationship, making it unique and separate from other academic subjects or courses one might study dealing with families. While these one-on-one and group interactions may appear to resemble therapy and often contain elements of relational theory, Doherty stresses the importance of family educators to remain objective and refer the family, when necessary, for additional counseling and therapy (1995).

While Doherty's hierarchy of family science was considered the norm for some time, things have recently began to change. Myers-Walls, Ballard, Darling, and Myers-Bowman (2011) offered a reconceptualization of that hierarchy by introducing the Domains of Family Practice model to better differentiate among family life education, family therapy, and family case management. Allen and Huff (2014) suggested that family coaching had emerged as another collaborative yet unique field of study and thus should be considered as a separate domain of practice.

In response to both, Allen and Huff (2014) introduced family coaching as a forth domain of family practice. The authors suggested that based on the results of a national study and the literature of family coaching, there is evidence to suggest the field of family life education make way for the inclusion of Family Life Coaching.

Family Coaching as a Domain of Family Practice:

Why? Purpose and goals of work with families	To partner with families to help them reach self-identified goals; families are involved as the partner and driver of the content.
What? Content base and foundation	Human development, strengths-based psychological theories and approaches; adult education; coaching psychology
When? The timing of work with families	Present and future focus; client identifies goals and works in here and now to reach future goals.
For Whom? Intended audience	Individuals, couple or family members who self-identify for services;
How? Techniques and methods used	Reaching goals through GROW, powerful questions, goal-driven work assignments, options and action steps

Allen and Huff (2014) conducted a national survey of 180 family science professionals in an effort to better understand opinions and experiences of family coaching. Recruitment efforts occurred through the National Council of Family Relations and the National Parenting Education Network. Mean age for the sample was 44.7 and 85 % were female participants. Additionally, 26 % of the sample held a Bachelor's degree, 52 % held a Master's degree, and 19 % held a Doctoral degree. Credential ranges and can be seen in the graph below.

Credential	n
Certified Family Life Educator (CFLE)	87
Licensed Marriage and Family Therapist (LMFT)	40
Credentialed Parent Educator	28

(continued)

Credential	n
Masters of Social Work (MSW)	15
Mental Health Professional, Other	11
Coaching Professional, Other	10
Educator, Other	8
Licensed Professional Counselor (LPC)	7
Family and Consumer Science Professional	3
Religious Affiliated Professional	3
Board Certified Coach (BCC)	2
International Coaching Federation (IFC) Certification	1

While the survey was designed simply to provide descriptive data and general perceptions, we found the results to be quite interesting and supportive of the field of coaching. 85 % saw the field as up and coming, and 49 % had already received some forms of coach training. While training levels varied significantly, a whopping 99 % of respondents felt it was important that family coaches were properly credentialed.

The survey also allowed for an open ended, qualitative question where we asked the participants if there was anything else they'd like to share. Indeed, there was! Sixty-eight respondents follow-up up with a response that fell into five themes:

(1) Need for Training and Credentialing;
(2) Goodness of Fit with Existing Family Practices;
(3) Opinions about Family Coaching Practice;
(4) Need for More Information; and
(5) Experiences with FC.

The quotes from the qualitative question helped paint a picture immersed in the opinions and experiences of the family science professionals that responded. Many shared strong opinions about the importance of training and credentials, and their strong concern of the lack thereof:

It should be well differentiated from the credentials that already exist. Coaching is a broad term that is applied to many fields (executive coaching, conflict coaching [mediation for one], etc) and specific credentials would also be good.

I am concerned about the lack of uniformity and guidelines for programs that certify coaches. I would love to see a process similar to the CFLE process

There are two associations who currently "oversee" the coaching field. Neither offers specific Family Life Coaching. I combined my formal educational experience with my coach training to create my services. I would be very concerned about the quality of education and experience of those who may seek to call themselves "family life coaches".

I would like to see more training opportunities for Family Specialist in the coaching arena.

My concern is a coach who starts out "coaching" but ends up trying to do therapy. Without training, they do not know the difference and proceed as if it is one in the same. Lately I am hearing more from clients who have tried coaching and are confused and dismayed by the outcome.

> I have serious reservations about coaching programs who do not use coaching skills and techniques in their course work. I also am concerned about online coaching programs that do not use video chat in their work. Coaching is more than active listening, reflection and advice-giving

Most of the other comments were positive in nature, and fit within the other four identified themes. Those comments included:

> Coaching is the natural application of CFLE's who actually execute and implement the knowledge with families. Most CFLE's are professors. To me, if you're a CFLE, you can coach. It's how you make money as a CFLE.

> I find it impossible NOT to coach families, couples, and individuals as I work with them in therapy. There exists a subtle balance (albeit necessary) between coaching and therapy—and knowing when to switch takes training, knowledge, and experience. My training in family systems is beneficial to coaching.

> I believe FLC is an up and coming field that needs attention from professionals to ensure it is viewed as a reputable source for working with families.

> We have witnessed thousands of couples enrich or restore their marriage using mentoring/coaching with over a 90 % success rate.

The conclusion we drew from this study was that there is a strong interest in family coaching among family professionals, but simultaneously, there is concern and need for rigor in credentialing and training. Although training programs specifically geared to family and parent coaching exist, they are few and there is little connection between those training programs and existing professional development organizations or family science credentialing process. Allen and Huff (2014) propose a need for graduate and certificate programs that offer consistency in training content. The training programs will best serve students and families if they are connected to a standardized credentialing system that provides oversight and national guidelines for family coaches.

Mechanics and Operations of Family Life Coaching

In addition to questions about the theoretical underpinnings of family life coaching, Tara Baker and I also asked several questions about experiences, pathway to FLC, training and credentials, types of issues covered in coaching, the process of coaching, outline of a typical coach session, how families respond, business and marketing, vision of future of the field, and any advice. I'm providing a brief summary of the data collected.

The majority of family life coaches interviewed had past experiences as parent educators, although a large majority also talked about their own role as parents being a key component of their professional training. All had a minimum of a bachelor's degree, and most had a master's degree or above. Additionally, all had received specific training on coaching as a supplement to their primary education having been in family science or education.

The business of family life coaching was a big topic; many felt that the work of coaching was a natural fit, but the business of coaching was a major learning curve. Marketing occurred mostly through word of mouth, website, and registries (IE, a registry affiliated with their training or credential) and most made free public appearances, such as workshops at schools and libraries as a marketing strategy. Most charged around $100 an hour for their services with a few offering the first session or a short first session for free. The experiences were mixed on place of service; about half were face to face and the other half were distance-based via phone or Skype.

As with the Allen and Huff (2014) results, there was a strong concern for quality of training and credentialing. Most identified a background in family science as critical, and a training emphasis on specific coach training as equally important. Overall, however, the majority described coaching as being a natural fit for people that are empathetic, motivational, and naturally curious.

Chapter Summary

This chapter summarized the theoretical underpinnings of family life coaching. While the field is young and still under development, the practice of FLC is built upon the fields of family life education and coaching psychology. The literature on FLC showcases theoretical underpinnings that include Ecological Theory, Positive Psychology, Adlerian Theory, Solution Focus Coaching, Adult Learning Theory, Humanistic Theory, Gottman's work on interpersonal relationships, and Bandura's Social Learning Theory. While these are theories identified by family life coaches interviewed for this book, this list is not yet conclusive. There is much more research needed to identify best practices of family life coaching, and the theories supporting those practices.

References

Allen, K. (2013). A framework for family life coaching. *International Coaching Psychology Review, 8*(1), 72–79.

Allen, K., & Huff, N. L. (2014). Family coaching: An emerging family science field. *Family Relations, 63*(5), 569–582.

Allen, K., & Baker, T. (2016). *Family life coaching: A grounded theory.* Manuscript in preparation.

Ansbacher, H. L., & Ansbacher, R. R. (Eds.). (1956). *The individual psychology of Alfred Adler.* New York: Harper Torchbooks.

Bandura, A. (1997). *Self efficacy: The exercise of control.* New York: Freeman.

Bandura, A. (1986). *Social Foundations of thought and action: A social cognitive theory.* Engle-wood Cliffs, NJ: Prentice-Hall.

Cooperrider, D. L., Whitney, D., & Stavros, J. M. (2008). *Appreciate Inquiry handbook for leaders of change* (2nd ed.). Brunswick, OH: Crown Custom Publishing, Inc.

De Shazer, S., & Berg, I. K. (1993). Constructing solutions. *Family Therapy Networker, 12*, 42–43.

Dreikurs, R. (1967). *Psychodynamics, psychotherapy, and counseling: Collected papers.* Chicago: The Adler School of Professional Psychology.

Doherty, W. J. (1995). Boundaries between parent and family education and family therapy: The levels of family involvement model. *Family Relations, 44*(4), 353–358.

Dreikurs, R. (1989). *Fundamentals of Adlerian psychology.* Chicago: The Adler School of Professional Psychology.

Gist, M. E., & Mitchell, T. R. (1992). Self-efficacy: A theoretical analysis of its determinants and malleability. *The Academy of Management Review, 17*(2), 183–211.

Gottman, J. M. (2011). *The science of trust: Emotional attunement for couples.* New York: W. W. Norton & Company.

Gottman, J. M. (1999). *The marriage clinic: A scientifically based marital therapy.* New York: W. W. Norton & Company.

Grant, A. M. (2006). An integrative goal-focused approach to executive coaching. In R. D. Stober & A. M. Grant (Eds.), *Evidence based coaching handbook: Putting best practices to work for your clients* (pp. 153–192). Hoboken, NJ: Wiley.

Grant, A. (2014). Autonomy support, relationship satisfaction and goal focus in the coach-coachee relationship: Which best predicts coaching process? *Coaching, An International Journal of Theory, Research, and Practice, 7*(1), 18–38.

Grant, A. (2015, February). *Putting the psychology into coaching, and the coaching into psychology: Lessons from the road (less traveled).* Presented at the 5th international congress of coaching psychology, San Diego, CA.

Hanft, B. E., Rush, D. D., & Shelden, M. L. (2004). *Coaching families and colleagues in early childhood.* Baltimore: Brooks Publishing.

Heimendinger, J., Uyeki, T., Andhara, A., Marshall, J., Scarbro, S., Belansky, E., et al. (2007). Coaching process outcomes of a family visit nutrition and physical activity intervention. *Health Education & Behavior, 34*(1), 71–89. doi:10.1177/1090198105285620.

Knowles, M., Holton, E. F., & Swanson, R. (2005). *The adult learning: The definitive classic in adult education and human resource development* (6th ed.). Boston: Elsevier.

Kolb, D. A. (1984). *Experiential learning: Experience as the source of learning and development.* Englewood Cliffs, NJ: Prentice Hall.

Lyubomirsky, S., King, L. A., & Diener, E. (2005). The benefits of frequent positive affect: Does happiness lead to success? *Psychological Bulletin, 131*, 803–855.

Myers-Walls, J. A., Ballard, S. M., Darling, C. A., & Myers-Bowman, K. S. (2011). Reconceptualizing the domain and boundaries of family life education. *Family Relations, 60*(4), 357–372. doi:10.1111/j.1741-3729.2011.00659.x.

Rogers, C. (1961). *On becoming a person.* Boston: Houghton Mifflin Company.

Rush, D. D., & Shelden, M. L. (2011). *The early childhood coaching handbook.* Baltimore: Paul H Brookes Publishing.

Rush, D., Shelden, M., & Hanft, B. (2003). Coaching families and colleagues: A process for collaboration in natural settings. *Infants & Young Children: An Interdisciplinary Journal of Special Care Practices, 16*(1), 33–47.

Seligman, M. E. P. (2002). *Authentic happiness: Using the new positive psychology to realize your potential for lasting fulfillment.* New York: Simon and Schuster.

Seligman, M. E. P., & Csikszentmihalyi, M. (2000). *Positive psychology. An introduction. American Psychologist, 55*(1), 5–14.

Seligman, M. E. P., Steen, T., Park, N., & Peterson, C. (2005). Positive psychology process: Empirical validation of interventions. *American Psychologist, 60*(5), 410–421.

Williams, P. (2003). The potential perils of personal issues in coaching. The continuing debate: Therapy or coaching? What every coach must know. *International Journal of Coaching in Organizations, 2*(2), 21–30.

Wildflower, L., & Brennan, D. (2011). *The handbook of knowledge-based coaching from theory to practice.* San Francisco: Jossey-Bass.

Part II
Application and Skill Development

Chapter 5
How to Coach Families

Theories are the backbone of family science as they help explain practice and suggest how to develop programs and services that change behavior. Part I provided the theoretical underpinnings of coaching psychology, family life education, and family life coaching. However, theory alone is not enough. To be an effective family life coach, one must base good practices upon theory.

This chapter focuses on the how-to of family life coaching, the process of coaching individuals, couples, co-parents, or a family dealing with family life issues. Readers learn about the core competencies of coaching, the process of coaching, and a case study is included so that students have an opportunity to witness a coaching session from start to finish.

> In coaching, you do not have to have the answer. In education, it usually is about an answer to something. And what can get a coach all stressed out is thinking they have to know the answer to something their client is struggling with. The gift of being a coach (at least with using AI) is you discover together the answer that is right for the parent and child. This is so freeing! As a partner to my clients we get to explore what is working or has worked and in this emerges the 'right' answer—which is often different for everyone. I love this about coaching! **Alice Hanscam, Family Life Coach**

Competencies of Family Life Coaching

In order to understand how practitioners coach, it is helpful to identify the coaching process. While there are many models of coaching and each model has a variety of steps, most include some variation of the following competencies.

© Springer International Publishing Switzerland 2016
K. Allen, *Theory, Research, and Practical Guidelines for Family Life Coaching*,
DOI 10.1007/978-3-319-29331-8_5

1. Setting the Foundation (ethics, coaching agreement)
2. Co-creating the Relationship (building trust, presence)
3. Communicating Effectively (active listening, powerful Questions)
4. Learning and Results (awareness, action steps, goal setting, accountability)

These competencies come from the International Coaching Federation (ICF, n.d.a), a professional association for coaches seeking to advance the practice of coaching. The ICF is one of many coaching organizations working to identify and promote professional competencies for coaches. The core competencies listed can be used as a framework for the skills and approaches needed for coaching professionals. The ICF core competencies were developed in order to support the greater understanding of skills used by coaches. Although they can be used as a guide for how to move through a coaching relationship, most models of coaching offer a step-by-step guide for coaching. Therefore the steps presented in this chapter are not directly from ICF, but rather they synthesis many models of coaching.

Steps of Family Life Coaching

The steps of family life coaching are really no different from the steps of other types of coaching, such as executive coaching, business coaching, or life coaching. Most coaching sessions are a goal oriented process whereby the coach helps the client identify solutions and action steps to meet that goal (Stober & Grant, 2006). Boiled down, the stages often look something like this:

1. Establishing a relationship
2. Solution or problem identification
3. Goals clarification
4. Action steps
5. Results, evaluation, and accountability.

Put another way, the coaching conversation includes a process where the coach engages in a conversation that begins to build rapport with the client. Using active listening skills, the coach begins to ask the client what it is they want to work on in the coaching session. The client is asked what they hope will come from the session in an attempt to clarify the goals of the client. Once the coach and client are aware of the client's goals, the coach begins to seek clarification and ask the client to identify steps for how they might reach their goals. This step is the heart of the coaching process. The client identifies action steps and puts together a plan to reach goals. The final step includes reviewing the process and talking about accountability for follow through. While this is a general overview of a typical coaching session, the steps are expanded below.

Step One: Building a Relationship

"Building the relationship is critical; this is about it is all about the relationship. Without it, you can't coach." **Alice Hanscam, Parent Coach**

During the first stage of coaching, an individual or family unit generally meets with a coach for as many sessions as needed to explore the nature of the coaching relationship and discuss the needs of family. Building a relationship is no small task; it takes time and skill. Rogers (1961), spoke of offering unconditional positive regard, being empathetic, and authentic as approaches to building rapport. What does building rapport look like? It looks like staying engaged, focusing on what the client is saying, and actively listening to the client. Although these tasks are important throughout the coaching process, they are essential in the early stages of relationship building. The step of establishing a relationship and getting to know each other is critical to the success of the coaching process. The quality of the coaching relationship has been found to have significant influence on the positive outcomes of coaching (Lai & McDowall, 2014). The building of rapport is a task in the early steps of coaching, maintaining a positive coaching relationship remains a priority of coaching throughout the coaching process.

Step 2: Solution or Problem Identification

In step two, which begins to happen in the first session and continues through each session thereafter, the client and coach begin to explore solutions. In the Appreciate Inquiry (AI) approach, this is considered the discovery phase. In the Discovery phase, the goal is to identify the best of what is possible (Cooperrider, Whitney, & Stavros, 2008). Coaching questions during this phase revolve around what has worked in the past, and recognizing the positive exceptions of the presenting problem.

Solution focused coaching is just that—focusing on the solutions of an issue rather than the problems. In a coaching environment, focusing on the problems is considered counter-intuitive (Hicks & McCracken, 2010). In my experience, this solution-focused process is not a process most families are familiar with. In fact, we all have a tendency to talk about what is wrong, and what we want to change rather than what is right and how can we do more of what works. Even more true is that we often have an interest in changing those around us, rather than focusing on what we have control to change in ourselves. Solution identification is often a new approach to individuals and families, and one that tends to encourage the family. Keeping the theme focused on solutions rather than problems creates an environment that allows for no one person to be the villain.

In this step, which is often occurring in tandem with building rapport, the client shares stories of accomplishments, history of the family, and identifies, either overtly or covertly, the strengths of family members. These are all important steps for the coach to not only get to know the client and their family members, but also to aid in the identification of possible solutions. After some time, the client and coach will begin to understand the problem, and will begin to identify what it is necessary to improve the situation.

Step 3: Goals Clarification

Setting and defining goals is a process driven by the client (Grant, 2006). When asked about goals, clients new to the coaching process may feel they need to have all the answers. This is not the case. Clients need to know that coaching is a process, and as such, together with the coach, the client will work through the process towards solutions. Goals clarification is the process in which the coach helps the client begin to identify a new vision for the future. What exactly they want their future to look like is the starting point, but soon clients begin to explore how that solution can become a reality.

The family's culture and beliefs must be taken into account before formulating goals when working with families. For example, cultural family norms for Jewish, Scandinavian, and African American families may be quite different from other (Western) norms (McGoldrick & Carter, 2001). Coaches will have an opportunity to get to know the client to some extent, but it is important to be aware of differences. Roger's (1961) spoke of the importance of being genuine. This includes asking questions and working to truly understand the lived experiences of the client.

In family life coaching, clients do not always know what will improve their situations. If they had the answers, they would implement the solution. In the world of coaching, many suggest having an expertise in content areas is not necessary (McLean, 2012). Although this may hold true in some areas of coaching, it is not true in all forms of coaching, and certainly not true in family life coaching. Grant (2006) suggests that coaches need content knowledge to help guide the process. In order to coach clients on family life issues, one must have knowledge on the content of family life. Having content knowledge in family life will help the coach ask better questions and create or co-create clarifications that might help the client find solutions based on evidence-based family life practices.

Teaching moments will arise during family life coaching sessions, enabling the client to recognize a behavior or identify a pattern they wish to improve upon or change. From there, a broad list of goals can be identified, written, and then narrowed based on the client's capabilities and eagerness to work on goals that are more urgent (Heimendinger at al., 2007). Raj and Kumar (2009) contend it is the job of the coach to assist the client in setting attainable goals that are further broken down at another time. Thus, although some of the goals may be long term (i.e., manage my children's routine and family tasks at home in the evenings without yelling and screaming), there are smaller, broken down tasks that will be addressed in order to reach the goal of a manageable household in the evening times (I will observe the circumstances in which I loose my cool for 1 week to better understand my patters of behavior).

Commitment to change is important in the initial stage of the coaching process. It is important for a coach to have a good understanding of Prochaska's stages of change model when assisting clients in setting goals. Although Prochaska's model grew from the mental health and addiction fields, it has been applied in practice and research in areas such as health and wellness, business, self-help, and coaching in management. Briefly, the stages of change include: pre-contemplation, contemplation, preparation, action, and maintenance (Norcross & Prochaska, 2002).

The pre-contemplative and contemplative stages are highlighted by a person's complete denial and/or lack of recognition that anything needs to change; or, they may believe perhaps some things need to change, but not right now (Norcross & Prochaska, 2002). Persons in the preparation stage of change have decided that they have concerns about some patterns of behaviors or thoughts, and are taking steps or making plans to take action. The action stage is characterized by goal setting, practicing new habits or behaviors, and changing thought patterns along with behaviors.

Understandably, not all family members can or are willing to recognize they may need to address certain issues at that particular time. This is one of the big differences of coaching and education. In education, we can simply tell the parent what they need to know/change/do. In coaching, the movement is guided by the client, and as such, we must honor where they are in that moment. So while education on a family life topic might provide insight, we must meet the client where they are.

Working with clients to resolve their ambivalence about changing a behavior or attitude is a part of the coaching process. For example, a client may express reluctance to alternatives to spanking or corporal punishment. In this example, the coach could facilitate self-discovery, and assist the client to identify areas where they are already successful in positive approaches to parenting and where they are not yet ready, to make a change. Ignoring where a client "sits" within the stage of change model would result in the assumption that all clients are at the same place and time with regards to how, what, and when they will choose to make a change in their lives. As such, we must be patient, work to help clients remember their dream or vision for the future, and assist them in identifying goals that will help them reach their solution.

Step 4: Action Steps

Once the goals have been set, the next stage of the coaching process begins—creating action steps. This is the stage where clients design their future. While in some cases this step might include acquiring new skills via direct instruction and education, the client guides this step. The coach might ask "so what steps do you think you need to take to get where you want to go", but it is the client that lists the steps. This is hard for anyone that has been an educator to adapt to a coaching mentality. We often come to this phase with a great deal of lived experiences, knowledge, and education that help us clearly understand what we think the client needs. However, this is not our process to take—it is the clients'.

> Coaches do not tell the client what to do or even give suggestions of what to do. This can be very difficult, but it is so important to remember! Tara Baker, Family Life Coach

During the action-planning step, coaches often facilitate the practice of new or existing skills. In-vivo practice, or practicing in the moment, has been suggested as an important component of family coaching (Beyer, 2008). One might assume that practicing parenting or relationship skills with a coach in the same room would be uncomfortable or awkward. However, a study on visit coaching with child welfare families found that parents reported feeling more connected to their coaches and the information made more sense when parents were able to practice skills and receive immediate feedback on their efforts (Beyer, 2008).

While education and practice can be a small part of the action planning, the goal is for the client to figure out what they are doing, what they are doing well, and what they are going to change. It is important to always remember there are things that are going well, and building on previous successes creates success in the latter parts of the process. Of course the client needs to make changes; they would not be in coaching otherwise. Therefore in the action-steps plan, the client can identify obstacles that must be overcome, and identify resources or supports for overcoming those obstacles. The action steps should all be congruent with reaching the goal identified by the client in step three.

The role of the coach in the action plan step is to support, challenge, and encourage the client. Although the actual action steps happen outside of the coaching session, the coach can ask powerful questions to help the client think through their action steps, so they leave the session with the best-possible plan for forward movement. Then, the clients go forth and take their steps!

Once the client has their list of action steps and has begun to complete them, some coaches offer free check-ins on an as-needed basis. These check-ins are most often emails, texts, or short phone calls that allow the client to ask for clarification, advice, or simply share positive results. While this is not a part of every coaching relationship, it is an opportunity to provide additional support to your client.

Step 5: Results and Evaluation

In the final step of the coaching session, the client and the coach evaluate how the action steps worked and determine next steps. Clients will report both successes and failures– in response, coaches should employ unconditional positive regard, empathy, and genuine caring attitudes towards the clients during feedback (Gockel, Russel, & Harris, 2008). However, McGoldrick and Carter (2001) caution that this response set should not be confused with becoming emotional or overly reassuring with clients when they experience frustration or failure, because this could be considered condescending or disabling. Thus, the overarching goal of the feedback and support offered by the coach is to encourage clients to be confident through increased self-reflection and self-correction (Raj & Kumar, 2009). Once again in this sense it is important for the coach to exhibit genuine, sincere, authentic regard to the client's progress.

Once clients are actively working towards their goals, a subset process begins whereby tasks and skills may be broken down to smaller tasks. Feedback is offered towards improvement; and clients put their knowledge, the existing skill set, and a new skill set to the test (Kaiser & Hancock, 2003; Raj & Kumar, 2009). This period also involves reflection with the coach, which gives the family members the opportunity to share how they feel about a task, and report a success. At this point, it is important for coaches to attend to their own interpersonal skills and behavior—to express warmth and empathy while also providing direct and specific feedback. Direction should be offered when a situation or skill is applicable to other situations—feedback must be specific and occur during the interaction for increased effectiveness (Kaiser & Hancock, 2003). Thus, in this subset process of practice, reflection, and feedback, there exists the opportunity for the clients to partner with the coach—and be continually aligned and supported in the coaching process.

It has been asserted that the coaching relationship must be cultivated continually, not just during the initial stage of the process (Gockel et al., 2008; Rush, Shelden, & Hanft, 2003). Thus, providing effective, specific feedback is only one part of the skill set needed for successful coaching. When discussing areas of need, tasks, or skills that may need more work, effective coaches must partner in this discussion, offering support and facilitating self-discovery (Gockel et al., 2008). Despite the appearance of the coach being an "expert," it is precisely the opposite dynamic that must occur between coach and client. Coaches must align themselves with the clients to ensure clear communication about goals, solicit feedback, and reflection in order to evaluate collaboratively whether mastery has occurred (Rush et al., 2003; Schwartz, 2002).

Following a few sessions of results and feedback, the direction of coaching sessions will take a turn. The client or coach will determine when it feels appropriate to evaluate the goals, progress made, and make adjustments to the plan. Eventually, there is informal and formal evaluation of the coach, the collaborative process, and the interventions (Gockel et al., 2008). It is important to note that results and evaluation and might happen at the begining of a session in relation to the previous session, as well as at the end of a session. For example, a couch might ask how the action steps went from a previous session, and might again inquire about how the action steps might look at the end of a session.

Informal evaluations occur during coaching sessions, requiring both finesse and excellent interpersonal communications skills on the part of the coach. During this type of interaction, a coach must solicit opinions and feedback from the client: the coach must have the maturity and self-confidence to hear the information that will be said, negative or positive. Kremenitzer (2005) contends that coaches working with families must be emotionally intelligent, and that this degree of intelligence can be honed with careful and intentional self-reflection and examination. Using this analogy, coaches must be able to perceive mood and emotional states in others and in self, remain neutral during unexpected events, and be able to hear information that may be initially uncomfortable. These skills are clearly well suited for informal evaluations, when a coach must ask for feedback, not knowing exactly what the response will be. Reflection and thoughtful responses to the feedback will allow for growth and collaboration as the relationship between client and coach progresses. This feedback will also aid the coach in their own growth of becoming a highly effective coach.

Essential Skills of Family Life Coaches

Listening

Listening is an essential element of effective coaching. In fact, some would call it the single most important skill of a professional coach. Listening is one of the components of Roger's (1961) skills to being an effective practitioner and is considered an essential element of building a coach/client relationship. Active listening is a technique often used in psychological training that requires the listener to reflect back to the speaker what they have just heard. Put another way, the listener mirrors back what the speaker has said through paraphrasing the client's comments. This process helps ensure that the listener truly understands the message of the speaker. Here is an example of an actively listening conversation.

Parent:	I swear, every time my teenager has her headphones on, she either doesn't hear me or ignores me. It makes me furious!
Coach:	It is really aggravating to you when she doesn't respond.
Parent:	Yes! More than aggravates. It makes me down right mad!
Coach:	Ah, so you are about at your wits' end with her not listening.
Parent:	Yes! Exactly. I just don't know how much more I can take.

Some communication programs use this model as a way to help family members truly feel as if the other person is listening. While active listening is one important listening skill, there are others that are relevant to coaching. Williams & Mendez (2007), provide a full detailed description of Whitworth, Kinsey-House, & Sandalh (1998)'s *three types of listening: listening to, listening for, and listening with.*

Listening to is much like active listening and includes listening to verbal and non-verbal communication patterns.

Listening for is slightly different, the coach is listening for what is important to the client. This could include listening for the client's values, agenda, or purpose. This is not the same as listening for a solution; *listening for* is more about trying to truly understand the client's experiences and the meaning given to those experiences. As Williams and Mendez (2007, p. 4) state, "it's about listening for possibilities, goals, dreams, and aspirations. It's about discovering, harnessing, and expanding on strengths and tools clients have".

The third kind of listening, *listening with*, explains how we listen. Whole-self listening means listening with our heart, intuition, and body. Many coaches use a technique where they use the client's own words to both help client know they are listening, and help the client get a better image of himself or herself. Language use is an important part of coaching, as is the process of self-disclosure. While the coaching session most often is about the client sharing their experiences, there are occasions when it is appropriate for the coach to share their own experiences: when it helps the client/coach connection or to help the client learn something new. This process should be limited to a few interactions, but is an important part of the listening process.

> Active listening is making sure that I truly hear what the parent is saying and not jumping in with my own ideas, but reflecting their idea. **Adrian Kalikow, Parent Coach**

Empathy

Another important element of coaching similar but different from listening is showing empathy. Empathy is simply the ability to understand another person, to see the world from their point of view. In a nut shell, that is what coaches do. They work to understand the client's experience. Evidence suggests that the use of empathy makes for a stronger coach (Brotman, Liberi, & Wasylyshyn, 1998).

Showing empathy helps the client feel safe to share, and it builds the relationship. What is empathy in a coaching relationship? It is the process of understanding the world from our client's point of view, and communicating that understanding back to the client. This process validates the client's experience, and fosters growth. It is important not to confuse this with feeling sympathetic with the client. To put yourself in someone's shoes does not require feeling sorry for the client. The act of feeling sympathy can sometimes affect the coaching relationship, and also block the potential for progress in the client.

Empower

While it sounds like a superhero skill, empowering is really just another way to say coaches help clients see their own abilities. Based on strengths-based approaches, empowering is the process of identifying strengths, abilities, and potentials the clients have. Empowerment is embedded in the philosophy that the client already possess these strengths and skills internally. People are not always great at seeing their strengths, so coaches help them extract these strengths from within. Helping clients get over self-doubt and increase positive self-talk and self-esteem can be a big booster towards effective change. Empowerment can happen through affirmations, helping the client generate new possibilities, and even offering resources or education are all ways to help empower a client to achieve success.

Ethics of Coaching

Professionalism of any helping industry must include a code of ethics. As such, Family Life Coaching must consider ethical standards of practice designed to provide guidelines and standard of conduct. A code of ethics is critical for the protection of families served and provides specific resource for practitioners. Many professional associations, especially those offering a credential, offer a standard code of ethics. The International Coach Federation Code of Ethics includes a philosophy and definition of coaching, as well as standards of ethical conduct (ICF, n.d.a, b). The Board Certified Coach Code of Ethics includes legal requirements, conduct standards, compliance ordinance, organizational policies, conflicts of interest and impropriety standards (CCE, 2010). National Council on Family Relations Code of Ethics includes ethical principles and relationship guidelines (NCFR, 2009). Most professional associations offer specific guidance, and therefore needs to be considered as part of the family life coaching process. No family life coach should be serving families without first studying and agreeing to a code of ethics.

Case Study

In order to best understand the skills and practice of coaching, a case study is being shared. This case study is designed to showcase the issues and complexities of family life coaching. This session is based on the lives of Patti and Jim and their two children, Jessica (16) and Beth (21). Beth is several hours away at college. Jessica and Beth get along as siblings, but have never been very close. Patti and Jim describe their marriage as happy, but both wish they had more time to spend together. Both spouses work; Patti only part-time because she "wanted to be home for her kids." Their daughter Jessica has been "quieter than usual" and growing distant from her parents. Patti and Jim are concerned, but say nothing they have attempted has helped. Feeling desperate, Patti says she went through Jessica's cell phone and found out that Jessica was having a relationship with another girl. Patti confronted Jessica, and admits to being "very emotional" during the conversation. Since then, Jessica's relationship with her parents has been even more strained. Neither Patti nor Jim approve, and have sought coaching to address the situation, because they believe they "failed" as parents and can still "change Jessica's mind" about her sexuality.

Coach: "Good morning, I'm so glad you came today. Thank you for filling out the forms I emailed you"

Patti: "You are welcome"

Coach: "Ok, great, were there any questions you had about the coaching agreement?"

Patti: "No, we are just hoping you can help us change our daughter's mind."

Coach: "Well before we dive into the work of coaching, I'd like to know if have you ever been to a coaching session before?"

Jim: "No, but when we were first married we went to a financial coach, where they told us how to budget our money for the things we wanted in life. I figure it will be sort of like that. We come in and talk about the problems we are having with Jessica and you can tell us how to change her mind. I do wonder, though, shouldn't Jessica be here for that too?"

Patti: "Jim! First we need figure out how we are going to address the situation, then we can bring Jessica in, right" (looking at the coach)

Coach: "Well first, I'm so grateful that you have both come today. It seems a very loving act to come to work on an issue that is clearly so important to you both."

Note: the coach is attempting to build rapport and make a connection with the new clients. The small talk that was initiated helps the coach better understand the situation, and she is listening on all three levels at this point to better understand the dynamics of this relationship and family life issue.

Coach: I do think it is important that we clarify my role and talk about our relationship. I just want us to be sure we are clear on our roles with each other, then we can delve into Jessica and whether or not to bring her in and how you might want to move forward. How does that sound?"

Patti: "Sounds good" [Jim nods in agreement]

Coach: First and foremost, it is important we all understand that the coaching process is a partnership together. I'm actually quite happy to be working with you as this is a partnership between me, the coach, and you both, the coachees. The process of coaching involves me doing a lot of listening and asking questions and you doing a lot of the talking and thinking. Together we will discover the values and strengths you each bring to the family and how to harness those strengths to come up with solutions to your problems. And if and when we all decide, Jessica may be brought into the coaching process as well. Are there any questions about our roles toward each other and the partnership?"

Patti: "No, not really."

Jim: "I think I understand."

Note: setting up the expectations is an important step in helping the clients know the boundaries and expectations of the relationship. The goal is to communicate the importance of the partnership.

Coach: "Ok, great, then let's move forward. On your intake packet, you mentioned that you recently found out your daughter is in a relationship with another woman, or teenager that is female and you are both trying to figure out how to deal with this. You mentioned a few goals on our intake about improving the relationship with your daughter, but rather than go over those goals specifically, I'm wondering if you can just fill me in on what has happened and perhaps what you want to talk about today"

Note: the intake packet is a nice resource to help provide background information for the coach, and it can also be a resource to helping clients focus on the most important points. Still, the clients should guide the session.

Patti: "Well, see it's like this. Our daughter Jessica has been quieter than usual and seems to be drifting away from me, from us. After a couple weeks of me trying to appease her, making her favorite meals, planning a movie together, and just some family time playing games I finally decided to check Jessica's cell phone and when I did I found evidence that she is in a relationship, (looks toward Jim) with another girl."

Jim: "Yes, and this is really weird. I just can't imagine this is real. I didn't believe it for myself when Patti told me. I mean a girl?!"

Coach: "So Jim, this is pretty unbelievable to you"

Jim: "Yes, I'm really at a loss"

Note: the coach used the active listening skill to connect with Jim as he expressed a powerful reaction to this situation.

Coach: "And Patti, it sounds like leading up the phone situation, you had tried hard to rekindle the connection with your daughter."

Patti: "Yes, but clearly that didn't work"

Coach: "Hmm. I'm not sure I understand what you mean that it didn't work."

Patti: Well, we are not feeling close to our daughter at all right now, so my attempts didn't work."

Coach: "Okay, I see what you are saying. But I'm not clear on how you think it would look like if you had success? How would you know that it worked?

Note: The coach is beginning to move towards solution clarification, or a better understanding of what the solution might look like.

Patti: "Oh, I guess if we had a positive conversation with Jessica that would be a good start. If we could just sit and talk with her, and she would help us understand"

Coach: "Thank you. That helps me know where you'd like to go. It seems like you, Patti, would like to have improved communication with your daughter. Is that right?

Note: while more attention can be paid on the vision for the future, this is the beginning of knowing what a solution, or goal might look like.

Patti: "Yes. Any communication would be improved".

Coach: "So communication. . .any communication. . . is the goal. That helps me understand. I still need more information. So you looked on Jessica's phone to see why she was being so distant and you found out that she is in a relationship with a girl, tell me, how did you approach Jessica about this?"

Patti: "Well, that is where I think I may have pushed her farther away, because I got very emotional about it. I mean a girl! This is ridiculous. What is she trying to prove?" "Is she trying to replace her sister Beth?"

Coach: "You seem pretty upset by this. It is hard for you to make sense of it, and you are wondering if the relationship with the other girl is an attempt by Jessica to fulfill her older sister's role in her life."

Patti: "Yes! I thought that maybe she was missing her and when I confronted Jessica about it, she went on and on about how her and Beth were never that close anyway.

Jim: "I think what my wife is saying is that they are both girls and perhaps Jessica is just confused and this other girl is giving Jessica attention right now and making Jessica feel special, so Jessica is just latching onto it, because she has always been like that. Not Beth. Beth has always been the oldest and always been more confident, maybe. You know Beth had boyfriends, and maybe Jessica is just acting out because she feels left out, not having a boyfriend, you know?"

Coach: "Um-huh. (Nodding). So one question you both have is if maybe your daughter's relationship with her sister has something to do with her sexual identify. Is that right?

Jim: "Well, we just don't know. We just don't understand this at all".

Coach: "So this is a big change for your family; something that was unexpected and you are having a difficult time making sense of it."

Patti: "Yes, and more than making sense of it. I'm not sure how to deal with it"

Coach: "Boy, parenting can be confusing on the best of days. When something this unexpected comes up, it makes it hard to know what is the right thing to do."

Patti: "Exactly. I never expected this, I expected that she was in a relationship but never with a girl. We have never approved of same sex marriages and we have made that quite obvious in our home. It even says in the bible, God made woman from Adam's ribs to give Adam a mate for life."

Jim: "Look we just need to nip this in the bud! She knows we disapprove of this relationship, she will get over it. She needs a distraction, maybe we can take her to Disney world or someplace far away." "Get her mind off of this and get her away from that girl."

Note: At times like these, coaches can be confronted with personal feelings or opinions that may not mirror that of the client. This is normal, but remember, we have to keep our own feelings in check. We also often come to the table with knowledge and education about family relationships that is important. In this situation, most FLC's understand the importance of support for LGBT youth, and might feel it important to share that information with the clients. While there is a time and place for education, it is important to find a good time. In this case, this is not the right time as the parents are upset and this could make for a difficult interaction. In the first session, this is a time to build the relationship. In this situation, it makes sense to look at past successes and move towards a goal of mending the relationship.

Coach: "I can tell this is an upsetting situation for you both, and I'm sure this is also very difficult for Jessica. I'd like us to switch gears a moment. I bet there have been other times where you had a challenge with Jessica and got past it. I'd like to learn more about those successes. Can you tell me about a tough time with Jessica and how you got through it as a family? Take your time and really think about what it was each of you brought to the presenting issue."

Patti: "Hmmm. Well this is hard. Let me see. (thinking, about 1 min passes).

Coach: "Take your time."

Patti: "I remember when Jessica was in the 7th grade there was this one group of girls that would taunt her. They called her names and one boy actually knocked her books out of her arms and left her to pick up everything on her own there in the hallway. She came home so upset. I sat on her bed and consoled her as she cried. I was supportive, and I think it helped. Oh why can't it work out that way this time? She doesn't even want me in her room"

Coach:	"So you were there for her, and were able to support her during a rough time. I can see that was an important time in your life. Jim, what do you remember about that time?"
Jim:	(thinking) "Not much, Patti has always been the one to help the girls when they have problems at school. I remember taking Jessica out for ice cream and she seemed fine then. Sure wish ice cream would help now."
Coach:	"Yup; we all wish parenting was as easy as ice cream sometimes [bit of a smile to form connection] Ok, Patti, what did Jessica do at school the next time those kids picked on her? What happened the next day?"
Patti:	"I remember she said she took another hall to the next class and I told her that was okay, to just stay away from them and to find a friend that wasn't associated with that group."
Coach:	"Patti, what led you to respond to Jessica in that way?"
Patti:	"You mean telling her is was okay to avoid them?"
Coach:	"Yes, can you identify where that belief comes from? Where did you learn to see conflict that way?"
Patti:	"Well, I am not sure. It seems like common sense. If someone or something was bothering me I would just avoid it."
Jim:	"That's the truth too. Patti, you avoid anything you don't like. Why just the other day you avoided Harriet at the grocery store because you said she is always so nosey and you didn't want to get into it with her, remember?"
Patti:	"Yes, I suppose that is true."
Coach:	"So Patti, in general, would you agree that one of your strategy is to avoid conflict?
Patti:	"Yes, I guess so. Conflict is messy and I get all flustered and really don't know what to say. I am one of those people that always thinks of the right thing to say after the fact. Even Jim and I don't have much conflict, I mean we have had our fights but we mostly just move on from them."
Coach:	"Being able to move on from a conflict is a strength. It shows the ability to move forward when faced with difficulties."
Patti:	"Well, I never thought of it like that"
Coach:	"Patti, what would you say are your most outstanding personality traits?"
Jim:	"Can I say something?"
Coach:	"Of course!"
Jim:	"I think one of Patti's outstanding personality strengths is her ability to juggle working and home making. She always seems to have time for me and the girls, whenever they need it."
Patti:	"Except now."
Coach:	"Hmm. This is interesting. Are you saying you don't have time for your daughter?"

Patti: "Well, I guess this isn't a timing issue. It is more that I don't have balance or that I just can't. . .or haven't had a conversation with her"

Coach: "don't sell yourself short just yet. We have only just begun, and you are here getting help. That tells me you are a supportive parent. I want you both to write down your best qualities. Take your time. Here maybe some scrap paper and a pen will help."

(A few minutes pass while Jim and Patti write down what they think are their most outstanding personality traits)

Coach: "Ok, well let's hear what you have written down"

Patti: "Well, I think I am a good leader. I can manage my time well. And I am a good cook. Cooking is fun for me. I get to be creative with what I make."

Coach: "So you are creative and have leadership. Thanks, Patti. How about you, Jim"

Jim: "Well, I think I have good work ethics. I am dependable and I am handy around the house."

Patti: "That is true, he fixes almost everything around the house."

Coach: You both seem to really be able to notice each other's strengths. That is a quality of a strong relationship. I don't see that with all my families, and I think that will help you get through this."

Note: The feeling in the room has moved. The tone was going in the direction of frustration and anger, but now both parents have softened and seem more open to the coaching process.

Coach: "Okay, let's look at Jessica's personality now. What would you say are her most outstanding personality traits?"

Patti: "Jessica is a good artist. She is very detailed and creative. She also is very giving. She gives so much away without a second thought about it.

Jim: "Jessica is also mature for her age and dependable. I can always count on her to get done whatever needs to be done."

Patti: "Yes, she is always there to take care of us too!"

Coach: "It is interesting to me how you both have such fond ideas of Jessica. Do you think she knows you think this way about her?"

Patti: "Gosh, I think she might have at one time, but we haven't really talked about that much lately. I am thinking maybe we need to let her know that we do see her good traits.

Coach: "So, you are starting to identify things you might want to try and do differently. What else might you try?"

Jim: "That is what we are here for. We'd love you to help us figure out what to do".

Note: the progression into action steps helps clients figure out forward steps. Sometimes during a first session, action steps may not be as fruitful or common as in later sessions. The first session is often about building rapport and helping the clients see a better future.

Coach: "Okay, well our time is almost up, but for today I want us to reflect on what we have discussed here. Both of you have identified areas you are good at, with yourself and within the family. You have also identified Jessica's strengths. You said earlier that you just wanted to have a conversation with Jessica. Let me ask, what do you think Jessica needs from you to feel willing to have that conversation?

Jim: "Excuse me, but how is this going to help us change Jessica's mind?"

Coach: "That is a good question Jim. Let's think about that a moment. What do you think will come about from us looking at each of your personality strengths?"

Jim: "Well, I am not so sure. I guess maybe we need to think about what each person is good at to remember how to love each other?"

Coach: "Exactly, Jim! You have been married a long time and have two almost-grown children. You are caring parents and a great family. You have had success with challenging situations in the past. So I'm wondering, how can you use the strengths you have identified to help you reach your goal of having a conversation with Jessica?

Jim: "Well, that is Patti's goal. I just want this whole thing to stop".

Coach: "It is frustrating for you, isn't it? Other than changing Jessica's mind, what else do you want? What would a good solution to this situation look like for you?

Jim: "Well, I want her to change her mind. But I also just want there to be less friction in the house."

Coach: "Less friction. More communication. That sounds similar to what Patti wants, a good conversation and improved relationship with Jessica."

Note: using the client's words here to reiterate the goal from before.

Coach: "So, you both have strengths to pull from. Jessica sounds like a great kid, and she clearly has two parents that are working to figure out how to move forward. So now I wonder. . .how do you want to move forward? What ideas do you have for making peace and having a good conversation?"

Patti & Jim: (looking at each other for a bit)

Patti: "Well, I think I could give her a little space, but also let her know that I would like to talk with her. I don't know, maybe I could invite her to lunch or even write her a letter"

Coach: "OK, now you are getting started with action steps for how to move forward. What else?"

Patti:	"Gosh. What else. I guess I could cook for her."
Coach:	"Anything else?"
Patti:	"I think what I'd like to do is bake her a treat, and put in a letter that I'd just like an opportunity to talk with her. I don't know if she'd be open, but I could try."
Coach:	"You remembered your cooking strength! Jim, how about you?"
Jim:	"I don't like this situation. I don't like it, and I want it to change, but I don't know how to change it. I really want you to tell us how to change it"
Coach:	"I appreciate your honesty. And I wish there was a magic wand. I will say that I do have some information about sexual identity and youth. I know we are about out of time today, but we could consider reviewing some resources or looking at ways other parents have successfully handled this kind of situation for guidance. The research on this topic is really geared toward acceptance of your daughter. Would you be open to that as either homework, or something we could go over next week?"
Jim:	"You know, maybe. I don't know. What if we let Patti try her idea, and then see what happens? If things are fixed, we won't even have to worry about it.
Coach:	"I like that you're supporting Patti's idea, and I hope it goes well. So Patti, you have a plan to try something this week. You shared several ideas. Is there one or two you want to try?
Patti:	"Yes, I do think baking a treat and writing a letter. That's what I'm going to try.
Coach:	"OK, so it sounds like you have a plan. Do you want to talk about when that will happen or what that will look like?"
Patti:	"Yes, I think it is worth a try. I think maybe I'll do it on Friday night. That will set us up for the weekend. And I am open to you idea of seeing what has worked for others, so I'd be happy to look at what you have as well".
Jim:	"Yeh, I'm fine with that"
Coach:	"OK, well you both have worked hard today. I feel like we are starting to know each other, and are moving forward. I also think Jessica has parents that love her and want the best. Patti, let's check in next week about how things went and in the mean time, I'll pull resources for you and send them to you in email. Does that work?"
Patti and Jim:	"Sounds good. Thanks, Doc!"
Coach:	"Great. Thanks so much for coming in today.

Chapter Summary

In this chapter, we began to explore the how-to of family life coaching. Family life coaches work with individuals, couples, and even whole families on family life topics. Family life coaches have content expertise on both family science and the coaching process. A typical family life coaching includes five steps in a single session.

1. Establishing a relationship
2. Solution or problem identification
3. Goals clarification
4. Action steps
5. Results, evaluation, and accountability.

While these steps typically occur in each session, the first few sessions focus mostly on building the relationship and establishing rapport. The intake process will be covered in detail in Chap. 6. Coaching is more than a coaching process; the coach must also have coaching competencies that facilitate the client growth and change. While there are a host of coaching competencies, the three most closely associated with family life coaching are listening, showing empathy, and empowering clients.

References

Beyer, M. (2008). Visit coaching: Building on family strengths to meet children's needs. *Juvenile & Family Court Journal, 59*(1), 47–60. doi:10.1111/j.1755-6988.2007.00004.x.

Brotman, L. E., Liberi, W. P., & Wasylyshyn, K. M. (1998). Executive coaching: The need for standards of competence. *Consulting Psychology Journal: Practice and Research, 50*(1), 40–46.

Center for Credentialing & Education. (2010). *Board Certified Coach (BCC) code of ethics.* Retrieved from: http://www.cce-global.org/Downloads/Ethics/BCCcodeofethics.pdf

Cooperrider, D. L., Whitney, D., & Stavros, J. M. (2008). *Appreciate inquiry handbook for leaders of change* (2nd ed.). Brunswick, OH: Crown Custom Publishing, Inc.

Gockel, A., Russel, M., & Harris, B. (2008). Recreating family: Parents identify worker-client relationships as paramount in family preservation programs. *Child Welfare, 87*(6), 91–113.

Grant, A. (2006). Solution-focused coaching. In J. Passmore (Ed.), *Excellence in coaching: The industry guide.* London: Kogan Page.

Heimendinger, J., Uyeki, T., Andhara, A., Marshall, J. A., Scarboro, S., Belansky, E., et al. (2007). Coaching process outcomes of a family visit nutrition and physical activity intervention. *Health Education & Behavior: The Official Publication of the Society for Public Health Education, 34*(1), 71–89. doi:10.1177/1090198105285620.

Hicks, R., & McCracken, J. (2010). Solution-focused coaching. *Physician Executive, 36*(1), 62–64.

International Coach Federation. (n.d.a). Core Competencies. Retrieved from http://www.coachfederation.org/icfcredentials/core-competencies/

International Coach Federation. (n.d.b). *The ICF code of ethics.* Retrieved from: http://www.
     absolutely-coaching.de/pdf/icf_code_of_ethics.pdf

Kaiser, A., & Hancock, T. (2003). Teaching parents new skills to support their young children's
     development. *Infants and Young Children, 16*(1), 9–21.

Kremenitzer, J. P. (2005). The emotionally intelligent early childhood educator: Self-reflective
     journaling. *Early Childhood Education Journal, 33*(1), 3–9. doi:10.1007/s10643-005-0014-6.

Lai, Y., & McDowall, A. (2014). A systematic review (SR) of coaching psychology: Focusing on
     the attributes of effective coaching psychologists. *International Coaching Psychology Review,
     9*(2), 118–134.

McGoldrick, M., & Carter, B. (2001). Advances in coaching: Family therapy with one person.
     Journal of Marital and Family Therapy, 27 (3), 281. doi:10.1111/j.1752-0606.2001.tb00325.x.

McLean, P. (2012). *The completely revised handbook of coaching: A developmental approach.*
     San Francisco: Jossey-Bass.

National Council on Family Relations. (2009). *Family life educators code of ethics.* Retrieved
     from: https://www.ncfr.org/sites/default/files/downloads/news/cfle_code__of_ethics_2012.pdf

Norcross, J., & Prochaska, J. (2002). Using the stages of change. *Harvard Mental Health Letter,
     18*(11), 5–7.

Raj, A., & Kumar, K. (2009). Optimizing parent coaches' ability to facilitate mastery experiences
     of parents of children with autism. *International Journal of Psychosocial Rehabilitation, 14*(2),
     25–36. Retrieved June, 15 2011, from http://www.psychosocial.com/IJPR_14/Optimizing_
     Parent_Coaches_Raj.html

Rogers, C. (1961). *On becoming a person.* Boston: Houghton Mifflin Company.

Rush, D., Shelden, M., & Hanft, B. (2003). Coaching families and colleagues: A process for
     collaboration in natural settings. *Infants & Young Children: An Interdisciplinary Journal of
     Special Care Practices, 16*(1), 33–47. Retrieved from EBSCOhost.

Schwartz, J. P. (2002). Family resilience and pragmatic parent education. *Journal of Individual
     Psychology, 58*(3), 250.

Stober, R. D., & Grant, A. M. (2006). Toward a contextual approach to coaching models. In R. D.
     Stober & A. M. Grant (Eds.), *Evidence based coaching handbook: Putting best practices to
     work for your clients* (pp. 17–50). Hoboken, NJ: Wiley.

Whitworth, L., Kinsey-House, H., & Sandahl, P. (1998). *Co-active coaching: New skills for
     coaching people toward success in work and life.* Lanham, MD: Davies-Black Publishing.

Williams, P., & Menendez, D. S. (2007). *Becoming a professional life coach: Lessons from the
     institute for life coach training.* New York: Norton & Co.

Chapter 6
The First Session and Intakes

> When we are no longer able to change a situation—we are challenged to change ourselves. (Viktor E. Frankl)

You have learned about coaching psychology, family life education, the foundations, applications, and skills of being a family life coach. The next step of learning to be a coach is to understand the process of coaching families. Coaching is a multi-step process and the first step includes the first contact, intake process, and the first session. While the work of building a coaching business happens before the coaching process, discussed in Chap. 13, This chapter provides an overview of coaching a client, including the first contact, intake process, and first session.

First Contact

You have been trained, you know how to coach, and now it is time to make your first contact with your new client. The first step in family life coaching involves finding clients. Best business practices suggest using a variety of marketing strategies to recruit families and individuals. These strategies include word of mouth, referrals from existing clients, website recruitment, and registries as part of a professional association or coaching registry. This is discussed in great detail in Chap. 13. Regardless of how a client comes to you, the first step is to introduce yourself and your services.

© Springer International Publishing Switzerland 2016
K. Allen, *Theory, Research, and Practical Guidelines for Family Life Coaching*,
DOI 10.1007/978-3-319-29331-8_6

I've been a coach for 6 years. The first three, I spent a lot of time on marketing by building relationships locally, talking at schools and libraries, taking information to fairs-I did it all. The last 2 years, no marketing other than Facebook. People find me now from word of mouth, Dr.'s offices, past clients, and workshops. **Alice Hanscam, Parent Coach**

Most first contacts come in the form of a phone call or an email, although contacts through social media are becoming common as well. In the first contact, clients will have questions about the process, outcomes, and the cost. Most coaches will benefit from having a website that offers an overview of the coaching process, as well as pertinent information about their business including location, type of coaching delivery (face to face or distance). Another new trend in both parenting education and family life education is partnering with family service providers, such as pediatricians, parenting education centers, social service providers, and educational settings to offer services to families.

Regardless of the clients are recruited, the first contact provides an opportunity for coaches to share the benefits and an overview of the coaching process. The initial call often comes in as either a cold call or referral. This is the coach's opportunity to explain the coaching process and begin to build the coaching relationship. Either the intake process or a practice session then follows this call.

Practice Session

Many coaches offer a free, short coaching session as a sample of the process. While this is not a standard service, some find this is a way to create buy-in from their prospective clients and helps them understand what to expect. A typical practice session is 15–20 min and includes the use of rapport building and powerful questions.

Intake

Much like other helping professions, most coaches utilize an intake process that allows the coach and client to get to know each other and more importantly, allows the coach to gain an understanding of the client's needs. A practice session can also accompany the intake, but more commonly, the coach uses an intake packet to gather information. Depending on the client, the intake can be completed prior to the first meeting, or it can be completed during the first coaching session.

I start with phone call, get basic information. I originally started with intake questionnaire. I found more often than not, they just brought it or forgot it, so I do intake in first call, the get to know you call, and continue it. I don't charge for first call. I get a fair amount of information in the first phone call. Tone wise; who is who and what is going one. Once we come together, I find out and focus on what is working. **Adrian Kalikow, parent coach**

Intake Packet

Most, but not all, coaches have their clients complete an intake packet that covers all elements and expectations of the coaching process. If the coach does not have a separate coaching agreement, this is the place to also include the coaching agreement. Each coach is responsible to create an intake packet that best represents the services and practices specific to the coach. Some coaches like short intake packets and then use the first session for exploring these items. Other coaches send out a full packet and ask for it back before the first session.

It is important to know your client and assess how they might best benefit from the intake packet. For example, I work with teen parents and I know from experience that these young parents are not likely to complete an intake packet on their own. Therefore I can use the first interview as the perfect place to learn more about the client by asking them questions from the intake packet. Once I have gained this knowledge I can follow up through social media and other technology to engage the client in the items that were left out but necessary for intake. Knowing your client can help you determine the best way to get the information you need to begin coaching.

Coaching Agreement

The agreement is the formal arrangement between coach and client. Typically, the coach can have a pre-written script, but the agreement needs to be both a mutual effort and a living document. The agreement will need to include confidentiality statements. There should be adequate space for the clients to add their own conditions, if they have any. This is where you identify the cost and frequency of the coaching sessions as well as the duration of the coaching agreement. McClean (2012 p. 128–129) identified the following components as important in a coaching contract: what is and isn't coaching, confidentiality, frequency of the coaching sessions, length of engagement, length of each session, cancellation policies, modality, location, price, client data, organizational information, measures of success and outcomes, feedback and observation practices, and the coaching process.

Guidelines

The guidelines are what the coach expects from the client. Guidelines can refer to the client/coach relationship, the coaching sessions themselves, or any other area the coach feels a need to address. For example, a coach may cover logistical items such as fees and appointments.

Client Information

Coaches need to collect the information needed to understand, as best as possible, the situation of the client. This is a typical client information sheet, including contact information, background, and other relevant details.

Background Information

Often presented as an open space for the client to write their story, the background allows the client the ability to give their coach a background story, a brief life summary of who they are as a person, and major life experiences to date. This allows the coach to get a "big picture" of the client.

Vision/Mission Statement

While most of us have not considered our personal vision or mission statement, some coaching intake packages include an opportunity for the client to provide a general statement about who they are and who they want to be. A mission statement provides a tangible, structured basis for behavior.

Solutions to Discover (Problems to Work On)

Clients come to coaching sessions for a reason—they want something to change. In this section, clients can describe the areas of their life that are causing them concern or stress as ideas for solutions.

Goals

Here the client combines the mission statement with the problem statement to create a set of goals for the coaching relationship. While clients might not know exactly what goals they want, this is an opportunity for them to begin to consider large and small, short and long term goals.

Sample Intake Form

Once a client has chosen you as their coach, the process of data collection and coaching begins. For most, the coaching session begins with an intake form. This is a sample intake form that I have been using for the past 3 years. I don't always include each section in my intake process, but my hope is this sample provides an overview to help you create your own intake form.

SampleWelcome/Intake Packet
Kimberly Allen, PhD
Raleigh, NC 27695

Date

Dear Client,

Welcome to coaching! I am so excited to be working with you in this process. As we talked about in our phone conversation, coaching is all about you getting where you want to be through personal exploration, goal setting, and action steps. It is my pleasure to work with motivated clients such as you as a partner, but please know that I view you as the expert on you. This process is about you leading the way by defining your own goals, developing your own definition of success, and helping me to support you on this journey.

I can tell you from experience that people have the best results when they are honest with themselves throughout the coaching process. I will do my best to be straightforward and supportive, and I will keep all our conversations confidential. Communication is key here, and I assure you that I will not be sharing your information with others.

AGREEMENTS
It is important that we agree to be:

- welcoming to new ideas
- working as a partnership
- supportive and respectful
- challenging in an encouraging way
- responsible for keeping the learning in motion
- accountable to our agreements

All clients should feel free to:

- Question!
- Say what works and what does not!
- Challenge!
- Be curious!
- Work to develop the most effective and rewarding coaching relationship for you.
- Notice and tell your coach what lifts your energy and what feels flat for you.

Based on our conversation, I would like to confirm our first meeting on [fill in the date and time]. The first session will be a time for us to go over coaching and it will be visioning session, so please hold 1.5 hours of your time for that session. All future sessions will last approximately 45 minutes. I am attaching a series of questions for you to complete as well. Please send those back to me 24 hours before our session. You will notice that the last page is a form to be completed before the following session as a way for you guide the conversation. Again, the more open and thoughtful you can be, the better the outcome.

Payment is due before the first session. The fee for this coaching process, which includes a visioning session and three coaching sessions and any correspondence in between, is $500.

Again, I am so happy to be working with you and I very much look forward to our first session. Please call with any questions.

Kim

Contact information here

Coaching Agreement

Please sign and date this page.

Confidentiality: I recognize that in the course of our work, you may give me a variety of personal and professional information. I will not at any time, either directly or indirectly, use any information for my own personal benefit, disclose, or communicate in any manner any information to any third party. I, Kim Allen, will not divulge that you and I are in a coaching relationship without your permission. I will hold everything that we say and do confidential unless you present as a physical danger to yourself or others. In this case, I will inform potential victims and legal authorities so that protective measures can be taken. In addition, you should know that unlike a physician or a lawyer our confidentiality agreement is not protected by law. Should it ever happen, I can not claim in court to be unable to divulge the contents of our conversations.

Nature of the relationship: You are aware that the coaching relationship is in no way to be construed as psychological counseling, psychotherapy, or any health-related service. In the event that you feel the need for professional counseling or therapy, it is your responsibility to seek a licensed professional. Coaching results are not guaranteed. You enter into coaching with the understanding that you are responsible for creating your own results. You are hiring Kim Allen, PhD for the purpose of advising and supporting you with respect to achieving your goals.

Client has read and agrees to parameters of Kim's coaching practice which have been outlined on the two previous pages:

Client signature: _____ Date: _____

Coach signature: _____ Date: _____

Personal Information

Date:_____

Name:_____

Complete home address: _____

Home phone: _____

Cell phone: _____

Fax: _____

E-mail address: _____

Website: _____

Occupation: _____

Student (what, where, year): _____

Work phone: _____

Work fax: _____

Date of birth: _____

Relationship status: _____

Family Structure (ie, names and ages of children, people that live in your home, etc):

_____

How did you find me ? _____

Vision and Mission Statement

While we most often think of companies and organizations as having vision and mission statements, it is sometimes a good practice to identify a personal vision or mission statement. A mission statement is simply a written description of what you are all about. There is no right or wrong way to create this, and it helps to consider your past successes, your core values, and goals. It can be long or short; the goal of this activity is simply to begin thinking about who you are and where you want to go.

Solutions to problems

This is your chance to let me know what you would like to change in your life. Coaching is often about growth and development, but it is also about finding solutions to problems in our lives. Here you can tell me what it is that brings you to coaching and any ideas you might already have for possible solutions. Don't worry if you don't have solution ideas just yet, we can always work on that together.

Goal Worksheet

The coaching process works best when each have an understanding of what you hope to accomplish. Once way to do this is by setting goals. On this form, please identify the goals you most achieve through the coaching process.Not everyone has a clear idea of goals and goals sometimes change in the coaching process. This isn't a document set in stone, but rather an opportunity for you to explore what you want from coaching. As such, so please write 3-5 of your family life, personal and/or professional goals. When you set the right goals for yourself, you will probably feel excited, a little nervous, and willing to get started. Your goals may evolve over time. This exercise is to give you a clear place from which to start.

The specific, measurable goal is:	Start date	Finish date
1.		
2.		
3.		

What are the benefits to you of accomplishing these goals? Put differently, what changes if you reach your goals?

1.

2.

3.

PERSONAL & PROFESSIONAL STRENGTHS
What do you consider to be your greatest strengths?

1.

2.

3.

MOST SIGNIFICANT PERSONAL & PROFESSIONAL ACCOMPLISHMENTS
What are you most proud of? Why?

1.

2.

3.

The First Session

Regardless of whether or not the intake packet was utilized, the first session is about building rapport and getting to know your client and their goals for coaching. This takes a bit longer, and as such, I typically allow for one and half hours or more to complete the process. The first few minutes almost always include small talk, and then a review of the coaching process. During this opening, it is important to build rapport. Rapport is the feeling of connectedness and harmony between a practitioner and the client (Morrison, 1995). Trust is a key component of the coaching process, and rapport helps build that trust.

The intake session is also a time to understand more about what the client (s) thinks and feels about their current life; what motivates or inspires the client, and specifics about the coaching process (Skibbins, 2007). Some coaches utilize assessments in the first session, such as a life satisfaction scale or a life balance scale. Others use visual imagery or the 4-D Appreciative Inquiry (AI) approach. Assessments will be covered in Chap. 7, and I will share both a visual imagery approach as well as a 4-D AI approach later in this chapter.

> ### Notes or Not?
> One question I hear often from students is whether or not to take notes. Each person needs to determine if note taking is right for them. I am a note taker, and writing key phrases and words helps me use the client's own language while I am actively listening or trying to help the client grow. Writing key phrases or words helps me focus on what is important to the client.

Language is connected to client success. If a client can clearly understand you and see that you understand them, it helps to create an alliance (Rogers, 1961). Mirroring the clients' language can accentuate the relationship, especially if you take verbal and non-verbal cues from your client and adjust accordingly (Morrison, 1995). Teenagers, for example, might not like the mirroring as much as other clients.

Notes are also valuable as a form of measurement for future references (Skibbins, 2007). It is important to remain alert and attentive, and taking notes requires a balance. As a courtesy, it is helpful to let the client know why you are taking notes, and it is best to be sure the note taking is kept to a minimum (Morrison, 1995).

It is also important to establish boundaries during the first session. The coaching process is about giving time for the client to explore, so it is important that coaches keep the session about the client and the client's goals. Clients might ask you personal questions, and it is the discretion of the coach to determine if and how the answer might benefit the client (Morrison, 1995). Beyond communication barriers, there are other pleasantries to consider; what to call each other, for example, can be addressed in the first session

The first session is about understanding the client, their vision for the future, their strengths, and their passions. While this could be done through a series of powerful questions, there are also activities, such as story telling and visualization, that help coaches better understand their client. The next two sections are about stories and visualization activities.

Future Self-Visualization Activity

My coach, Dr. Andrea Shaw, used this visualization process with me during my intake session. I found the process to be incredibly impactful, and it is an activity I use often when training family life education students.

Instructions Explain to the client that you are about to take them on a mental journey; one that help them better visualize what life might look like if they achieve their goals. Encourage them to find a comfortable position and let them know that they might want to have paper and pen nearby so at the end of the experience they can jot down anything they noticed and wish to record. Using your own words, say something along the lines of the following script:

Script "I invite you to close your eyes, if you're comfortable with that. If not, just allow a gaze. Notice the chair in which you are setting. Notice how your body feels inside the chair. Notice where there's constriction and where there is ease. Let your awareness settle on the breath. Breath in, and out. In and out.

As you are breathing, begin to notice your thoughts, letting them come and go at own pace. Trust yourself to notice and rest in awareness. Perhaps you find this a relief-you don't have to fight or follow thoughts. For right now, you have nowhere to go and nothing else to do. You can allow your full presence into this experience. As your body relaxes, notice what happens to your breathing

I invite you to imagine that you can transport yourself into the future. You can choose the time frame, 1–5–10–20 years. Choose a specific time and then imagine you can transport yourself to that time in the future in any way, real or imagined. If you like fast cars, you can drive, or if you've ever wanted to fly on the Concord, here is your chance. If you'd prefer an imaginary or whimsical method, ride a magic carpet or go in a special traveling machine. Whatever transportation calls you forward. Allow yourself to feel safe taking that ride into the future. You're traveling in time and space to the most optimal place you can possibly conceive of in your best future.

Now you find yourself arriving in a new place and time. The time you pick, and the place you are in the future. Begin to notice the surroundings where you've landed. Notice the landscape. Notice the weather. What do you see when you look out there?

Now you begin to notice a dwelling. This is the dwelling of your future self, the most desirable version of you that you can imagine. Maybe it is a dream house, or maybe it is the place where your dream life happens. Approach the dwelling knowing that your future self is on the other side of the door. You notice that to the side of the door there is a basket. This is a special basket, one that allows you to leave any aspects of you or your current life that you no longer want to carry with you. Begin to leave behind the things that cause you stress. The items that cause you pain. And if you change your mind later on, you can always retrieve anything you left in the basket.

Go to the door. When you knock on the door, your future self opens the door and you greet each other. You see now your wise, future self. Notice your appearance; see your energy, and the feeling of space. How does it feel? What is different about your future life, or your future dwelling?

Go in, look around and then find a place for a comfortable conversation. Ask your future self the questions you need answers to. What did you do to get to this place, or this way of being? Take time, and listen to what your future self has to say. *__Given the way you know yourself__*, what is said about what you most need to remember regarding how to get from where you are now to where you are in the future.

What advice is given? Then feel free to ask any other questions you may have.

It is time to return. You find yourself giving thanks for spending this time together. Take in the surroundings once again before you prepare to leave. Now you can return in your chosen transportation. Begin to travel back.

I'm going to count from three to one so you can comfortably return...

3. feeling your body; feel yourself again in your chair.
2. allow awareness of your breath and a sense of whole awareness
1. as you are ready, allow your eyes to open"

> Take a moment. I'm going to be quiet for a moment. Please use this time to Give yourself to jot down what that experience was like for you, what stands out in the memory of this experience. (Adapted from Andrea Shaw, Ph.D.)

Once completed, the coach and client have a discussion about the events that occurred in the visualization process. This activity is especially useful at helping a client gain a better understand of their own wisdom, as well as a way for the coach to gain a better understanding of the client's process and feelings of self.

Appreciative Inquiry 4-D Model of Intake

We have established that the first session is important for helping clients visualize their ideal life. As we learned in Chap. 4, Appreciative Inquiry (AI) can be explained best in a 4-D Cycle: Discovery, Dream, Design, and Destiny (Cooperrider, Whitney, & Stavros, 2008).

Discovery is helping the client understand the strength they are bringing into the coaching session. This is not only a great way to help build a rapport, it also provides valuable insight and information about the client. This happens by asking the client to identify some peak times in their lives. Name times, places, and events when all was right with the world, and life was as it should be. As they share insights from these events, the coach can begin to identify strengths, values, and what is most important to the client. This information can be useful to both coach and client as they move through the coaching process.

Dreaming is understanding further the client's idea of where they want to go. While this information comes regularly throughout the coaching process, dreaming, or imaging what might be, can be especially useful at the start of a coaching relationship for two reasons. First, it aids in the process of rapport building and second, it helps the client and coach better understand where the clients wants to go. While there are many activities that can help a client better understand what can be, one activity that has been widely used to help clients dream is the Future Self Visualization process mentioned above. Other approaches would be asking a client to describe what success would look like.

The **Design** and **Destiny** phase are less common in the first session, but are opportunities to design action steps, known in AI as possibility statements or design principles. Some AI coaches have the clients write out a statement of the ideal family life, and begin the process of identifying a path to completion. The statement of an ideal life activity has been useful for clients to better visualize what family life could look like if goals are met and honors the client's current experience by allowing them to understand they hold the wisdom and the answers. While this activity may not work for all clients, it is an example of dream activities that help to better understand the client and help the client better understand themselves.

Finishing the Session

The first session is about discovery and process, but clients want and deserve results. Actions steps and evaluation are still a part of the first session. An important component of any coach session is the accountability step, which often looks like action steps that will be taken outside of the coaching session as homework. Ideally, the homework will be a result of the process of dream and design, and will likely need a bit of accountability language on the part of the coach.

Action steps need to be identified and designed by the client. It is often a tendency of educators and counselors to assign homework. Clients might even come to the session expecting action steps to be identified by the coach. In the coaching process, however, it is important to allow the client to identify the activities they will complete as well as the process for how those activities will be completed. It is the coaches role to have the client identify the coaching steps and an accountability process for those action steps.

Williams and Menendez (2007) describe accountability as a step in the coaching process. They suggest that accountability doesn't necessarily have to be related to performance, but rather it could be about changing behavior or increasing aware-ness of thinking patterns. Coaches, then, must ask for direction in a new way, a way that engages the client. For example, "what might be your first step towards creating the change you want to see?" This question encourages clients to think about themselves and how they want to move forward. Accountability doesn't stop at the coaching session; accountability continues. "How would you like to be held accountable for this work?" This question again places the onus back on the client reminding them that the work is theirs, and what they choose for accountability needs to be followed through. If the accountability is directed to the client, the chances of success are even higher. A coach is not the task-master but rather the provocateur helping the client identify goals, action steps, and accountability that the client owns.

Case Study

Desiree is a single mom of two young boys, 16 months and 3 years. She is feeling overwhelmed—she works a full-time job and a part time job to support herself and her kids. Her support system is consists of her grandmother, who watches the children while she is at work. Desiree is confident in her abilities as a mother, but wants guidance in organizing and balancing her life. She remarks that she never takes any time for herself; that she is always "running around doing something for the kids." She says she has no interest in dating, as it is "a waste of time," although admits it would be nice to have a partner to help her out. This is the first family life coaching session.

Coach: "Hello Desiree. How are you doing?"

Desiree: "Okay. How are you?"

Coach: "I am well today. I'm really happy you called. When we talked on the phone last week, it seemed you were really busy, so I am extra glad you made time for coaching"

Desiree: "Yes, I went back and forth about whether or not I even have time for this. I swear, my life is crazy right now!"

Coach: (somewhat playfully) "So I bet you are really hoping this is worth you time, then?"

Desiree: (laughing) "exactly!"

Coach;   "Were you able to bring with you the intake packet I emailed you?"

Desiree: "Actually no, I was not. I am so sorry. I must have left it in the diaper bag."

Coach: "That is okay. The first meeting is usually where I describe the coaching relationship, where we exchange our expectations, and also where we begin to understand some of your goals and strengths. I will ask questions. Lots of questions to help me get to know you better. It will be good to do it in person. I know I explained some of this on our short intro call last week, but do you have any questions?"

Note: The coach does not judge or make the client feel bad, but reframes as an opportunity to build the relationship.

Desiree:	"No, I am looking forward to this. I haven't done anything for myself in a very long time."
Coach:	"Great, then let's get started. I might ask some of the questions on the intake, but we don't have to stay on that script. Just let me know if something comes up or you'd like to move in a different direction. It would help me to get a bit of information from you to start the process. Does that work?"
Desiree:	"Sure"
Coach:	"Okay so let's start with our agreements. We are working as a partnership. This is a big part of coaching—I'm not the expert on you, you are. So it is important that we see this as teamwork. My role in the relationship is to help you define your own goals and then you decide how you want to get there. Your role is to be open minded, and willing to make any changes you decide to make. We need to agree to support each other, be respectful, and sometimes, I will challenge you and ask you to be accountable for our actions. What do you think about that?"
Desiree:	"That sounds good. I agree to all of that. In fact I am looking forward to learning something."
Coach:	"Terrific! Well, let's begin with the confidentiality coaching agreement; everything you say will be completely confidential between you and me. Our conversations will remain confidential including any mention to anyone about a coaching relationship unless. There is one exception. I am a mandated reporter, which means if I detect physical danger to you or others, I will need to report that. Also, I am not practicing psychotherapy so if I see any problems that may present as needing psychological counseling, I will refer you to someone else. We've already talked about fees, frequency and length of sessions, but do let me know if you have questions about that"
Desiree:	"Nope. I think we are good. Do I need to sign the coaching agreement?"
Coach:	"Yes, thank you. If you don't have any questions let's begin with page 5, the Goal Worksheet."
Desiree:	"Okay, hmmm, a measurable goal. That one is kind of tough. It's hard to measure not being overwhelmed. Well, first and foremost I would like some balance in my life."
Coach:	"Balance! Yes, I think that is a word I've heard from you a couple of times already. That must be important to you."
Desiree:	Yes!"
Coach.	"So how would you know if you were balanced? What would balance look like to you?"
Desiree:	"Hmm. What would it look like? (thinking). . .that would look like me not being so stressed and actually enjoying time with the kids instead of just rushing around from one place to the next."
Coach:	"OK, so a calmer, less rushed life. What else? Tell me what that would look like, enjoying time with the kids."

Desiree: "Oh, I don't know, taking them to a park for an hour. Pushing them on the swings. Making dinner for my grandmother and us all sitting down together instead of me rushing out the door."

Coach: "So having time to enjoy your family sounds important to you. Is there anything else you want to add to your goals?"

Desiree: "Yes I would like an evening out every once in a while."

Coach: "What does once in a while look like to you?"

Desiree: "Well, I don't know maybe once a month to start. I mean every week would be nice but let's be honest. I work all the time. It's not possible."

Coach: "Okay, once a month for an evening out. What would you do on that evening out?"

Note: in the first session, the goal is to better understand the client's vision and goals. However, sometimes clients benefit from a bit of stretching, or really encouraging them to think a bit more.

Desiree: "Maybe see a movie, get a manicure or my hair done. That sounds nice. I don't have too many friends because I work all the time, but having dinner with a friend too. Maybe someone from work."

Coach: "So quality family and personal time seem to be important, and part of that balance might include having friends to socialize with...is that right?

Desiree: "yes, I think so. I think that is what I'm looking for"

Coach.   "So tell me about a time when you felt balance...when you had quality time with your family and for yourself. What did that look like?"

Desiree: "Gosh. I don't know. Let me think. Honestly, ever since I had the kids, I haven't felt balanced".

Coach: "So having kids has made balance hard. Go ahead and tell me about a time when you felt balanced"

Desiree: "well, I guess before I had kids, I had more free time, and could spend more time doing what I wanted."

Coach: "ah, so you have had success! I knew it! (smiles)."

Coach: "I think it is important to recognize that you have been successful before. And not that long ago, really. You oldest is three, right? (Desiree nods). I feel encouraged, and confident you can get there again.

Desiree: "oh, that feels good. Thanks for believe in me (laughs)"

Coach: "Okay let's talk further. What are the personal or professional benefits you would receive from accomplishing these goals—spending fun time with your kids, enjoying a meal with your grandmother, and getting out for an evening once a month."

Desiree: "Benefits, hmmm. Well I think it would help my relationship with my kids. I love them so much but I am always so busy I feel more like a planner than their mother. We could run, laugh, and play together. It would bring me joy."

Coach: "That does sound lovely. Okay what about dinner with your grand-mother, how will that benefit you?"

Desiree: "Well, I could say thank you. She watches the kids all the time and I can't really pay her much for her help. I would love to show her how much I appreciate her help. I think dinner would do that."

Coach: "Yes, an act of service to say thank you for all you do, a celebration of her devotion to you and your children."

Desiree: "Yes, she really is the reason this all works so smoothly."

Coach: "Sounds like she is a big support. Let's move onto page 6. What would you say are some of your personal and professional strengths?"

Desiree: 'Well, let's see. I am determined and unafraid. I am a hard worker, articulate, and I persevere, never give up. That is how things got to this place. I got to make the best life for my kids. They are my life. I am not gonna let them ever give up. Things are hard, suck it up and make it work. It's do or die. I do."

Coach: "Wow, I see your passion. You must have something deep inside of you that fuels this passion."

Desiree: "Yes, passion. I got that too! That comes from my hard upbringing. It was do or die then. That's when I learned it and I am never gonna give up."

Coach: "Wow, you were able to spin that to a positive! That is a sign of resilience, and certainly is a strength. What would you say are the most significant personal and professional accomplishments in your life?"

Note: rather than dwelling on past experiences that are likely emotionally charged, the coach identifies the strength and moves forward.

Desiree: "My children. Their father and I are not together, and he ended up moving back to his home, out of state. So they don't see him too often. So for now, that's my role"

Coach: "Okay, what else?"

Desiree: "My jobs. I always have a job. Gotta put food on the table and I want my family to live in a respectable place. It doesn't have to be "all that" but I don't want any crime or danger for my children and grandmother."

Coach: "Desiree, I'm seeing a lot of strengths in you, and your self awareness is impressive. I think that will aid in you reaching your goals. I think we have spent a lot of time going over these questions already. This next section has some more thoughtful questions to get you thinking in a way that will hopefully get our work together successful. Are you OK to keep going?"

Desiree: "Sure. In a weird way, this is kind of fun. I don't really think about this stuff too much"

Coach: "Great. First question—If there were no obstacles in the way, what dream would you like to make happen?"

Desiree: "Well, I have always wanted to get my degree. I couldn't do it now, not with the children and work but that would be one big dream I have always had. I only got my Associates degree. I would love to have a 4 year degree from a University."

Coach: "I have to say, I am feeling really excited for you about that. We'll come back to that as I don't want to lose that goal. Second question—What parts of your current job or life activities do you enjoy the most?"

Desiree: "I like being the "go-to" person at work, and music. I love music. I also like to see the results of my work. Like my second job; I'm a maid. I mean it's just a means to an end but it is nice to see it all clean when I am done. It is also flexible. I only do it every other week. But I like that there is a visual result. It makes me feel like I did something worth doing."

Coach: "Okay, sounds like you enjoy the fruits of your labor."

Desiree: "I guess I do. That's what I am missing about my kids. I miss seeing them and playing with them and enjoying them."

Coach: "How have you been motivated in the past to reach difficult goals, or challenging things? How can we best utilize that motivator now?"

Desiree: "Well, I think by focusing on the end result. I like to see that result and if I start to get discouraged I just remind myself what it will look like when it is done and I plow through. Do or die."

Coach: "Uh-huh. Do or die. I suspect you will choose do. So what do I need to know about you that will help me the most in coaching you?"

Desiree: "Gosh. I don't know. I will say that I've already spent more time thinking about all this today than I have in a long time. That is good. OK, you should know that I am direct and to the point. I don't beat around the bush. I work for results and I expect results. Also I'm always aware of time. So as not to put a burden on you or anything but time is money."

Coach: "This is very helpful Desiree. I have enjoyed getting to know you today. My intake sessions usually take a full hour and half, but I know you said you just have less than an hour today. I don't typically assign homework, but since our time is short, I have an exercise I'd like you to do at home if you are willing. I think this will help you to determine which way you want to go and you seem like the type of person that is willing to do some hard work to get to the end. I feel that a values activity may help you determine how best to spend your time, thus freeing up some time for your goals. Are you open to doing some homework?"

Desiree: "Yes, I hope I have time. How long will it take?"

Coach: "It shouldn't take more than 20 to 30 min. It is called the Values Process Activity. If you want to do the second page, Magical Moments, go ahead but you don't have to. Okay?"

Desiree: "Sure. I'm sorry I have to go, but I'll be sure to do this activity.

Coach:	"I really respect that you have taken time out of an already busy day to work on your balance. I like you and thank you very much for taking time to meet with me."
Desiree:	"Yes, this has already been helpful. I'm leaving on a high"
Coach:	"Okay. It was nice meeting you Desiree. Just to be clear, you are going to complete the values process activity, and then at our call in 2 weeks, we'll go over that?"
Desiree:	"yes, sounds good. Thanks, coach!"

The first session is truly about getting information, understanding the client and his or her goals, and building the relationship. Communication skills are very important, and will be discussed more in Chap. 8. Keeping the focus on the client, and encouraging them to drive the process is critical in coaching, although in the first session, the coach has specific information to gather, making this session more driven by the coaching than subsequent sessions. The next chapter will focus on the process of gaining additional information in through assessments and on other models of coaching.

Chapter Summary

The coaching relationship begins with the first session. Having a clear and consistent process for setting up the coaching relationship is key to success. The coaching agreement is the formal arrangement between coach and client that includes confidentiality statements, guidelines, and client information. The agreement often comes as part of an intake packet, and the intake process can either happen independently before the session or as part of the first session. The first meeting is primarily about defining the coaching process and building a rapport. If following the appreciative inquiry process, the first session will focus on discovery, which is a process where the client and the coach better understand past successes.

References

Cooperrider, D. L., Whitney, D., & Stavros, J. M. (2008). *Appreciate inquiry handbook for leaders of change* (2nd ed.). Brunswick, OH: Crown Custom Publishing, Inc.

McLean, P. (2012). *The completely revised handbook of coaching: A developmental approach.* San Francisco: Jossey-Bass.

Morrison, J. (1995). *The first interview.* New York: The Guilford Press.

Rogers, C. (1961). *On becoming a person.* Boston: Houghton Mifflin Company.

Skibbins, D. (2007). *Becoming a life coach.* Oakland, CA: New Harbinger Publications, Inc.

Williams, P., & Menendez, D. S. (2007). *Becoming a professional life coach: Lessons from the institute for life coach training.* New York: Norton & Co.

Chapter 7
Models of Coaching and Assessments

> If you change the way you look at things, the things you look at change.
> (Wayne Dyer)

Chapter 7 provides an overview of research-based assessments that are helpful in coaching families. To further illustrate the importance of assessments, readers will be required to complete their own strengths-based assessments and familial assessments to help them better understand themselves as a coach and to provide practice on the use of assessments.

Assessments identified in this chapter include Strengths Finder, Styles of Conflict Management, Styles of Decision Making, Communication, Interpersonal Strengths Model, Learning Style Inventory, Assessing Parenting, Keys to Interactive Parenting Scale, Relationship Satisfaction Survey, and more.

Assessments in Family Life Coaching

Across the various disciplines of coaching, assessments are regularly used to help clients. The term assessment means evaluation, or estimation, and includes a broad spectrum of evaluation tools that help provide information about a person (Hunsley, 2002). Assessments bring awareness about who people are, what is important to them, and in what direction to go while gaining personal insights and clarity designed to help people reach their goals. Formal assessments have been well-researched and proven to be scientifically valid and reliable, while informal assessments have not undergone extensive evaluation (Neukrug & Fawcett, 2010). Formal assessments often require specific training and credentials of the facilitator

© Springer International Publishing Switzerland 2016
K. Allen, *Theory, Research, and Practical Guidelines for Family Life Coaching*,
DOI 10.1007/978-3-319-29331-8_7

(APA, 2000). Although informal assessments have not undergone extensive testing, their results can still provide insights and encourage the process of self-discovery.

As Neukrug and Fawcett (2010) discuss, assessments have been around for centuries; the first evidence of testing goes back to ancient times and has been a staple of the coaching industry since its inception. Business and industry began using situational testing on potential employees and budding managers back in the 1930's to help decisions on hiring practices. The first psychologist used assessments to help them understand intelligence, cognitive abilities, and career aptitudes, but practitioners around the same time began using informal assessments called clinical interviews to help them understand how to best treat their patients.

Today, assessments are used for identifying abilities, including achievement and aptitude testing; personality assessment; and informal assessments for a host of issues (Neukrug & Fawcett, 2010). As family life practitioners, there are questions to consider when identifying assessments for our clients.

- How will the assessment be use?
- How valid or reliable is the instrument?
- How will the administration of an instrument impact my client?
- Are there privacy or developmental concerns?
- Is the tool fair or culturally competent?
- Am I qualified to use this tool?
- What about FERPA and HIPPA laws?

Although many of the assessments highlighted in this chapter are free and openly available to practitioners, it is important to do your own research on the tools you use to make sure they are appropriate for your clients and that you are qualified to use the tools. Confidentiality is also an important consideration, and one that should be covered with the clients you serve. Most of the assessments presented here are informal and are not used for diagnostic purposes, but for self-growth for you and your client. There are ethical considerations for use of assessments, and it is the responsibility of the practitioner to make sure to follow all rules and ethics of the governing body of your professional association or accreditation.

Coaching Assessments

In this section, a short overview of a few of the top assessments used in the field of coaching and family science will be reviewed. These assessments I have commonly found in coaching and family life books, but this is not a complete listing nor is this an endorsement for any of the assessments. It is the responsibility of the coach to research and find assessments that are appropriate for your clients. However, my hope is that this will be an overview of the possibilities you might use to help your client gain insight and ideas for how to best move forward, as well as a glimpse of a few assessments to use when coaching parents and families.

VIA Character Strength Inventory

Values in Action (VIA) inventory (Peterson & Park, 2009; Seligman & Peterson, 2004) is a free, online survey designed to identify character strengths, or attributes of human excellence that facilitate human flourishing. More than two million people from all around the world have tested this survey, which is part of the positive psychology movement. The survey consists of 120 questions on a variety of topics designed to help individuals identify their greatest strengths. Scoring is done through a Likert scale ranging from most like you to least like you.

Once the survey is completed, a report will be generated that identifies all 24 strengths, ranging from the highest to the lowest. Based on the results, individuals can learn how to utilize their strengths to reach their potential. The scale gives results in many categories, including strengths in youth, parenting, work, and general. Their website has many resources for professionals that serve families and individuals. http://www.viacharacterblog.org/resources-for-professionals/

Strengths Finder

Strengths Finder 2.0 (Rath, 2007) is an assessment tool designed to help in the identification of strengths. Donald O. Clifton, Tom Rath, and scientists from the Gallup Company developed the program in 1989, and it has gone through several iterations of improvements. The survey is completed online through a series of questions answered by the client. Questions, such as "I like to jump right into things" are asked to help identify the top 5 strengths out of a possible 34.

Once completed, the system sends a report of the top five character strengths identified. The survey is accompanied by a book that provides a detailed description of all the strengths, ideas for action based on the strength, and tips for working with others that may have that strength. The same company has expanded to include an assessment for youth ages 10–14 called Strengths Explorer.

Satisfaction with Life Scale

The Satisfaction with Life Scale by Ed Diener (Diener, Emmons, Larsen, & Griffen, 1985) is a five question assessment that includes a 7-point Likert scale with 1 = strongly disagree to 7 = strongly agree. The scale is designed to measure global judgments of a person's life satisfaction and takes about 1 min to complete. While this measure does not specify satisfaction with life domains, it does help the coach understand emotional wellbeing.

1. In most ways my life is close to my ideal.
2. The conditions of my life are excellent.

3. I am satisfied with life.
4. So far I have gotten the important things I want in life.
5. If I could live my life over, I would change almost nothing.

To score the assessment, add up the numbers from your answers, which will give you a range of 5 to 35. Scores of 21–25 are considered normal. This scale has been empirically validated (Diener et al., 1985) and can be followed up by additional probing questions to help better understand the results. Follow up questions could include "what could you do differently to increase towards your ideal life?" and "which areas of your life are you more satisfied with".

Psychological Well-Being Scale

The Ryff and Singer (1998) scale measures multiple facets of well-being includes self-acceptance, ties to others, autonomy of thought, ability to manage complexity, pursuit of life purpose, setting meaningful goals, and growth and development. Diener et al. (2009) developed a shorter version of the scale, which is presented here. Similar to the Satisfaction with Life Scale (SWLS), the Psychological Well Being Scale uses a 7-point Likert scale with 1 = strongly disagree to 7 = strongly agree.

1. I lead a purposeful and meaningful life.
2. My social relationships are supportive and rewarding.
3. I am engaged and interested in my daily activities.
4. I actively contribute to the happiness and well-being of others.
5. I am competent and capable in the activities that are important to me.
6. I am a good person and live a good life.
7. I am optimistic about my future.
8. People respect me.

To score, add the numbers, which will range from 8–56. The higher the score, the higher the feelings of well-being. This scale provides a reliable snapshot of a client's overall feelings of well-being. Similar to the SWLS, this scale could be followed up with additional probing questions, such as "what activities make you feel most engaged" and "what are you optimistic about for your future".

Life Wheel Assessment

An assessment that has gained great popularity in the coaching industry is a tool designed to help individuals develop a clearer idea of their life balance.The Life Wheel Assessment, Wheel of Life Assessment, Life Balance Wheel—although there are a large variety of titles, names, trademarks, and websites, the overall idea is the same.

On a scale of 1–10, coaches have clients identify their current satisfaction level on the following eight areas of life:

1. **Family:** quality of relationship with family members, quality and quantity time spent, happiness with partner
2. **Health/Wellbeing**: fitness, nutrition, stress, healthful living, wellness
3. **Work/Career**: job satisfaction, workplace relations, use of talents, joy of work
4. **Recreation and Fun:** hobbies, travel, vacation, laughter, adventure, activities
5. **Friends and Social Connection:** community involvement, friends, feelings of connectedness
6. **Personal Growth and Development:** opportunities for growth, intellectual challenges, education, self-efficacy
7. **Family Resources:** financial planning, time management, goal setting, life transitions
8. **Life Fulfillment/Spirituality:** life purpose, stewardship, feelings of spirit

Life Wheel Assessment

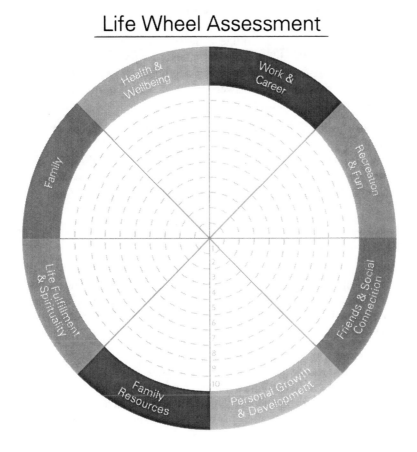

To score, simply plot out each section from the 1–10 rating for each level. For example, if a person gets a 7 on work and career and a 9 on recreation and fun and a 10 on friends, you would put a dot at the 7, 9, and 10 levels. Connect all dots to create a circle. The final result will be a wheel with varying levels of satisfaction. Although there is no ideal, balance is considered valuable to most. Areas with the lowest satisfaction rate could be considered important for coaching practices and client goals.

Learning Style Inventory

This assessment is based upon the work of psychologist David Kolb's learning styles. Kolb believed that learning is a process by which knowledge transferred through a person's experience (McLeod, 2010). This assessment is used to determine the learning style of a respondent based upon answering specific questions about your own specific preference of being educated (McLeod, 2010). The Learning Style inventory focuses on how people learn by identifying which category best suits their learning style . This is relevant to family coaching because it can be used to determine a possible career choice, to assist with educational issues with children, or for clients to process how they take in information. This assessment is currently administered online, the respondent answers a series of questions. Answers are then scored to determine which of the four quad-rants a participant falls into.

1. **Divergent**-(Feeling and watching): Sensitive, using imagination to solve problems
2. **Assimilating**-(Watching and thinking): Logical, interest in abstract ideas
3. **Converging**- (Thinking and doing): Practical, using technical skills
4. **Accommodating**-(Feeling and doing): Hands on, relying on intuition

Relationship Assessment Scale

The relationship assessment scale (Hendrick, 1988) is a short, 7-items inventory designed to measure relationship satisfaction. This instrument has been validated. Using a 5-point Likert scale with $1 =$ Low to $7 =$ High, individuals answer the following questions:

1. How well does your partner meet your needs?
2. In general, how satisfied are you with your relationship?
3. How good is your relationship compared to most?
4. How often do you wish you hadn't gotten into the relationship? (R)
5. To what extent has your relationship met your original expectations?
6. How much do you love your partner?
7. How many problems are there in your relationship? (R)

To score this scale, simply add the scores (4 and 7 are reverse scored). The higher the score, the more satisfied the relationship. This can be useful in coaching individuals or couples on relationship issues. Follow up questions could help further growth and exploration. For example, if a client states their partner is not meeting their needs well, a follow-up question could be "how has your partner met your needs in the past?" or "how could your partner better meet needs your needs in the future?"

Parent Satisfaction Scale

The Parent Satisfaction Scale (Guidubaldi & Cleminshaw, 1985) is a short, 10-item inventory designed to address perceptions of the parent-child relationship. This instrument has been validated and is free to use and requires no training. Using a 4-point Likert with 1 = strongly disagree to 4 = strongly agree, individuals answer the following questions:

1. I wish I did not become impatient so quickly with my children.
2. I am upset with the amount of yelling I direct towards my children.
3. I wish I were more consistent in my parenting behaviors.
4. Sometimes I feel I am too critical of my children.
5. I feel uncomfortable with the way I often discipline my children.
6. I wish I were a better parent and could do a better job parenting.
7. I am satisfied with my child-rearing skills.(R)
8. I wish I gave my children more individual attention.
9. Sometimes I feel I should provide more supervision for my children.
10. I am satisfied with the amount of time I can give to my children. (R)

To score this scale, simply add the scores (7 and 10 are reverse scored). The higher the score, the more positive the perceptions of the parent-child relationship. Parent and family coaches can use this to help parents identify their perceptions of the parent-child relationships and can be used for further exploration. For example, if a parents answers that they are upset with the amount of yelling they direct towards their children, then the coach could follow up with a strengths-based questions about times when the parent has been successful, and thus can begin to increase perceptions and identify strategies for improved parent-child interactions.

Parenting Style Assessment

What's your parenting style (Pitzer, 2001) is part of the Parents Forever Line Course for parents. This 32 question inventory is divided into eight sections asking parents to identify the statement most like them in each question. For example, Group one questions are:

1. I believe children should be seen and not heard.
2. I enjoy the chaos of parenting.
3. I believe children can be children and also practice civility.
4. My children keep to themselves and don't bother me much.

After one question in each group has been marked, the scores are tallied based how many 1s, 2s, 3s, and 4s. The Four styles of parenting identified in this instrument are Dominating (authoritarian), Permissive, Positive (authoritative), and Unengaged. There is a description of each of these parenting styles. Once completed, the coach can engage with the client about their parenting style, and ask questions to help the client better understand how their parenting is impacting their children. For example, on a parent that scored high on unengaged, a coach could ask, "how do you think you children would respond if you became more engaged?

Models of Coaching

In addition to assessments, there are coaching models that are standard practice in many coaching programs. As with the assessments, I have not included all models, but rather a few of the models I have found to be most prominent in the coaching industry and ones that fit best with family life coaching. Models covered in this chapter include GROW, PRACTICE, James Prochaska's readiness for change model, and although it has been reviewed in Chap. 4, I am also including a recap of Appreciative Inquiry.

GROW

Arguably one of the most common and most used models of coaching (McLean, 2012), the GROW model was developed by Max Landsberg (1999) and was first published by John Witmore (2009). The model has four stages and was developed primarily for the process of goal setting and problem solving. The four stages include:

Goal setting
Reality checking
Options
Will

Goal Setting refers to the trajectory of the coaching process as it relates to the goal the client sets for him or herself. Coaching questions relevant to the goal setting stage include questions such "what do you want to focus on;" "how do you want to spend your time today;" and "what outcomes might help you consider this a success?"

Reality Checking is a about becoming aware of the client's situation while helping the client learn to self-evaluate. Questions relating to reality checking include questions such as "when has this happened in the past;" "what have you done this week to move towards your goal;" and "what are the results of your work?"

Options is the process of generating options and brainstorming. In this stage, the client begins to explore solutions. Questions relevant in this stage include "what else can you do;" "who can help;" and "what are the pros and cons of this option?"

Will is the final step of the GROW model. This is where the client makes her or his action plan for forward movement. The questions that support the will stage include: "what do you need to do to reach your goal;" "what obstacles might get in the way;" and "what is your first step?"

Although this approach is highly popular in the coaching field, there are some limitations. McLean (2012) states that GROW model focuses so heavily on one individual session, making it difficult to focus on a longer term framework and it lacks focus on obstacles and resistance.

PRACTICE

Stephen Palmer (2007) created the PRACTICE model of coaching as an adaptation of Wasik's (1984) approach. While the two have many similarities, the primary difference between the two is that the PRACTICE framework has a solution-focus element. PRACTICE stands

Problem identification
Realistic goals (include SMART goals)
Alternative solutions generated
Consideration of consequences
Target solutions
Implementation of
Chosen Solutions
Evaluation

The PRACTICE model is a solution-focused model, but unlike purely solution-focused processes, the original version of the PRACTICE model includes problem identification. Palmer (2011) went on to consider replacing the P to "presenting issues" (p. 156). Coaches can use this model to help guide a process in a solution-focused manner.

Prochaska's Model

James Prochaska's model of coaching (Prochaska & DiClemente, 1982) comes from his early work on the study of the psychotherapeutic theories. Change is hard for many people, especially changing behaviors in the family life realm. Understanding the process of change, including the stages of change, can help a coach assess the likelihood of success based on how likely the client is to change. Some clients will come in ready to take action; others might just be at the beginning of the change process. Prochaska's broad approach to change methodologies informs components of a fundamental coaching process. The model includes five levels of change:

1. **Precontemplation:** the client is not ready to change.
2. **Contemplation:** the client is unsure about change.
3. **Preparation:** trying to chance.
4. **Action:** practices new behaviors.
5. **Maintenance:** commitment to sustaining new behavior.

Although not an original stage, a sixth stage of relapse is assigned when the client reassumes old behaviors. This work emphasizes elements of coaching methods such as the understanding that complexities are at play whenever a client begins the change process (McClean, 2012). While there are limitations to the model, such as it provides little guidance for individual coaching sessions, it is considered a foundational coaching model and helps coaches understand the nature of change further. This model is cited often as one of significant influence in the coaching realm.

Appreciative Inquiry

Appreciative inquiry model (Cooperrider, Whitney, & Stavros, 2008) describes a process of engaging clients to produce positive change. This model of inquiry uses a strengths-based approach to human behavior change based on four principles. Those principles lead to the 4-D model of inquiry: Discovery, Dream, Design, and Destiny.

In the **Discovery** stage, clients reflect what is concerning them, and more importantly, identify signature strengths that have lead to success in the past. Discovery is the process of learning about and beginning to understand the best of a person's experiences. It is during Discovery that the family coach begins to better understand the client through shared stories, interviews, and conversations. In the **Dream** stage, the client is encouraged to visualize, and truly begin to paint a mental image of what is possible. In order to achieve a dream, the client must first understand what it is they want, hence the Dream stage: visualization and dreaming.

In the **Design** stage, clients develop concrete ideas for how to move towards their dream. The client, with guidance from the coach, begins to design action steps that help them reach their desired goals. Finally, the **Destiny** stage is when the client begins to feel the movement towards the goal. In this phase, the client is actively participating in moving towards their goal.

Case Study

Ron is a 45-year-old male who is struggling in his retail business career. He is extremely unhappy in his job and cannot seem to shake it. His unhappiness is affecting his family life. There have been several occasions when his bad moods made it unbearable for his wife, Sarah, and their three kids to enjoy time together. He wants a job that allows him flexibility to be with his family and provides enough money and benefits to support his family, while also giving him a reason to get up and go to work in the morning. Ron is frustrated because he did not finish his college degree, which hampers his job searches, but he does have many years of experience. His wife is well educated and has a great job. He does not know which direction to move but he knows he does not want to work in retail any longer. Therefore, Ron has sought coaching in order to better determine how to address his situation. This is session number two of the coaching process.

Coach: "Welcome back, please come in. How are you today?"
Ron: "I guess I am okay, but the job search is not going to well. I am not sure how many more times I can make the drive into work."
Coach: "It sounds like you are at your wits end."
Ron: "Yes, I definitely feel that way."
Coach: "So last week during our session you shared some of your goals, strengths, and accomplishments. You had homework—to complete the VIA survey. How'd that go?"

NOTE: accountability is one role of the coach. Seeing where the client is and how the action steps identified in the previous session can be helpful for the coach. It is important to be mindful that the client is the driver of the session, and it is not appropriate to place negative judgment if the client completes or does not complete tasks. Rather, it is good to explore the reasons why and work on a new strategy in the current session.

Ron: "Pretty good, I guess. I have my results."
Coach: "Good. You completed the survey. Would you like to go over the results? If you recall, the purpose of that activity was to define your values and that will help you identify which jobs to look for. If I recall, you said you wanted a job that aligns with your values and your strengths, and I think your words were that your current job is 'obviously not' something you value."
Ron: "You got that right!"
Coach: "So, you completed the strengths-based VIA Character survey. What did you find out?"
Ron: "Well, it wasn't so bad. My wife and I did it together, and we weren't too surprised. My top strengths were judgment, perseverance, fairness, humor, and prudence. My bottom was appreciation of beauty, which my wife wasn't too happy about." (he is joking)

Note: Sometimes joking is a coping mechanism and sometimes it is just a part of a person's regular speech. Humor, and other coping mechanisms can be pointed out, but at this point, the goal is still on understanding the client and building relationship. Therefore the coach plays into the humor.

Coach: "Well, maybe that's because you value her beauty so much you don't even notice the other beauty around you." (joking back)

Ron: "Yea, I should have told her that!"

Coach: "So judgment, perseverance, fairness, humor, and prudence. What does that tell you about yourself?"

Ron: "I kind of get why I've stayed at my job so long—perseverance, judgment. . .those kind of fit with me not leaving."

Coach: "Interesting. You have really persevered in your job, that's for sure. Any thoughts about what this could mean for a new job, or a direction to go?"

Ron: "We talked about that after we took the test. I don't think I can be a stand up comedian, so I'm not sure how to work in the humor, but I do think something where I can take time and think things through would be good."

Coach: "What kind of job would be one where you can think things through?"

Ron: "Beside college professor? (Another joke). I was thinking about management. I've certainly been managed a great deal, and I have had a few times when I was not really a manager, but more of a team lead and I liked that."

Coach: "OK, I can sure see how that fits with judgment, prudence, even humor"

Ron: "Yea, I think everyone likes a funny boss. Or maybe not. . .I'm not sure."

Coach: "I tell you what, I think it is a great step that you are taking a look at how some positions might fit better with your strengths!"

Note: Remembering to reinforce the positives helps, especially when working with a discouraged client. While giving positives, it is also important to not place judgment on the clients specific decisions as we want to support the client's path, not our own ideas of where the path should lead.

Ron: "Yea? Good. Now how do I get that new job?"

Coach: "Great question. My guess is you have much better ideas about that than me! But I do have that other assessment we talked about. Besides continuing with the assessments, is there anything in particular you would like to focus on, a new goal that came to mind, or something that has moved to the forefront of your priorities? I am just wanting to make sure this session is heading where you want to go"

Ron: "No, just want to get out of this dead end job and figure out what it is I want and can do."

Coach: "Okay, well let's get started then. I'd like to talk about VIA more a bit later, but first I would like for you to do another activity called the Values Process Activity. There are two parts and we can do the first part here in the session. Are you okay with that?"

Ron: "Sure."

Coach:	"Here is a pencil, pen, and paper. The first step is to create a large circle in the center of the paper. This circle is your circle. Think about this question: when you are at your best, what is created in your life?"
Ron:	"Hmm. When I'm at my best, people laugh."
Coach:	"What else?"
Ron:	"Umm... happiness. I feel happy when I'm at my best."
Coach:	"Great. Write those answers inside the circle. Take your time. What else is created in your life when you are at your best?"
Ron:	"Peace, joy. Contentment."
Coach:	"you are coming up with a strong list. Can you list a few more?"
Ron:	"OK, when I'm at my best, we all get along, I feel good about myself."
Coach:	"Peace, getting along. It sounds like you value those things. Now draw four lines coming out of the circle to the edges of the paper. Sort of like a sun with only four rays, one on top, bottom, and each side. Pick a quadrant and title it IN. This section is going to label what has to happen for you to be at your best. What supports you living in the Circle?"

Example:

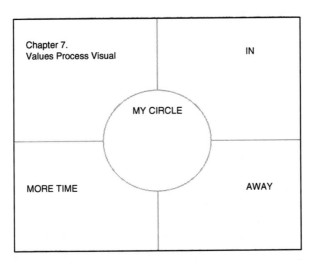

Ron:	"I'm not sure I understand. Can you give me some examples?"
Coach:	"Sure, so what supports you living at your best might be getting enough sleep, or working hard. Does that help?"
Ron:	"Yes, okay. Playing my banjo. Listening to music. Quiet time to myself, family time, not being overscheduled-too much to do really makes it hard to be content for sure."
Coach:	"Great, what else is necessary?"
Ron:	"Working on the house, and being outside. Taking my wife on a date. Having plenty of downtime together as a family."
Coach:	"I keep hearing you mention family"

Ron: "Absolutely. They are the most important".

Coach: "Let's continue. In another quadrant title it AWAY. This is the section where you will label things that take you away from the circle. That keep you from being your best"

Ron: "Well, my job right now. That is a huge part of getting farther away from the circle."

Coach: "Yes, what about your job takes you away from the circle?"

Ron: "Well, it is not challenging. I deal with idiots all day long, people don't put any effort in their work. They are all lazy and do the bare minimum. Every single one of them. The customers are rude and treat me like a dog. Honestly sometimes I feel like I can't depend on anyone. It's like they are children and won't lift a finger unless I ask, even though they have worked there for months and know exactly what needs to be done. It's ridiculous!"

Coach: "Okay, so, feeling overwhelmed and having too many demands. And not being able to feel supported at work. Depending on people who won't carry their own weight. Those all sound like it would be extremely difficult to stay in the circle with so many unreasonable stresses."

Ron: "Yes, no circle while working in retail for me. And the bosses are just as bad. They go around and tell everyone it is their fault for not having a product or being prepared when it is really a collective issue. The bosses should be helping everyone but they just walk around all high and mighty barking orders. It is not a good place to work."

Coach: "I do hear your frustration, Ron. All the more reason to keep going! Let's continue and see where your values activity leads us. In the next quadrant I want you to explain what it would take to get you to have more time in the circle."

Ron: "Okay, let's see. Quitting my job and finding another one. Planning a monthly date with my wife. A family night once a week would be good too. Playing music with some friends."

Coach: "So, we have now done two assessments. What are you thinking?"

Ron: "Well, I had never thought about what qualities I have and how to use those in a job."

Coach: "So you are learning about yourself, how is that for you?"

Ron: "Ya, it is actually making me stop and think about what direction to go. I can tell you that I'm thinking in a whole new way."

Coach: "I'm glad you are feeling like you are making progress."

Ron: "Yes, what should I do with my values paper?"

Coach: "We are going to keep exploring. We can put the two results side by side and see what happens."

Ron: "I'm already seeing things in a new way. I really want a job where people care, and where my hard work is just like everyone else's hard work. You know what I mean? I don't want to be the person working the hardest, or I mean, the only one working. I want a place where everyone works hard".

Coach: "So it sounds like hard work is a value."
Ron: "Yea, I think that is almost as important as what I do."

Note: for the sake of space, we are stopping after the use of an assessment. The session would continue and the action steps would ideally lead to Ron identifying a plan for reaching his goal.

Chapter Summary

There are a mountain of assessment resources for coaching clients that are designed to help clients and coaches discover strengths, abilities, and personality characteristics. There are visual activities, assessments for parenting, relationship, and family values...the list goes on and on. This chapter was intended to provide a few examples of the gamut, but family life coaches will need to seek our quality resources based on the specific needs of the clients served. Below are a few websites from the tools mentioned here.

VIA Character Strength Inventory

http://www.viacharacter.org/www/The-Survey

Strengths Finder

http://strengths.gallup.com/110440/about-strengthsfinder-20.aspx

Satisfaction with Life Scale

http://internal.psychology.illinois.edu/~ediener/SWLS.html

Psychological Well-Being Scale

http://www.liberalarts.wabash.edu/ryff-scales/

Life Wheel Assessment (one of many examples)

http://www.healthsystem.virginia.edu/pub/worklife/selfscreeningtools/personal-assessment-wheel.pdf

Learning Style Inventory

http://www.odessa.edu/dept/govt/dille/brian/courses/1100orientation/
learningstyleinventory_survey.pdf

Parent Satisfaction Scale

https://www.cyfernetsearch.org/sites/default/files/PsychometricsFiles/Parent%
20Perfomance.pdf

Parenting Style Assessment

http://www.extension.umn.edu/family/parents-forever/docs/parenting-style-assess
ment.pdf

References

American Psychological Association, (APA). (2000). Report of the task force on test user qualification. Retrieved from: https://www.apa.org/science/programs/testing/qualifications.pdf

Cooperrider, D. L., Whitney, D., & Stavros, J. M. (2008). *Appreciate inquiry handbook for leaders of change* (2nd ed.). Brunswick, OH: Crown Custom Publishing, Inc.

Diener, E., Emmons, R., Larsen, R., & Griffen, S. (1985). The satisfaction with life scale. *Journal of Personality Assessment, 49*, 71–75.

Diener, E., Wirth, D., Tov, W., Kim-Prieto, C., Choi, D., Oishi, S., et al. (2009). New measure of well-being: Flourishing and positive and negative feelings. *Social Indicators Research, 39*, 247–266.

Guidubaldi, J., & Cleminshaw, H. K. (1985). The development of the cleminshaw-guidubaldi parent satisfaction scale. *Journal of Clinical Child Psychology, 14*(4), 293–298.

Hendrick, S. S. (1988). A generic measure of relationship satisfaction. *Journal of Marriage and the Family, 50*, 93–98.

Hunsley, J. (2002). Psychological testing and psychological assessment: A closer examination. *American Psychologist, 57*(2), 139–140.

Landsberg, N. (1999). *The toa of coaching: Boost your effectiveness at work by inspiring and developing those around you.* New York: Haper Collins.

McLeod, S. A. (2010). Kolb – *learning styles*. Retrieved from http://www.simplypsychology.org/learning-kolb.html

McLean, P. (2012). *The completely revised handbook of coaching: A developmental approach.* San Francisco: Wiley.

Neukrug, E. S., & Fawcett, R. C. (2010). *Essentials of testing & assessment: A practical guide for counselors, social workers, and psychologists* (2nd ed.). Belmont, CA: Brooks/Cole Cengage Learning.

Palmer, S. (2007). PRACTICE: A model suitable for coaching, counseling, psychotherapy, and stress management. *The Coaching Psychologist, 3*(2), 71–77.

Palmer, S. (2011). Revisiting the 'P' in the PRACTICE coaching model. *The Coaching Psychologist, 7*(2), 156–158.

Peterson, C., & Park, N. (2009). *Classifying and measuring strengths of character.* In S. J. Lopez & C. R. Snyder (Eds.), *Oxford handbook of positive psychology* (2nd ed., pp. 25–33). New York: Oxford University Press. www.viame.org

Peterson, C., & Seligman, M. E. P. (2004). *Character strengths and virtues: A handbook and classification.* New York/Washington, DC: Oxford University Press/American Psychological Association. www.viame.org

Pitzer, R. (2001). *What is your parenting style? A parenting styles self- assessment.* St. Paul, MN: University of Minnesota Extension.

Prochaska, L. O., & DiClemente, C. C. (1982). Transtheoretical therapy: Toward a more integrative model of change. *Psychotherapy: Theory, Research, and Practice, 19*, 276–288.

Rath, T. (2007). *Stengthsfinder 2.0.* New York: Gallup Press.

Ryff, C. C., & Singer, B. (1998). The contours of positive human health. *Psychological Inquiry, 9*, 1–28.

Wasik, B. (1984). *Teaching parents effective problem-solving: A Handbook for professionals.* Unpublished manuscript. Chapel Hill: University of North Carolina.

Whitmore, J. (2009). *Coaching for performance* (4th ed.). London: Brealey.

Chapter 8
Family Communication and the Power of Questions

Nichole L. Huff, Ph.D., CFLE

Good communication is the staple of a happy, healthy family. In this chapter, we will review literature on family communication, discuss effective communication techniques (such as reflective listening), and review solution-focused communication approaches. Also, we will explore the use of powerful questions and how asking a series of questions can help a client clarify or discover something new, provide a new insight, or evoke a clearer vision. Family coaches can use these communication strategies to help clients explore their options and dig deeper.

This chapter includes a series of powerful questions students can use as they practice family life coaching. Students can pull powerful questions from other strengths-based approaches, such as solution-focused brief therapy or motivational interviewing. Further, at the end of the chapter, sample questions are categorized around the five elements of a coaching session:

1. Problem Solving
2. Goals Clarification
3. Exploring Options
4. Action Steps
5. Results/Evaluation

This chapter will help readers better understand the types of questions to ask at various stages of the coaching process while it provides experiential activities to practice as part of the process of learning to ask powerful questions.

The Power of a Question

Many coaches understand the format and process for coaching, yet knowing what to say or what to do at a particular time can be stressful. A strategy family life coaches can use to increase their coaching confidence and effectiveness is to understand the power of questions to evoke cognitive and behavioral changes.

© Springer International Publishing Switzerland 2016
K. Allen, *Theory, Research, and Practical Guidelines for Family Life Coaching*,
DOI 10.1007/978-3-319-29331-8_8

But what makes questions so powerful?

It seems that Socrates correctly pegged the power of a question to evoke discussion, prompt reflection, and spark ideas during communication exchanges. Family life coaching is no exception. Like Socrates, coaches must engage clients in ongoing conversations driven by the use of powerful questions. The most effective family practitioners (e.g., coaches, therapists, counselors, educators) are those who recognize and incorporate powerful questioning techniques into their work with families. The *use of questions* may be the single most important catalyst for promoting client change, more so than nearly every other pedagogical or clinical strategy used by family professionals.

> The answers you get depend on the questions you ask. *Thomas Kuhn*

In the text, *Coaching Questions: A Coach's Guide to Powerful Asking Skills*, Tony Stoltzfus (2008) outlines five key reasons for coaches to "ask instead of tell" (p. 9). These reasons are summarized below and have been expanded to directly apply to family life coaching.

1. *All Information Rests with the Client*

Clients are the experts on their lives. It's important for family life coaches to remember that it is the client who knows the intimate details of a given situation— not the coach. We will continue to discuss the notion of client expertise later in this chapter by learning to take a curious or "not-knowing stance" using a solution-focused approach.

2. *Asking Creates Buy-In*

According to Stoltzfus (2008), "Coaching starts with the assumption that the key to change is not knowing what to do—it's being motivated to do it" (p. 9). By asking questions, coaches prompt the client to generate their own ideas and solutions to reach goals or solve problems. "Asking creates buy-in," continues Stoltzfus, "and buy-in gets results."

3. *Asking Empowers*

Asking implies that you value someone's opinions and you take them seriously. This sends a powerful message that promotes client self-confidence—a key catalyst to change. The coaching process, like other strengths-based approaches, assumes that the client often knows what to do; they either lack the confidence to take action or they've lost sight of their capacity to be successful.

4. *Asking Develops Leadership Capacity*

To foster leadership capacity, Stoltzfus (2008, p. 9) explains:

Leadership is the ability to take responsibility. A leader is someone who sees a problem, and says, "Hey—someone needs to do something about this! And I'm going to be that someone." Simply asking, "What could *you* do about that?" moves people away from depending on you for answers, and toward taking leadership in the situation. Asking builds the responsibility muscle, and that develops leaders.

5. *Asking Creates Authenticity*

Taking the time to ask questions and—most importantly—*listen to the answers*, communicates interest, authenticity, and transparency. This not only builds trust and rapport in the client-coach relationship, but also fosters a more transformational change process for the client.

> The wise man doesn't give the right answers, he poses the right questions. *Claude Levi-Strauss*

Exploring Effective Communication Practices

Before we examine communication approaches to use during family life coaching sessions, we should first consider *family communication.*

> Any problem, big or small, within a family, always seems to start with bad communication. Someone isn't listening. *Emma Thompson*

Regardless of how one defines family, communication is at the core of is functional existence. While all families communicate differently, finding common-alities among communication patterns helps researchers and practitioners learn ways to strengthen family relationships (Huff, 2014). Family communication can be comprehensively defined as "the process of developing intersubjectivity and impact through the use of codes among a group of intimates who generate a sense of home and group identity, complete with strong ties of loyalty and emotion, and experience a history and a future" (Noller & Fitzpatrick, 1993, p. 14).

One theoretical model that specifically depicts this is the *Theory of Family Communication* (Koerner & Fitzpatrick, 2002).

Theory of Family Communication

Introduced in 2002 by Ascan Koerner and Mary Anne Fitzpatrick, the *Theory of Family Communication* asserts that family communication is highly patterned. Individual and interpersonal relational schemas influence the way members of a family typically communicate with one another; these relational schemas coalesce to form a family communication *type* (Koerner & Fitzpatrick, 2002) or *climate* (Barbato, Graham, & Perse, 2003).

As Barbato and colleagues (2003) highlight, the family communication climate remains the primary context in which children's communication values are shaped. The authors tout that "the family is the most important socialization agent that children experience... Moreover, parents provide opportunities to teach and reinforce communication skills. One of the lessons that children learn is how communication is used in interactions to help achieve personal goals" (p. 124).

The theory of family communication, sometimes referred to as *Family Communication Patterns Theory (FCPT)*, views family communication as involving norms of parental control and supportive messages that critically influence child socialization. According to Koerner and Fitzpatrick (2002), parent-child interactions "not only allow children to develop the ability for self-regulation, but also force parents and children explicitly to acknowledge, discuss, and renegotiate the rules and norms that govern their interactions and relationships" (p. 89).

Relational schemas, family communication patterns, and family types represent the three main components of family communication theory.

Relational Schemas

In FCPT, individual and interpersonal *relational schemas* influence the way members of a family typically communicate with one another (Koerner & Fitzpatrick, 2002). Relational schemas in the family are organized from general to specific: (1) what a person knows about relationships in general, (2) what a person knows about family relationships as a type, and (3) what a person knows about relationships with other members of his or her own family. Relational schemas include knowledge about the degree of *intimacy* within the family, the degree of *individuality* within the family, and factors external to the family, such as societal or cultural *influences*.

Family Communication Patterns

Over time, repeated communication exchanges form family communication patterns that fall along a continuum between two broad categories: *conformity orientation* and *conversation-orientation* (McLeod & Chaffee, 1972). The over-arching goal of both orientations is to promote family harmony; however, the means by which this is done differs greatly (Koerner & Fitzpatrick, 2002).

In *conformity-orientation*, as the name suggests, parents exert authority to promote child conformity. In *conversation-orientation*, parents more actively engage in conversation and negotiation with their children. Conformity orientation places an emphasis on harmony through obedience, whereas conversation orientation promotes the open exchange of ideas and feelings.

In an earlier study by Koerner and Fitzpatrick (1997), which helped to empirically pave the way for the theory of family communication, the authors examined the impact of family communication patterns on family conflict styles. They found that conflict avoidance was negatively correlated with conversation orientation but positively correlated with conformity orientation. This suggests that the more conversation-oriented a family, the less likely family members are to avoid confronting conflict when it arises.

Family Types

Because conformity- and conversation-orientations fall along a continuum, each dimension can be further divided into a typology comprised of four family types: consensual, pluralistic, protective, or laissez-faire (Koerner & Fitzpatrick, 2002). A family's communication type is based on the combination of low or high patterns of conversation and conformity.

Consensual families have communication patterns that are both high in conformity and conversation. Parents remain the ultimate voice of authority, but only after real-time communication exchanges occur between the parent(s) and child during which ideas, feelings, and reasons are considered. Parents strive for a combination of openness and conformity.

Pluralistic families—those low in conformity but high in conversation—stress the relationship between the child and concepts or issues. While parents may offer opinions on directives, they leave most final decisions up to the child.

Protective families—those high in conformity but low in conversation—stress obedience and conformity between the child and parents. Minimal conversation is permitted and little room is left for negotiation.

Laissez-faire families have little to no consistent communication norms. Both conversation and conformity are low. Because there is often little parent-child communication, parental neglect or apathy often exists.

Family Types in Family Communication Patterns Theory

Conversation Orientation

	High	Low
Conformity Orientation — High	*Consensual* Strive for a combination of conformity and openness	*Protective* Stress a relationship of obedience and conformity
Conformity Orientation — Low	*Pluralistic* Ideas exchanged, but parents are not final authority	*Laissez-Faire* No consistent norms; little parent/child communication

Promoting Strengths-Based Communication Practices

In relationships, what often distinguishes happy and thriving couples or families from those experiencing relational distress is the effectiveness of their communication skills.

> Communication is the one crucial ingredient that defines a relationship. Once a relationship is established, however, communication remains the key skill for maintaining intimacy. In fact, the quality of communication becomes more important as the level of intimacy in a relationship increases. (Olson & Olson, 2000, p. 23)

There is no greater sabotage for success (including successful communication) than negative thinking. According to the text, *Empowering Couples: Building on Your Strengths*, by Olson and Olson (2000):

> It is not your actual circumstances that cause your emotions, but your thoughts or attitudes about those circumstances. And you have total control over your thoughts and attitudes. As Henry Ford wittily observed, *"Whether you think you can or you think you can't, you are right."* So, although you cannot control your emotions, you can learn to choose the thoughts that produce them. (p. 181)

As a strengths-based professional, reminding clients that they have the **ability** to control their actions is a powerful tool. However, many people (individuals, couples, families) have lost sight of their capacity for success. One of the major roles of coaches, clinicians, and educators is helping clients regain sight of their strengths.

Couples and families without healthy communication patterns are more likely to experience strained relationships. As a family coach, utilizing strengths-based communication techniques in the coaching process can help to accentuate client strengths and generate client ideas that will lead to more transformational, long-lasting changes in thinking and behavior.

Let's explore one strengths-based model for fostering client change that uses powerful questioning—the solution-focused approach.

The Solution-Focused Approach

Solution-focused practice (whether it be therapy, counseling, social work, coaching, or family life education) centers around two basic premises: hope and respect. *Respect* for clients—for their stories, challenges, strengths, perspectives—and promoting client *hope*—especially relating to their capacity for long-term success.

Steve de Shazer and Insoo Kim Berg were key players in the expansion and global dissemination of the solution-focused approach (Visser, 2013). Central tenets of the solution-focused (SF) process—many of which are shared with the family life coaching process—include:

- Maintaining a future focus
- The use of powerful questioning
- The importance of exceptions and "success"
- The belief in client resourcefulness
- An emphasis on the pragmatic
- Respecting a client's expertise regarding his/her experiences
- Recognizing that solutions are not necessarily connected to problems
- A reliance on the client to evaluate progress and decide on termination of services

One of de Shazer's most important contributions to the SF process was emphasizing the importance of the professional in *creating an expectation of change*. By using powerful questioning, de Shazer began asking clients questions that implied change was undoubtedly going to happen. This questioning technique contributed to the client's increased trust in the change process (Visser, 2013).

While some narrative or dialogue-based change approaches focus on past events or motivations, SF approaches emphasize current strengths, experiences, and future activities based on recent successes. SF professionals recognize the distinct importance of the client's past, present, and future (particularly with regard to client resourcefulness, and goal-setting), but primary focus is placed on a future orientation. According to Thomas (2013), SF approaches "use goal setting to reinforce the value of all three chronological categories: hindsight (drawing from past successes), insight (making sense of experience in the moment), and foresight (planning future actions)" (p. 49).

The SF process creates a co-learning environment where curiosity drives the conversation and learning occurs through interaction (Thomas, 2013). Family practitioners *lead from one step behind*, meaning that "rather than pushing, cajoling, or pulling their clients in certain directions," instead they gently tap the client on the shoulder and ask "whether she noticed the beautiful sunset in the sky or that tiny wild flower swaying in the breeze" (Berg & Dolan, 2001, p. 3).

The SF approach is "not just a technique, but it's a willingness to learn from clients, as they are the driving force of this, and some sense of humility, of modesty. It's not about us, it's about the clients and it's about their life and how to make their life better" (Berg & Wheeler, 2006, p. 6).

> We can't solve problems by using the same kind of thinking we used when we created them. *Albert Einstein*

To better understand the natural application of a solution-focused approach, below is a 2015 article published by the National Council on Family Relations in the *NCFR Report: Family Focus on Communication*. In this article, Huff not only illustrates the ease of using a SF approach, but also possible neuro-social benefits of asking positive, strengths-based questions.

> *The following article is reprinted with permission from the National Council on Family Relations. It first appeared in the June 2015 edition of the NCFR Report. Dr. Huff served as the invited Guest Advisor of this special edition.*

Communicating Exceptions: Considering Neurosocial Effects of Solution-Focused Practice

Nichole L. Huff, Ph.D., CFLE

Recently my seven-year-old brought home her school progress report. Penned underneath the list of grades was a single comment that read, *"Addison is progressing, but she continues to have trouble focusing and staying on task."* Needing a more detailed explanation, I requested a parent-teacher conference. The following week, as the teachers began to expand on the presenting problem—which has presented itself off-and-on all year despite our many attempts at resolve—the Solution-Focused practitioner in me found myself reframing the conversation. *"Yes, I understand your concerns, but..."* (There was a lot of 'yes-butting' on my part.) *"...I need for you to try communicating the exceptions."*

As a concerned parent, I needed to hear that there were exceptions to the problem; and as a strengths-based family professional, I knew that by highlighting these exceptions, we could better identify situations and strategies that promoted her success in the classroom. Once I shared the principles behind my request, not only did the focus of our conversation shift, but our thought-processes did as well.

This allowed us to identify those moments, *regardless of how small or seemingly insignificant*, when the problem wasn't a problem. By communicating when Addison was succeeding (which happened to far outweigh the times she wasn't), we learned more about what made these situations different; and once we better understood the exceptions, we could—quite simply—*do more of what worked*.

The Importance of Examining Exceptions

In the 2001 book, *Tales of Solutions: A Collection of Hope-Inspiring Stories*, Insoo Kim Berg and Yvonne Dolan discuss a simple assumption of solution-focused practice: *There are exceptions to all problems.* Although our parent-teacher conference was a simple 20-minute conversation, I believe it speaks to the essence of brief, solution-focused communication practices used by strength-based educators, therapists, coaches, and other family professionals. In the above example, it wasn't that our daughter had trouble concentrating at all times; rather, she had trouble concentrating in certain situations based on specific contextual markers that we better understood after we examined the differences between the times when she was successful at staying on task and the times she wasn't successful.

By utilizing solution-focused communication techniques, such as asking about exceptions, family practitioners help to accentuate client strengths and generate client ideas that lead to more transformational, long lasting changes in thinking and behavior (Hanna, 2014). However, according to Berg and Dolan (2001), because many professionals are not trained to look for exceptions, they can miss opportunities to enhance client motivation and build effective working relationships. Understanding this solution-focused tenet is key for affecting change: people often lose sight of their capacity for success in the midst of challenging circumstances; thus, one of the major roles of the solution-focused professional is helping clients regain sight of these strengths during brief communication exchanges.

As Berg and Dolan note, because solution-focused approaches are foundationally strengths-based, practitioners assist clients with two major objectives: (1) communicating exceptions to presenting problems (i.e., when the problem isn't a problem, or when the problem could have been a problem but wasn't) and (2) communicating existing internal and external resources on which the client can capitalize in order to sustain change. By communicating exceptions, clients articulate their present and future capacity for success by connecting it with past accomplishments.

Neural Effects of Strengths-Based Communication

So why don't these and other communication approaches always promote sustainable changes? Research suggests that the insights and behaviors learned during clinical interventions may not have long-lasting results because they are not sufficiently integrated into the everyday operational states of the brain (Atkinson et al., 2005). In general, people want to think about (and talk about) their problems. Atkinson and colleagues recommend that professionals help clients cognitively transform bad communication habits by helping them practice changing their attitudes and emotional states. Asking clients to communicate in terms of solutions is one tool that professionals can employ to help clients practice thinking differently. By repeatedly asking clients to communicate in novel and positive ways, we can assist them in retraining how their brains process, approach, and resolve problems.

Retraining the brain is possible through a process called neuroplasticity, which is the brain's ability to modify itself in order to adapt to new, changed, or challenging experiences. From a family science perspective, without neural flexibility, we couldn't make the social or emotional adaptations necessary to accommodate our shifting social roles and/or evolving relational dynamics (Huff, Werner-Wilson, & Kimberly, 2014). Neuroplasticity grants narrative and solution-focused communication approaches the potential to impact cognitive processes such as affect, meaning, memory, and rewards (Hanna, 2014). When people retell their stories in happier, resolved, or positive ways, they use language to actively create their reality; this shifts their perceptions and definitions of what is both real and possible (Berg & Dolan, 2001).

Neurosocial suggestions for family professionals should be considered. Neuroscientists Richard Davidson and Bruce McEwen (2012) note that structural and functional changes in the brain, including increasing neuroplasticity, have been observed with reflective, communication-based therapies and interventions. Rossouw (2013) stresses the implications of solution-focused work for practitioners, explaining that neural imaging scans show how new firing patterns emerge when a client is given specific instructions to think about or is asked to communicate his or her thoughts regarding possible solutions to a presenting problem in writing. Rossouw adds that current helping professionals are uniquely positioned in this post-"decade of the brain" era, and are thus charged with applying neural principles to the facilitation of relational wellness strategies. This is enhanced by a better understanding of brain processes and evidence-based practices.

Implications for Family Practitioners

While research continues to empirically examine the efficacy of using strengths-based communication to facilitate sustained neural changes, family professionals should consider neurosocial implications of using solution-focused approaches. Although an isolated intervention cannot change neural firing patterns, prompting someone to think about and discuss negative situations in novel ways does activate new firing patterns. Solution-focused practitioners ask questions to foster goal setting and promote client change, which helps clients communicate a preferred future (opposed to a 'problem-free' future). Rossouw suggests that in order to establish new neural patterns, an activation period of 6–8 weeks is needed. These findings may be particularly relevant for family practitioners such as educators, therapists, and coaches who provide consecutive talk-based sessions in one-on-one or group settings over an extended period of time.

Because using a solution-focused approach requires thoughtfulness about the use of language in our daily lives, family professionals can utilize communication techniques to provide insight, help clients clarify or discover something new, or evoke a clearer client vision. Three communication strategies to do this include *visualization, recognition,* and *expansion.*

Visualization Insoo Kim Berg suggested that sometimes it's better to begin with the ending of the story. Beginnings are riddled with problems, whereas endings have the expectation of resolution. As family professionals, we can help clients more clearly identify attainable end goals. One way to do this is to ask clients to communicate their visions for success apart from present-day problems or obstacles.

Recognition Because solution-focused practitioners assume that there are exceptions to all problems, this guiding principle helps us to assist clients in searching for those times when, simply, *the problem isn't a problem.* Communicating exceptions also help clients recognize existing strengths to better align them with their vision of success. Clients often have the skills they need to be successful; they have just lost sight of their competence.

Expansion As the solution-focused mantra asserts: *"It's easier to do more of what works than it is to try and fix what doesn't."* Once clients have communicated times when the problem isn't a problem, it becomes important for them to then communicate what about those particular circumstances is different. Solution-focused professionals promote future client success by having clients identify what currently "works" in order to expand upon existing change strategies that have proven successful.

Conclusion

As a strengths-based family professional, I have tried to train myself to focus on the positive attributes of situations. Solution-focused practice requires that professionals believe the best in others—exploring negative *actions* instead of assigning blame or attributing negative behaviors to pathology, character flaws, or malice (Berg & Dolan, 2001). This extends the benefit of the doubt rather than assuming the worst of clients, subscribing to the belief that generally people do the best they can in any given circumstance given (1) the context of the circumstance; (2) their available resources at the time; and (3) the knowledge, capacity, and experience they bring into the situation. As such, it is the solution-focused practitioner's responsibility to use communication techniques to encourage clients to reflect on and communicate about a given circumstance.

To revisit my parent-teacher conference example, I knew that asking the teachers to look for my daughter's successes would help them begin to see more successes in her. I also knew that it would shift both the direction of our conversation and our cognitions toward optimism. At the time I felt discouraged, having an identified problem in hand for which no one was offering any solutions. Simply making me aware of the problem didn't help me identify ways to combat it (nor did it help me understand when, where, and why the problem was reoccurring). Like many of the families we serve, I was a parent who needed to feel hopeful. By exploring resourcefulness and communicating exceptions, however, I began to feel encouraged; solution-focused communication helped to draw attention to the possibility of personal agency within an experience of positive change.

Selected References

Atkinson, B., Atkinson, L., Kutz, P., Lata, J., Lata, K. W., Szekely, J., & Weiss, P. (2005). Rewiring neural states in couples therapy: Advances from affective neuroscience. *Journal of Systemic Therapies, 24*, 3–16. doi:10.1521/jsyt.2005. 24.3.3

Berg, I. K., & Dolan, Y. (2001). *Tales of solution: A collection of hope inspiring stories.* NY: W.W. Norton.

Davidson, R. J., & McEwen, B. S. (2012). Social influences on neuroplasticity: Stress and interventions to promote well-being. *Nature Neuroscience, 15*, 689–695. doi:10.1038/nn.3093

Hanna, S. M. (2014). *The transparent brain in couple and family therapy: Mindful integrations with neuroscience.* NY: Routledge.

Huff, N., Werner-Wilson, R., & Kimberly, C. (2014). Electrical brain activity, family functioning, and parent–adolescent conflict communication. *Contemporary Family Therapy, 36*, 409–416. doi:10.1007/s10591-014-9307-5

Rossouw, P. J. (2013). The neuroscience of talking therapies: Implications for therapeutic practice. *The Australian Journal of Counselling Psychology 13*, 40–50.

Used by permission from the National Council on Family Relations.

Applying a Solution-Focused Approach

Using a SF approach requires a thoughtfulness about the use of language in our daily lives. Key communication techniques that guide the practice of a SF approach include taking a "not-knowing" stance, asking questions, and using silence and tentative language.

Taking a "Not-Knowing" Stance

Solution-focused practice, like family life coaching, requires a professional to believe the best in others. Insoo Kim Berg believed that people act out of good intentions (even if their actions are met with "less than" outcomes). By using phrases like "You must have good reasons to..." in sessions, Berg explored negative actions instead of assigning blame or attributing negative behaviors to pathology, character flaws, or malice (Berg & Dolan, 2001; Thomas, 2013). As the Huff (2015) article above asserts, SF professionals extend the benefit of the doubt rather than assuming the worst of their clients, subscribing to the credence that *generally* people do the best they can in any given circumstance given (1) the context of the circumstance; (2) their available resources at the time; and (3) the knowledge, capacity, and experience they bring into the situation.

Because SF practitioners are not necessarily privy to the context of the client's circumstances, their available resources or strengths, or their knowledge, capacity, or experience, it is important that SF professionals assume this "not-knowing" posture. This means that SF professionals have an intonation of curiosity in their approach as they "lead from behind." According to Berg and Dolan (2001), the SF approach "recognizes that clients are the experts on their own lives and know what will best fit their needs" (p. 95), being consistent with the assumption of respecting and accepting client values and beliefs while making it possible for practitioners to ask questions rather than tell clients what to do.

Asking Questions

Because SF approaches are strengths-based, it is important that practitioners use powerful questioning techniques to assist clients in identifying (1) exceptions to presenting problems (i.e., when the problem is not a problem, or when the problem could have been a problem but wasn't) and (2) existing internal and external resources on which the client can capitalize in order to sustain change.

Exploring exceptions and resourcefulness through questions brings attention to the possibility of personal agency (i.e., the client's ability to choose and act) within an experience of positive change (Thomas, 2013). SF practitioners ask questions to foster client goal setting, which helps clients create a preferred future (oppose to a "problem free" one). An example of such a question is, "How will you know things *will* be better?" This wording implies that change is going to happen, opposed to "How would you know things *could* be better?" According to Visser (2013), "The latter formulation is conditional; it leaves open whether the change is going to happen or not" (p. 14).

Examples of SF question types include exception, miracle, scaling, and coping.

Exception Questions
– "What is different about the times when this is less of a problem? What did you do that was helpful?"

Miracle Questions
- "Suppose by some miracle, this was no longer an obstacle. How would things be different?"

Scaling Questions
- "On a scale of 0–10, where 10 means you feel that life is going was well as it could be and 0 means you feel like this is the worst day of your life, where would you say you are in relation to 10 right now"
  [Client responds, by saying "5-and-a-half."]
  "What would it take to move you from a 5-and-a-half to a 6?" "How would you know you were at a 6? What about your current situation would be different?" "What kept you from saying 4 or 5?"

Coping Questions
- "How have you managed to prevent things from becoming worse?"

Using Compliments

Through the use of intentional questions, SF practitioners also use *compliments* to help identify strengths, resources, and capacity. *"That's great! How were you able to do that?"* According to Berg and Dolan (2001), "How" questions tend to emphasize clients' resourcefulness and ingenuity, while "why" questions challenge clients' motivations (p. 12). "How" questions are used because they tacitly compliment the client.

Using Silence and Tentative Language

Solution-Focused practitioners (e.g., clinicians, educators, coaches) should also maximize *silence* when working with clients in order to allow time for reflection on questions and consideration of possible solutions. Because so many of the questions we ask are initially met with, "I don't know," silence creates *conversational pressure*, or the practitioner's respectful anticipation of a response (Thomas, 2013).

The use of *tentative language* (or hedging) is another communication technique used in SF approaches to promote conversation and collaboration during sessions. This includes phrases such as "Perhaps...," "I wonder...," or "It seems like...," that often precede questions and are spoken with a tentative inflection.

Using "Suppose..." is a more specific form of hedging that assists clients with maintaining a future focus. It fosters client's use of imagination by embedding a future-focused premise into a question (Thomas, 2013).

Reflecting on the Domains of Family Practice

While it's helpful for family life coaches to be aware of other strengths-based approaches to consider during the coaching process, it is also important to reflect on the domains and boundaries of family practice, especially how it applies to family coaching (Allen & Huff, 2014; Myers-Walls, Ballard, Darling, & Myers-Bowman, 2011). As discussed in other chapters of the book, while there are parallels between family coaching and family therapy, for example, family practitioners must know when they are within the boundaries of their practice and training, and when referral is necessary.

Additional Communication Strategies

In addition to the communication practices previously discussed in this chapter, there are other communication techniques family coaches can used to "decrease the likelihood of resistance and increase change talk" (Delgadillo, 2015, p. 256). Two additional approaches include *reflective listening* and *motivational interviewing.*

Reflective Listening

Reflective listening (RL) is used to respond to client responses in order to build empathy. It involves "listening carefully to clients and then making a reasonable guess about what they are saying; in other words, it is like forming a hypothesis" (Sobell & Sobell, 2008, p. 3). The professional then paraphrases the client's comments back to them (e.g., *It sound like this situation makes you feel frustrated.*). Unlike the other communication approaches discussed in this chapter, reflective listening is not a powerful questioning technique, but rather it is a communication skill that capitalizes on using empathic statements that demonstrate active listening.

According to Sobell and Sobell (2008), reflective listening can be helpful in getting clients to state their arguments for change (i.e., *have them 'give voice' to the change process*). Further, reflections also validate what clients are feeling and doing to communicate that the professional understands what the client has said. When reflections are correct, clients usually respond affirmatively; however, if the reflection is wrong, clients are typically quick to disconfirm the hypothesis.

Examples of Reflective Listening Prompts
– "I get the sense that...."
– "What I hear you saying is. . ."
– "It sounds like...."
– "It seems as if...."

- "So on the one hand, it sounds like... Yet, on the other hand..."
- "It feels as though..."

Motivational Interviewing

Motivational interviewing (MI) is "a form of collaborative conversation for strengthening a person's own motivation and commitment to change" (MINT, n. d.). It is a person-centered change strategy often used by counseling and health professionals in order to address a client's ambivalence regarding change. Professionals who use MI pay particular attention to the language of change, using strategic communication techniques (including questioning) to strengthen an individual's motivation for and movement toward a specific goal. More specifically, MI is used by professionals in order to elicit and explore a person's reasons for change within an atmosphere of acceptance and compassion (MINT, n.d.).

In the book, *Motivational Interviewing*, Miller and Rollnick (2013) explain how the use of perceptive reflections is a key tool for "change talk" that when communicated directly from the client, rapid progress generally occurs in the desired direction.

To promote change, MI follows four basic steps to help clients reach goals: engaging, focusing, evoking, and planning. Professionals first *engage* clients in talking about issues, concerns, and hopes in order to establish rapport and trust. Practitioners then use *focusing* to narrow the conversation, thus helping clients identify habits or patterns they wish to change. To *evoke* a client's motivation for change, MI works to increase the client's sense of the importance of change, their confidence about change, and their readiness to change. The professional then works with the client to *plan* pragmatic steps for implementing the desired change.

Although MI demonstrates respect for the client, it is less self-directed than family life coaching or a solution-focused approach. However, this lends itself to increased applicability in healthcare settings, for example, when it is more within a professional's domain of practice to address unhealthy behaviors (e.g., smoking, obesity, substance abuse) without being first identified by the client.

MI relies more on reflective listening statements than questions to promote change; however powerful questioning is an important communication tool in the approach. Examples of MI question include (Sobell & Sobell, 2008):

- Asking permission

  - *Do you mind if we talk about [insert behavior]?*

- Evoking change

  - *What would your life be like 3 years from now if you changed your [insert risky/problem behavior]?*

- Exploring importance and confidence (similar to scaling in the SF approach)

- • *What would need to happen for your importance/confidence score to move up from a [insert #] to a [insert a higher #]*

– Open-ended

- • *What would you like to see different about your current situation?*

Asking Powerful Coaching Questions

Like solution-focused practitioners, family coaches use powerful questions to help clients explore their options and dig deeper. Family coaches use questions to clarify or discover something new, provide a new insight, or evoke a clearer client vision.

As a family coach, it is important to understand types of questions to ask at various stages of the coaching process. Consider sample powerful questions (Stoltzfus, 2008) as divided by the five elements of a coaching session:

1. Problem Solving
2. Goals Clarification
3. Exploring Options
4. Action Steps
5. Results/Evaluation

Problem Solving

– What would make this a lasting difference and not just a permanent one?
– What outcome would make this conversation a great success?
– What makes this change difficult?
– Do you need to change your situation, or change the way you respond to it?
– What in this situation is within your control, that you can realistically change?
– What do you excel at? What are your best skills?

Goals Clarification

– What will be different as a result of working in this area?
– Where would you like to be with this in three to six months?
– How can we make that goal measurable so that you know when you've achieved it?
– Be specific: what will be different when you've reached this goal?

Exploring Options

– What have you tried already? What difference did those actions make?
– What have you seen others do that might work for you?
– If you had access to unlimited resources and knew you couldn't fail, what would you try?
– What if the obstacle were removed? What could you do then?
– Who could help you achieve this goal?
– What could you change about *you* that would change your situation?

Action Steps

1. Use "Could Do" questions to explore possibilities.

   • What could you do? What else could you do?

2. Use "Want To" questions to ask client to choose an option.

   • Which of these options do you want to pursue?

3. Use "Will Do" questions to ask for commitment to a specific step.

   • What will you do, by when? What step will you take first?

Results/Evaluation

– What do we need to focus on today to keep you moving toward your goals?
– How can you keep yourself motivated?
– What are some ways you want to keep track of progress?
– What are the most important takeaways for you from this conversation?

Practice

As noted in the Huff (2015) article reprinted earlier in the chapter, research suggests that the insights and behaviors learned during clinical interventions may not have long-lasting results because they are not sufficiently integrated into the everyday operational states of the brain. Atkinson and colleagues (2005) propose that "bad emotional habits can rob people of what's most important to them in life—nourishing intimate relationships. Many people develop bad emotional habits when they are very young, and go through their whole lives crippled by these habits" (p. 13).

However, professionals can help clients cognitively transform bad relational habits by helping them *practice* changing their attitudes and emotional states. Repetition is necessary for long-term success. Communicating through powerful questioning is one tool that can help clients practice thinking differently.

Chapter Summary

At the heart of family functioning is good communication. Chapter 8 covers the theoretical underpinnings of family communication and addresses how those theories can be applied in family life coaching. Strengths-based communication strategies of reflective listening, motivational interviewing, and asking powerful questions, for example, can help a coach better understand and create an environment conducive to client change. Solution-focused strategies center around hope and respect, two competencies at the heart of family life coaching.

Recommended Readings

Berg, I. K., & Dolan, Y. (2001). *Tales of solutions: A collection of hope inspiring stories.* New York: W. W. Norton.

Berg, I. K., & Steiner. T. (2003). *Children's solution work.* New York: W. W. Norton.

Stoltzfus, T. (2008). Coaching questions: A coach's guide to powerful asking skills. Virginia Beach, VA: Stoltzfus.

Szabó, P., & Meier, D. (2008). Coaching plain & simple: Solution-focused brief coaching essentials. New York: W. W. Norton.

References

Allen, K., & Huff, N. (2014). Family coaching: An emerging family science field. *Family Relations, 63*(5), 569–582. doi:10.1111/fare.12087.

Atkinson, B., Atkinson, L., Kutz, P., Lata, J., Lata, K. W., Szekely, J., et al. (2005). Rewiring neural states in couples therapy: Advances from affective neuroscience. *Journal of Systemic Therapies, 24*(3), 3–16. doi:10.1521/jsyt.2005.24.3.3.

Barbato, C. A., Graham, E. E., & Perse, E. M. (2003). Communicating in the family: An examination of the relationship of family communication climate and interpersonal communication motives. *Journal of Family Communication, 3*(3), 123–148. doi:10.1207/S15327698JFC0303_01.

Berg, I. K., & Dolan, Y. (2001). *Tales of solutions: A collection of hope inspiring stories.* New York: W. W. Norton.

Berg, I. K., & Wheeler, J. (2006). Riding the underground railroad. *Solution News, 2*(3), 3–6.

Delgadillo, L. M. (2015). Coaching and financial counseling communication skills: A comparative analysis. *Family and Consumer Sciences Research Journal, 43*(3), 259–268. doi:10.1111/fcsr.12101.

Huff, N. L. (2015). Communicating exceptions: Considering neurosocial effects of solution-focused practice. *Family focus on effective communication* (NCFR report FF64), F5–F7. Minneapolis, MN: National Council on Family Relations.

Huff, N. L., Werner-Wilson, R., & Kimberly, C. (2014). Electrical brain activity, family functioning, and parent-adolescent conflict communication. *Journal of Contemporary Family Therapy, 36*(3), 409–416. doi:10.1007/s10591-014-9307-5.

Koerner, A. F., & Fitzpatrick, M. A. (2002). Toward a theory of family communication. *Communication Theory, 12*(1), 70–91. doi:10.1111/j.1468-2885.2002.tb00260.x.

McLeod, J. M., & Chaffee, S. H. (1972). The construction of social reality. In J. Tedeschi (Ed.), *The social influence processes* (pp. 50–99). Chicago: Aldine.

Miller, W. R., & Rollnick, S. (2013). *Motivational interviewing: Helping people change*. New York: The Guilford Press.

MINT (Motivational Interviewing Network of Trainers). (n.d.) B. Miller, & S. Rollnick (Eds.). Retrieved from http://www.motivationalinterviewing.org/about_mint

Myers-Walls, J. A., Ballard, S. M., Darling, C. A., & Myers-Bowman, K. S. (2011). Reconceptualizing the domain and boundaries of family life education. *Family Relations, 60* (4), 357–372. doi:10.1111/j.1741-3729.2011.00659.x.

Noller, P., & Fitzpatrick, M. A. (1993). *Communication in family relationships*. Englewood Cliffs, NJ: Prentice-Hall.

Olson, D. H., & Olson, A. K. (2000). *Empowering couples: Building on your strengths*. Minneapolis, MN: Life Innovations Inc.

Sobell, L. C., & Sobell, M. B. (2008). *Motivational interviewing strategies and techniques: Rationales and examples*. Retrieved from http://www.nova.edu/gsc/forms/mi_rationale_tech niques.pdf

Stoltzfus, T. (2008). Coaching questions: A coach's guide to powerful asking skills. Virginia Beach, VA: Stoltzfus.

Thomas, F. N. (2013). *Solution-focused supervision: A resource-oriented approach to developing clinical expertise*. New York: Springer.

Visser, C. F. (2013). The origin of the solution-focused approach. *International Journal of Solution-Focused Practices, 1*(1), 10–17. doi:10.14335/ijsfp.v1i1.10.

Chapter 9
Relationship Coaching

You can discover more about a person in an hour of play than in a year of conversation. (Plato)

At the core of every interpersonal conflict is a relationship issue. Good relationship skills can be applied to any relationship. The information covered here is specifically about couple relationships, but most relationship concepts can be translated into all human relationships, which can be useful for both coaches and the clients they serve. The literature presented in this chapter comes primarily from relationship education literature. There are a few models and articles about relationship coaching in the coaching psychology literature (see Ives, 2012), but the bulk of relationship research and evidence-based practices has occurred in family science. In this chapter, we will look at the history of relationship education, identify components of a healthy relationship, and apply relationship coaching to a case study.

Why Relationship Coaching?

Relationships are a natural part of the life cycle and the human experience. Roughly 80 % of Americans report currently being in a romantic relationship or actively looking for a partner (Madden & Rainie, 2006). I often ask my students to think back to when they fell in love for the very first time, and I will ask you the same questions. Do you recall the feelings of falling in love? What about the actions of falling in love? How did you spend your time? How did you think about the person with whom you were falling in love?

When I ask these questions of budding coaches and family life educators, they answer the same as when I ask the young families I coach. With smiles on their

© Springer International Publishing Switzerland 2016 161
K. Allen, *Theory, Research, and Practical Guidelines for Family Life Coaching*,
DOI 10.1007/978-3-319-29331-8_9

faces, sometimes with a giggle, they talk about feelings of elation and belonging; of long walks and hard to end phone calls. They talk about wanting to spend every waking moment together; wanting to be with the new person in which they are falling in love. Without exception, the answers are similar: spending great amounts of time together, learning more about their partner, and sharing meaningful experiences are the common responses. They often recall the warm and happy feelings of sharing and receiving small gifts of affection, time, and service. Falling in love was pure bliss, many say.

As they are basking in the memories of falling in love, I often ask, "then what happens?" As you can imagine, many say something like..."life happens. We get busy. We go back to our routines. Kids happen."

Sustaining the romance of falling in love is not easy, yet we have evidence of successful relationships and a good body of literature designed for practitioners to help couples. A relationship, if it succeeds past these wonderful moments of falling in love, becomes one of many priorities and unfortunately, sometimes it falls completely off the priority list. For couples in this situation, it is possible they will seek the help of a relationship coach.

History of Marriage and Relationship Education

During the past two decades, the research on couple's relationships has strongly impacted our understanding and abilities to be able to assist couples wanting to work on their relationship (Fincham & Beach, 2010). However, there has been a long road to better understanding how to help couples improve relationships. Marriage education formally began in the early 1970s. Before that point, couples could go to a professional counselor or to a religious leader for help. There were very few options for help if couples where experiencing difficulty with their marriage and simply wanted education (Gottman & Notaruis, 2002). In 1973, the Association for Couples in Marriage Enrichment (ACME) was created in an effort to house an umbrella organization for non-professional marriage initiatives (Doherty & Anderson, 2004). Although there was concern from the marriage and family professionals about the potential risks to couples, this movement has led to one of the most prevalent and well-funded initiatives in counseling history (Doherty & Anderson, 2004).

The trend of growing research and programming for professional couple educators continued into the 1980s. Marriage researchers that had been evaluating programs in the late 1970s were soon applying their research to marriage education programs (Doherty & Anderson, 2004) and marital research saw an explosion (Gottman & Notaruis, 2002). There was not only an increase in traditional marriage research, but also an increase in racial and cultural variations of family and gender roles (Carlson, McLanahan, & England, 2004; Gottman & Notaruis, 2002).

Even with the increased research on cultural and gender differences, the mainstream research that was turned into marriage education programming was consistently conducted on white-middle class families (Gottman & Notaruis, 2002). Many of the most well-known marriage education programs on the market today were developed in the late 1970s and 1980s including Relationship Education (RE), Prevention and Relationship Enhancement Program (PREP), Couples Communication, and Pairs.

The culture of the 1980s was not conducive to human growth and development due partly because the cultural emphasis on consumer goods and the politics of pharmaceutical companies made business difficult for mental health professionals (Doherty & Anderson, 2004). In particular, marriage and family therapists were working to be recognized by insurance companies to get reimbursement. Under the medical model, insurance companies have never really recognized educational programs or prevention methods, making it difficult for mental health workers to include these resources to their families (Doherty & Anderson, 2004). What was attractive to researchers was the topic of divorce prevention, which ended up being a large piece of marriage education programs. By the early 1990s, Gottman was publishing his findings that predicted divorce with 94 % accuracy based on relationship interaction patterns (Gottman & Notaruis, 2002).

All the flurry of the lay-led marriage movement, the movement of peer training rather than professionals offering training, of the 1970s slowed down in the 1980s (Doherty & Anderson, 2004). Many community-based programs were experiencing low attendance and the momentum was lost. With the exception of pre-marital programs in the faith-based community, churches temporarily stopped placing an emphasis on marriage education as a service for families or as a topic for sermons.

The culture of divorce and feminism also contributed to the slowdown in marriage education in the 1980s. By the early 80s, divorce rates were at record highs, and for the first time in history, more couples opted for divorce than reconciliation. This was seen by many in the women's movement as a step forward towards women's empowerment. As Carlson et al. (2004) explains, divorce gave women an option to be in a relationship where they had power, or to leave that relationship if an egalitarian role was not available. The idea that two-parent families were better than single families was no long longer a dominant opinion, giving women power to raise children on their own. Historically, women had not been granted choice in their relationship status, and this new ideology was empowering for many women.

It was not until the 1990s that renewed energy for marriage education surfaced. Family researchers began to discover that divorce had negative repercussions for families, particularly children, and the political climate once again began to focus on family wellbeing (Doherty & Anderson, 2004). These two factors created a demand for marriage education to resurface over the next decade.

National and state-wide movements have been fueled by both the State and National government policy and community groups, including faith-based and social service groups. Most notable is the federal government's commitment to fund healthy marriage initiatives across the U.S. The U.S. Department of Health and Human Services Administration for children and families announced a 5 year, $500+ million dollar grant initiative to support healthy marriages (ACF, 2006). The government released this funding in order to combat risk factors and increase protective factors for child-wellbeing based on the premise that children fare better when parents are married to each other. The funding was available primarily to organizations working with low-income families, but there are also large amounts of funds available to communities working to implement marriage initiatives. Much of the research and evidence-based practices of relationship education available now came from the ACF Funding.

John Gottman and the Gottman Institute

John Gottman is perhaps the single biggest contributor to the field of marriage education and couple relationships. For four decades, Gottman has researched nearly every element of couple development. The Gottman Institute, located in Seattle Washington, is a research lab, a professional training facility, and a center that provides services to families. Gottman's research has taught professionals in the field about best practices for program development by researching what makes a relationship successful and what is harmful.

The principles and lessons Gottman shares with his audiences come from decades of research. For example, Gottman and Driver (2004) sought to understand how regular every-day positive events improve humor and affect during negative events. Participant couples volunteered to spend 24 h in a laboratory "apartment" doing "normal" activities. Although 12 hours of tape was captured, the focus in this study was the dinnertime conversation. Couples were asked to talk about a confliction topic, and researchers observed the interaction.

The results showed the way couples interacted in mundane events affected what happens during conflict; the more positive daily interactions, the more healthy the conflict. In a similar study, Gottman, Coan, Swanson and Carrere (1998) found the only predictor of marital stability and satisfaction was positive affect during conflict and that humor and affect is also a prominent characteristic of senior couples still in their first marriage. Couples who like each other and express that affection by being happy around each other do better in conflict.

This research, and other similar studies conducted by Gottman and his colleagues have shaped the direction of marriage education. The core of most marriage education places emphasis on communication. Gottman has identified both risk and protective factors in marital satisfaction specifically in the realm of communication. The risk factors are the negative interactions a couple experiences during conflict. While conflict is normal, how a person responds to conflict is of critical importance.

Gottman and Silver (1999) identified four specific negative interactions:

- criticism
- contempt
- defensiveness
- stonewalling

Gottman referrers to these behaviors as the Four Horsemen of the Apocalypse as these are especially harmful to couples. The first is *criticism*, which is simply a complaint disguised in an assault on the partner. Example: "you said you would put your dirty socks in the hamper, but I guess that would be expecting too much, wouldn't it?" Really, there is a complaint here that could easily be expressed as "please put your socks in the hamper" without the mean-spirited commentary often used by couples in conflict. For more information about the four horsemen, see Gottman and Silver (1999). The remaining three become more destructive in nature until finally, a partner will disengage all together, or stonewall their partner. These four communication styles are destructive to relationships, and many marriage enhancement programs teach skills to avoid these dangerous communication tactics.

Gottman's work has also given professionals information on what helps a relationship succeed. Protective factors for a marriage are plenty, but Gottman has formed them into seven principles, which he teaches in his book The Seven Principles for Making Marriage Work: A Practical Guide from the County's Foremost Relationship Expert (1999). Those principles are

- Creating a love map
- Nurturing fondness
- Turning toward your partner
- Partner influence
- Problem solving (includes communication)
- Overcoming gridlock
- Creating a shared meaning

Utilization of these seven principles can save relationships by focusing on creating happiness and connection in the marriage. Gottman noted that it takes five positive experiences to negate one negative. So for couples that are happy together, there are five times as many positive interactions as negative ones. Positives can include something as simple as a warm welcome home when a partner arrives to a date night. In fact, it is the little everyday moments that truly make a difference in relationship satisfaction, so the more daily positives, turning towards each other, the happier the relationship.

Gottman has turned his research on marital satisfaction, divorce prediction, and the effects of childbearing into a marriage program for new families. The Bringing Baby Home Program (Gottman & Gottman, 2007) is designed for couples that are expecting a child. The 2-day educational workshop provides basic skills training and is followed by a support group for 6 months. This program helps parents understand the issues surrounding the transition into parenthood, which has been associated with relationship satisfaction decrease (Shapiro & Gottman, 2005). Results on the evaluation of the Bringing Baby Home program showed that couples participating in this program are more likely than the control couples to report higher levels of relationship satisfaction, lower levels of postpartum depression, and have a more positive affect with their partner (Shapiro & Gottman, 2005).

Howard Markman and Scott Stanley, PREP

Other researchers that have made developments in the field of relationship education are Howard Markman and Scott Stanley. Markman and Stanley's research is
based on marital success and distress studies conducted at the University of Denver.
Their research has yielded a great deal of interest from both the professional and
lay-led communities as their research describes protective factors and risk factors
for marriage and divorce. The research of Markman and Stanley come from a
variety of studies and experiences with couples. In general, these researchers found
that people are happy with their partners and want their relationships to work. For
example, they conducted a phone survey to 947 adults to find out the perception of
relationships among couples (Stanley, Markman, & Whitton, 2002). They found
that the couples that reported dedication to their relationship had stronger and
happier relationships. They also inquired about topics couples argue most about
and found that couples argue most about money, followed by children, household
labor division, careers and finally, in-laws.

When asked about factors that help a relationship succeed, couples reported that
the more they contributed to the relationship, the happier the relationship and
sacrifice played a large role (Stanley, Whitton, Low, Clements, & Markman,
2006). For example, when it came to division of chores, this study showed that
the more equitable, the happier the couple. When one person in the relationship
made a sacrifice for the other, it also fostered happy relationship. The message is
one of balance, of give and take. This research suggests that couples that share the
responsibilities and are king and generous have happier relationships.

Like Gottman, Stanley and Markman found the following danger signs in
unsuccessful relationships: withdrawal, escalation, criticism, loneliness, belittling,
holding back feelings, uneven perceptions. Much of their work focuses on communication and conflict (Markman, Stanley, & Blumberg, 2010). Couples who
exhibited negative reciprocity, poor affect management and withdrawal during
conflict where most likely to have a troubled relationship. They also found that
communication, conflict, and commitment are fundamental to relationship success.
Their research showed that negative communication is linked with lower relationship satisfaction and higher rates of divorce. Negative communication is also linked
with thoughts and talk of divorce. Their findings on communication are significant
because their applied program, PREP, focuses heavily on the communication skills
of partners.

Based on the data they had collected over the years, the authors created a
program to help couples improve their relationship. Research on marriage shows
that the interactions between couples is predictive of outcomes, therefore Markman
and Stanley designed their Prevention and Relationship Enhancement Program
(PREP) to prevent marital distress and divorce by providing training on how to
have more positive interactions in relationships. Their book, *Fighting for Your
Marriage*, has become a best seller and has reached mass audiences (Markman

et al., 2010) and led them to become arguable the most well-known research and programmers in the field of marriage education and divorce prevention.

National Extension Relationship and Marriage Education Model

When couples are at that point to seek help from a professional, things have typically gone wrong in their relationship. Historically, professionals that work with couples focus on helping the couple communicate better and deal with the difficulties of their relationships. Communication has been established as the cornerstone of all relationships, and more information about family communication is found in Chap. 8.

While focusing on positive communication is useful, working with couples to develop a healthy relationship is much, much more than communication training. How relationship coaching can and should differ from therapy or counseling is the process of helping clients focus on the strengths of their partner while creating goals to help achieve a shared vision.

Before working with couples, however, it is important to understand the research and dynamics of couple happiness and wellbeing. Researchers and Family Life Specialists with the National Extension Relationship and Marriage Education Network (NERMEN) reviewed the relationship literature on predictors of relationship quality and from that research, built a model of relationship and marriage education (Futris & Adler-Baeder, 2013). Theoretical underpinnings of the NERMEN Model include Ecological and System Theories, Life Course Theories, Social Learning Theories (see Chap. 3), Spillover Theories, Social Exchange Theories, Attribution Theories, and Feminist Theory.

Based on the research, their model includes seven components of a healthy relationship development. While written to support program development of community-based relationship and marriage education as part of family life education, the NERMEN concepts covered here are relevant and important for family life coaches. In order to help a client through the process of relationship coaching, it is critical to have foundational knowledge of healthy relationships and information on how to help couples improve their relationship. Therefore I present the seven core component of the National Extension Relationship and Marriage Education Model.

Choose
Care for self
Know
Care
Share
Manage
Connect

Choose to Make the Relationship a Priority

Choice is the spice in life and some would argue the answer to most struggles. Making a choice to be committed to making your relationship a priority is a critical factor in healthy relationships. Coaches can help their clients understand if and how to make their relationship a priority.

A metaphor for choosing to make a relationship a priority is like going on a float trip. One could ask their client, "Have you ever been floating? What do you need for a float trip?" The answers may vary, but the bottom line is that people will describe the tools they need to be successful.

Bill Doherty talks more about making a choice to prioritize the relationship in his book, Take Back Your Marriage (2001). He refers to a relationship as a river with currents taking you downstream. Regardless of your affection, hope, or intentions, the current will carry you aimlessly unless you paddle. Couples must paddle and work on the float trip in order to have success.

A major part of the relationship work is focusing on strengths. Coaching places a lot of focus on strengths, and relationship coaching is no exception. When couples focus on what is frustrating them or on what doesn't work, it brings out the worst. Recall the phrase, "what you focus on grows." This suggests that what we put our attention and energy on is what becomes the focus. So couples that focus on keeping score or noticing what is wrong tend to be less happy. Asking couples what is working, or what has worked in the past switches the focus to strengths. Continue to move the process forward by helping the couple envision a healthy future together.

Choosing is relevant for both participants in a relationship, but is also relevant to singles that are in the process of becoming a couple. Many young couples preparing for their lives together might choose to seek help from a coach in an effort to prepare for success. The topic covered in this chapter is relevant for both types of clients.

Care for Self

The literature on healthy relationships suggest that we are best in our personal relationships when we care for ourselves. Although this is not news to most people, knowing what to do doesn't always lead to doing what is right. Physical, social/emotional, and spiritual health are all essential elements of a healthy relationship (Futris & Adler-Baeder, 2013). This is true of all relationships; parenting, career, romantic…we are all better people when we have taken the time to care for ourselves. This is not the same as being selfish; this is having a system in place to care for our basic needs such as sleeping, eating healthy, exercising, and down time.

Ask your clients to think about how they felt the day after a sleepless night or when they felt themselves coming down with a cold. They are probably not their best selves, which is often when conflict arises. We can help clients understand they can HALT and reflect on their mood to help understand their feelings.

- Hungry
- Angry
- Lonely
- Tired

The science of positive psychology shows focusing on the positive is key to social and emotional health. Seligman (2002) refers to paying attention on a daily basis of what went well. In fact, clients can begin to train themselves to focus on the positive by asking themselves or each other what went well on a daily basis. Positives can also come in the form of noticing strengths. Remember the VIA character strengths identified in the assessments chapter; couples can identify each other's strengths as well as their own to help them better understand each other. Helping clients identify their own health and wellbeing can truly impact all elements of their life satisfaction, including their relationships.

Know Your Partner

We already discussed the importance of couples truly spending time and energy getting to know each other. For couples that are forming, it is important to know enough about each other to decide to engage in a relationship. Rather than simply letting life happen, couples do best when they continue to learn about each other throughout the life of the relationship.

At first glance, it might seem as if being together for months, years, and even decades would account for knowing each other. But that is not necessarily true; we are evolving humans that have daily experiences impacting and helping us grow. Sometimes, couples grow apart. Having a strategy and maintaining the connection with our partners is essential, and often times couples do not realize this.

As coaches, we can help clients understand this concept and work to design meaningful time spent together. John Gottman (2015), a world-class researcher of marriage and relationships, refers to the importance of Love Maps. Knowing our partner's love map is the process of becoming intimately familiar with the details of our partner's life. Couples need to spend time together, much like they did in the early parts of the relationship, so they can continue to know their partner. It is possible, even common, for couples to get so caught up in the day to day of life to they lose information about each other. The love maps brings couples together and are formed through a process of discovery. Like the paddle, it takes work, time, and shared experiences.

Care for Your Partner

How do you know someone cares? What are the actions or behaviors in a caring relationship? Care is the very essence of what most people think about when they think about being in a healthy relationship-doing nice things for someone, spending quality time together, and being helpful are just a few. Care refers to the behaviors that lead couples in a positive direction, such as kind, nurturing, and fruitful interactions. Similar to knowing your partner, care for your partner is commonly found in all stages of relationship development. Loving actions, tender moments, and more positives than negatives are the very essence of care. Gottman's research (2015) shows a magic ratio of positives to negatives that can predict the course of a relationship. In the healthiest of relationships of Gottman's study, there was a ratio of 5 positives to every one negative interaction. For every one argument or negative interaction, a couple needs five moments or experiences that help bring them together.

In coaching couples, one might encourage both parties to begin to observe the positives of a relationship, then coach them to focus more intentionally on exhibiting positives. We are humans, and as such, we are often in the habit of noticing what is wrong. However, we can learn to focus on what went well; what is good and that can make a tremendous impact on a relationship. As simple as it sounds, this task does not come easily to people that are hurt, disappointed, or even discouraged by their relationship. For these couples, change is often slow and well earned.

An assessment tool that is highly popular among relationship coaches and educators is Gary Chapman's The Five Love Languages (2007). Understanding our own and our partner's love language can help make sense of interactions in the relationship. **The five love languages include quality time, words of affirmation, gifts, acts of service, and physical touch.** What sometimes happens is that one member of a relationship will have a type of language different than their partner. They give a gift they would love, but their partner might not speak that language. This is part of the love map; knowing if a partner feels most loved with words of affirmation will help them know what to do to speak that language.

I have a friend who loves little gifts. Getting a little tinker toy or action figure or book makes his day! He spent his life giving little tinker toys to his wife, who was always grateful for the thoughtful gift, but never understood why he continued to give gifts. She knew how important spending quality time together was, so she often arranged for special moments together, which he enjoyed, but often wondered why she never reciprocated with little gifts. Once they understood each other's love language, he began organizing the quality time together and she rarely showed up without a gift. They were finally speaking each other's language.

Regardless of our love language, spending quality time together and showing affection, appreciation, and kindness are critical to happy, healthy relationships, and should be the focus on coaching interventions. Helping people understand how important showing caring actions are can make the difference to a relationships.

Shared Experiences

Although care is about the behaviors one person can show to another, share is about meaningful shared experiences together. I can show loving behaviors towards my partner by sending sweet texts throughout the day or offering to watch his favorite show. Those are individual behaviors. Share is about the time and experiences my partner and I spend together. It takes two people to share.

While grand gestures and highly romantic moments might be the connotation of what it takes to create a healthy relationship, researchers Janice Driver and John Gottman suggests just the opposite. "The mundane and often fleeting moments that a couple experiences in their everyday lives may contribute to the health or deterioration of a relationship" (Driver & Gottman, 2004, p. 301). The playful everyday moments tend to serve as protectors for couples. Couples that have more positives than negatives in their everyday lives tend to have more positive affect during conflict.

A quality partnership most often begins with a strong friendship, and includes three critical elements of sharing: time together, shared couple identify, and nurturing positive interactions. Often, life becomes busy and we forget to take time to nurture the relationship. Shared experiences, either grand events or simple moments, are the heart of happy relationships. As coaches, helping couples better understand and move towards positive shared experiences can help a couple begin to focus more on the positive.

Manage Relationship Differences

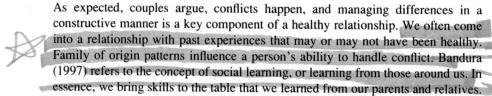

As expected, couples argue, conflicts happen, and managing differences in a constructive manner is a key component of a healthy relationship. We often come into a relationship with past experiences that may or may not have been healthy. Family of origin patterns influence a person's ability to handle conflict. Bandura (1997) refers to the concept of social learning, or learning from those around us. In essence, we bring skills to the table that we learned from our parents and relatives.

When I teach the Healthy Relationship and Marriage Education training, I have participants stand in a line based on where they believe they fit on a continuum of 1–10; 1 raised in a peaceful home and 10 raised in a highly conflictual household. We then process what this means for them in their current situation. More often than not, adults raised in a high conflict home do not want this for their current family. They want the skills and ability to work through troubled times with a calmer, less heated process. Many do not know how to make this happen as it was a skill they never learned.

Certainly, people want and do better, and succeed more readily when they are raised in a low-conflict environment (Cowan, Cowan, Pruett, & Pruett, 2005). However, without the skills for good communication and conflict management, many couples struggle with how to manage their relationship differences. Gottman and Silver (1999) identified four negative patterns of conflict: criticism, defensiveness, contempt, and stonewalling. Evidence of any one of these "horsemen" need to be challenged as they make the task of healthy relationship quite challenging.

Tips from Gottman's Research include

- Softening startups
- Repair attempts
- Finding common ground
- Forgiveness

Softening a startup refers to the approach a partner uses when beginning a conversation that is conflictual in nature. For example, rather than saying "You always..." a soft start up might be "Is this an OK time to talk? I feel as if I need to let you know how I feel about..." Repair attempts include accepting responsibility for our part of the conflict, being open to what our partner says, and soothing ourselves so that we are more calm and open to the solution.

Finding common ground and forgiveness are not new, but couples still need to be reminded and coached sometimes for how to find common ground or forgive. For more information, or a resource for couples dealing with conflict, I recommend John Gottman's book, The Seven Principles for Making Marriage Work (1999). This book works much like a series of assessments, with information on how to make improvements for each assessment. For example, the activity, Assessing your marital conflicts questionnaire has couples identify whether issues or solvable or perpetual. The activity allows for discussion about the issues, but then points to the key to conflict resolution. Each chapter is filled with many activities and assessments that could be useful to relationship coaches.

Connect with a Supportive Community

The last concept identified by the National Extension Relationship and Marriage Education model is the importance of connecting with others. When families have support from the people around them, they do better. Bronfenbrenner ecological theory (1979) helps us understand the importance of systems, and this is true in relationships. Over the past decade, research on relationships has shown an importance of connecting with others as an essential element of couple happiness (Doherty & Carroll, 2002). Having friends to support the relationship can help reduce stress and increase relationship resilience (Cohen & Hoberman, 2006). Brothers, Behnke, and Goddard, (2013), suggest the following for couples:

- Engaging in social support systems
- Being connected to sources of meaning or purpose
- Reaching out to others and offering support

How to Coach for a Healthy Relationship

While these components of a healthy relationship are uniformly true of most couples, it is important to recognize that familial stress truly impacts couple happiness and wellbeing. Risk factors of healthy relationships include economic stress, gender distrust, multiple partners and blended families, substance abuse, and many others. As coaches, we must understand that the more risk factors at play, the higher the stress levels and likelihood of relationship problems. This doesn't mean that stressful relationships are hopeless; just the opposite. There is support in the literature that suggests couples can learn skills and improve the quality of their relationships (Futris & Adler-Baeder, 2013). This is encouraging as many couples just need support, guidance, and help reaching their goals. When coaching couples, consider the following:

Dream the dream: couples often understand what they don't want or don't accept, but might need help identifying what they do want. In Appreciative inquiry language, work with couples to help them:

1. *Discover what it is working in the relationship*. Even relationships that need lots of change have positives, so begin by finding what's right. You could ask them "what does it look like when things are at their best?"
2. *Dreaming of what might be* helps couples visualize the future they wish to see. Although this might play out as what they would like to see different in the partner's behavior, help them to focus on the dream scenario of what could be. "What would it look like if things were as you would have them be?"

Keep the eye on the prize: it is easy for couples to get off topic, and begin to share frustrations or examples of what they would like to change in their partner. The coach can help the couple stay on track by reframing the language back to the dream, or the goal set by the couple. "I'm wondering if this discussion is helping you get to your goal. How might we move back towards designing your destiny?"

Practice makes perfect: some couples come with few skills, which makes it difficult to achieve movement. As a coach it is important to help them identify and practice some of the evidence based skills identified in this chapter. This could happen in a session, but could also be used as homework.

Bring in the resources: as couples learn new methods of communication and better skills for cultivating happiness, they might need resources. Below are resources that could help couples learn and practice the skills needed to cultivate happy relationships.

Model of Relationship Coaching

While there is a dearth of literature on coaching couples or relationship coaching, Ives (2012) reflected on his process of coaching individuals that are single and looking for partners. In his experience, the focus is on relationship attitudes, skills, and goals. By working with individuals to explore their attitudes and perceptions of relationships, clients are better prepared to engage in a relationship. Ives suggested coaches also work to help clients identify clear goals and effective action plans. By working on both personal development (relationship skill development) and goal setting, a positive opportunity for relationship satisfaction is created. His GREAT model of relationship coaching includes:

Goal. Setting a goal.
Reality. Understanding the current situation
Exploration. Gaining of experiences, perspectives, and attitudes
Action Plan. Identify strategies to reach goal.
Take Action. Implement the action plan.

Many relationship coaches, however, work with couples already in a relationship. The research on the effectiveness of relationship coaching is sparse, but a

Google search on "relationship coaching" and "couples coach" produces a large number of hits. Most of the websites are practitioners currently offering relationship-coaching services. I personally completed couples coaching with my husband and had success at identifying the strengths of our relationship and directions for how to move forward with the positives of our life. Clearly, there is a major gap in the research and training on relationship coaching, but I include it as a new and growing approach to serving families.

Sexuality Coaching

Although technically sexuality coaching is a separate field of coaching, anyone that chooses to focus specifically on relationship coaching should have some training in sexuality. Patti Britton, a clinical sexologist, wrote a book in 2005 designed to show family practitioners, such as therapists and counselors, how to grow their practice by offering sex coaching. Her book shares information on the differences of therapy and coaching, and suggested that coaching is about the future and goal setting, not about emotions and the past. Like relationship coaching, there is a vast gap in the research on the effectiveness of sex coaching, but there are training schools and a plethora of sex coaches marketing their services on the internet.

Case Study

Emily and George, a couple in their early thirties, is seeking coaching to "revive" their relationship. Both spouses say they are still in love with one another, but have been "in a rut" after 9 years together. Emily says the marriage has functioned more as a partnership in the last few years, with little time or energy to devote to romance, dates, or getaways. George agrees, saying he wishes things were more like the "early days." The couple has decided to try for a baby, but wanted to get their marriage back on track before taking the next big step. They have been in the coaching process for 1 month.

Coach: "Good evening. How are you both today?"

Emily: "Pretty good. We're ready to work on this some more."

Coach: "Great! Let's jump right in. The last time we met, 2 weeks ago, Emily you had expressed a desire for more romance and intimacy, and George you had expressed boredom with the "routine" of your marriage. You both came up with a plan and agreed that you would engage in a weekly date, at home or out and to specifically not talk about work. I'm so curious...how did the past 2 weeks play out?"

George: "The first week went pretty well in that I think we were both pretty excited to put emphasis on ourselves and going out together. I picked the date place and I think we both liked it."

Coach: "Well that sounds promising! What did you like about it?"

George: "I liked the atmosphere, it was intimate. We went to an Italian restaurant, had a really nice and special meal with wine and appetizers. Afterward we went to a movie. The movie was okay but I really enjoyed spending time together and not talking about what we needed to do at home."

Coach: "That sounds very nice George, how about you, Emily?"

Emily: "I really enjoyed the movie and dinner too! The food was really good and I got something I usually don't get, stuffed peppers. I think I enjoyed the movie more than George but overall I think it was a great date."

Coach: "Great, what about after the date? What happened when you got home?"

Emily: "When we got home we kind of fell into our routine roles, taking care of housework and honestly I believe the mood changed from what it was on the date, however we still had a nice intimate night."

George: (chuckling) "Yes."

Coach: "Well it sounds as if you are both happy with the way the night went. How about Emily's date the following week?"

Emily: "Well, I thought it would be fun to go on a picnic and since we both had Saturday free, I wanted to take the whole day and devote it to us. I picked out a nearby state park and packed a cooler and picnic basket. I made some sandwiches and George helped put some of the things together too. We drove out there and parked. It was a beautiful day and a nice park, (looking at George) lots of vegetation and very peaceful."

Note: At this point, the coach is listening for the non-verbal's, such as love languages and if both are feeling as if things are moving in a positive direction.

George: "Yes, it was quite nice. I brought along the camera and I am so glad I did because I got some nice pictures of a woodpecker and a piece of amethyst quartz."

Coach: "Tell me more. What went well? What was your favorite part?"

Note: Coach is using Seligman's what went well strategy and Gottman's focus on positive interactions to help them focus on the positives.

Emily: "My favorite part was holding George's hand and day dreaming on the blanket of bringing our future children there to play."

George: "My favorite part was being able to sit beside my sweetheart without any distractions."

Coach: "Wow! This sounds like a win-win situation. Just the sound of your voice I can hear a joy with each other. How are you feeling about the relationship now?"

Emily: "Well personally I felt so connected to George. We spent the entire day together talking about our new experience and I couldn't wait to get home."

George: "Me too. It really felt like it did in the "early days" of our romance. It was a really nice date." (Turns to Emily and smiles)

Coach: "What a great amount of progress you have both made in 2 weeks. I remember last time, you each took a moment to talk about how you would like to see your future together. How do these past few experiences fit with that vision?"

Emily: (smiling) "Really good. I can't wait to see what our next date night will bring."

Coach: "What about you George, how do you feel about the past 2 weeks?"

George: "Good, and happy."

Coach: "Okay, so now that the past 2 weeks have gone well, what would you like to focus on for today? What goals would you like to reach for our next meeting?"

Emily: "Something that has been on my mind the past 2 weeks as we moved forward toward our date nights is that there is still so much I don't know about George. I mean I know him and I believe we have the same values but when I think about getting pregnant and trying for a baby my mind begins to whirl."

Coach: "Okay, so are you saying you are curious about what George will be like in the father role?"

Emily: "Yes, I know he has told me some things about when he was a child and how he was raised and I wonder how much of that I really know and does he really know about me and my childhood (looking to George)."

Coach: "Well Emily that is a valid question, bringing a child into a relationship can bring lots of uncertainty. George, what are your thoughts on this topic?"

George: "I'm not sure really. It doesn't seem weird to understand things better, but I'm not sure I have the questions Emily does. I figure we can manage once the baby arrives. I am more concerned about having enough money and insurance."

Coach: "Well it sounds like you both have curiosity about what to do next in preparation to growing a family. Would you like to make this your topic for today? Or would you like to explore other ideas?"

George: "I would like to keep our date nights as one of our goals and begin exploring what else we need to do in preparation for a child, whatever that might be. I mean, things feel good now, but how do I know things will stay like this?"

Emily: "I agree George. I would like to have our new goal be determining what is important to us about family and parenting and understanding the finances involved."

Coach: "Okay, well I think this is a great next step. I think we are all in agreement that in addition to continuing to work on staying connected, the next goal would be understand your family values and financial responsibilities toward raising a family. This goal is still quite broad, may I suggest breaking it down into smaller goals. Or maybe we could break it into a part that would you like to focus on for this week?"

George: "I think I will need more time to understand the financial aspects so if Emily doesn't mind, maybe we could explore some of our family values while I research more about insurances at work."

Coach: "How does that sound to you Emily?

Emily: "Yes, I think that is fine."

Coach: "OK, good. George, I'm just having a thought, and I want to share that with you, if you don't mind.

George: "Sure"

Coach: "If you are working on researching insurance, how will you be able to devote time for understanding each other's family values, and work, and a date night this week?"

George: "Hmmm. Well. I don't think it will be a problem. I can research at work some and ask around some of my coworkers. Then we can talk more about family values in the evening. That show we were watching just ended. Maybe we could talk about it that night. Emme?"

Emily: "Yes, I am fine with that. But I am not quite sure how to figure out our family values. How do we do that? I mean I really want to stay home with the kids, that's what my mom did and that would mean a big financial cut in our budget. Is that even a possibility George?"

George: "I didn't realize you wanted to stay home. I'm not sure. This could get interesting. Would you quit your job?"

Emily: "Well, I don't know but if I am having a baby someone needs to take care of it. And I would like to nurse. I would need to be home for that, right?"

George: "You know I would rather you stay home with the baby then me but what else do we need to do? Can we still go on vacations? What about date night?"

Coach: "I think you both have very valid concerns. Starting a family is a big step. Tell me about people or resources in your community that will be a part of your life when the baby comes"

 Note: Knowing that the importance of community, the coach is able to help guide the process by helping the clients see that it takes a village. This redirection helps two ways; helps them see the bigger picture and helps them move past a potential conflict by identifying more resources.

Emily: "Hmmm. I am not sure. My mom is only 45 min away, maybe we could use her. George?"

George: "Yes that sounds okay but (shakes his head)

Coach: "Am I sensing some confusion George?"

George: "Uh, I don't know"

Coach: "Okay, well name a feeling you are having right now."

George: "Ummm.....overwhelmed."

Coach: "Emily, do you sense George's feelings right now?"

Emily:	"Yes, whenever he is overwhelmed he rubs his forehead like that. So I always just drop the subject when he does that. I don't want to overwhelm him, maybe he isn't ready for this. George?"
Coach:	"Having a baby is a big commitment. It can certainly feel overwhelming."
George:	"Yup. I don't know. I am really ready. I want to have a family with you, Emily. I love you, Emme. It's just 1 min we were talking about our great dates and now Emily is quitting her job, her mom is coming to watch a baby, and I don't even know if I can afford a family yet"
Coach:	"I see, so you are feeling scared because it is a lot and you are not even sure if you can afford this."
George:	"Yes! I want to be able to afford it. Diapers, and doctors. And what if something bad happens I can't fix."
Coach:	"Wow, yes George. There is a lot of unanswered questions there. (waits about 20 seconds to let the feelings be felt) Okay, let's refocus again on our goals for this week. Emily and George, you are both very concerned about starting a family and what that means and looks like to you. Before our session ends today, let's set a reasonable goal about your desires of having a family for this week and this week only. It doesn't have to be big. Just a small step to further gain understanding about what it is you really want and need for your desires to come true. I have an activity. Here is a marker and paper. What do you most want to work on for our next meeting? Take your time and really think this through." (Coach takes notes while Emily and George write and think for about 2 min)
Coach:	"Okay, let's see what you have come up with."
Emily:	"I think George is right, we should at least have an idea of cost, cost for pregnancy, birth, and first year of a baby's life. I wrote down research finances of childbirth."
George:	"I wrote down researching finances too."
Coach:	"I noticed you changed your focus Emily. What made you change?"
Emily:	"I see how important that is to not only George but the entire situation and if I am going to leave my work temporarily maybe there is something I can get from my job before I leave that will help with the financial aspect of my pregnancy."
Coach:	"Okay, George is there anything you want to add."
George:	"Yes, I think Emily will be a great mother and I can't wait to take our brood to the park and hold hands and take pictures together. It is a dream of mine to have a happy family."
Emily:	"Really, George? It makes me so happy to hear you say that"
Coach:	"That was very nice George. So this week, you are each going to continue your date time. Right?"
Emily:	"Yes, that's right".
Coach:	"So for the record the goal for this week is to further understand, investigate, and research the financial aspect of pregnancy, childbirth, and raising a family. Is there anything else you would like to add?"

Emily: "Nope. I think that is it."
Coach: "George?"
George: "No. That is plenty for this week."

Note: the coach would continue to work with clients to identify action steps for reaching the goal and identify way of accountability. While resources did not come up in this session, the coach might begin to look for resources or assessments to have on hand for future meetings.

Chapter Summary

Relationship coaching requires specific content for helping couples make meaningful changes. The science of love and relationships has grown greatly in the last few decades, and there are plenty of evidence-based practices that coaches can help clients implement to improve their situation. What was not mentioned here is the world of literature on how a happy, healthy relationship impacts children. As the Healthy Relationship and Marriage Education Training materials (n.d.) show, child safety, child permanency, and child-wellbeing are all tied to healthy relationships. Chapter 10 will focus on parent coaching and will provide many tips on helping parents, but the foundation for children lies in their parent's ability to co-parent. Of course not all children have interaction with both parents, but for those that do, healthy co-parenting is a recipe for positive outcomes.

Further Reading[1]

Chapman, G. (1995). *The five love languages: How to express heartfelt commitment to your mate.* Chicago: Northfield Publishing.
Doherty, W. (2001). *Take back your marriage.* New York: Guilford.
Gottman, J. M., & Silver, N. (1999). *The seven principles for making marriage work: A practical guide from the county's foremost relationship expert.* New York: Three Rivers Press.

References

Administration for Children and Families. (2006). *Healthy marriage demonstration grants.* Retrieved from http://www.acf.hhs.gov/grants/open/HHS-2006-ACF-OFA-FE-0033.html
Bandura, A. (1997). *Self efficacy: The exercise of control.* New York: Freeman.

---

[1] There are a plethora of resources for families available from the National Extension Relationship and Marriage Education Network website: http://www.nermen.org/NERMEM.php

Britton, P. (2005). *The art of sex coaching: Expanding your practice.* New York: Norton and Company.

Brothers, S., Behnke, A., & Goddard, W. (2013). *Connect: Engaging in a positive social network of support.* Retrieved from http://www.fcs.uga.edu/docs/Nermem_08_Connect.pdf

Carlson, M., McLanahan, S., & England, P. (2004). Union formation in fragile families. *Demography, 41,* 237–261.

Chapman, G. (2007). *The five love languages: How to express heartfelt commitment to your mate.* Chicago: Northfield Publishing.

Cowan, C. P., Cowan, P. A., Pruett, M. K., & Pruett, K. (2005). An approach to preventing coparenting conflict and divorce in low-income families: Strengthening couple relationships and fostering father's involvement. *Family Process, 46,* 109–121.

Cohen, S., & Hoberman, H. M. (2006). Positive events and social supports as buffers of life change stress. *Journal of Applied Social Psychology, 13*(2), 99–125.

Doherty, W. (2001). *Take back your marriage.* New York: Guilford.

Doherty, W., & Anderson, J. (2004). Community marriage initiatives. *Family Relations, 53,* 425–432.

Doherty, W. J., & Carroll, J. S. (2002). The families and democracy project. *Family Process, 41,* 579–589.

Driver, J. L., & Gottman, J. M. (2004). Daily marital interactions and positive affect during marital conflict among newlywed couples. *Family Process, 43*(3), 301–314.

Fincham, F. D., & Beach, S. R. H. (2010). Marriage in the new millennium: A decade in review. *Journal of Marriage and Family, 72,* 630–649.

Futris, T. G., & Adler-Baeder, F. (2013). *The national extension relationship and marriage education model: Linking research to relationship and marriage education.* Retrieved from http://www.nermen.org/NERMEM/Nermem_01_Intro.pdf

Gottman, J., & Notaruis, C. (2002). Marital research in the 20th century and a research agenda for the 21st century. *Family Process, 41,* 159–197.

Gottman, J., & Silver, N. (2012). *What makes love last?* New York: Simon & Schuster.

Gottman, J. M. (2015). *Principia amoris: The new science of love.* New York: Routledge.

Gottman, J. M., Coan, J., Carrer, S., & Swanson, C. (1998). Predicting marital happiness and stability from newlywed interactions. *Journal of Marriage and the Family, 60,* 5–22.

Gottman, J. M., & Driver, J. L. (2004). Daily marital interactions and positive affect during marital conflict among newlywed couples. *Family Process, 43,* 301–314.

Gottman, J. M., & Gottman, J. S. (2007). *And baby makes three.* New York: Three Rivers Press.

Gottman, J. M., & Silver, N. (1999). *The seven principles for making marriage work: A practical guide from the county's foremost relationship expert.* New York: Three Rivers Press.

Ives, Y. (2012). What is relationship coaching? *International Journal of Evidence Based Coaching and Mentoring, 10*(2), 88–99.

Madden, M., & Rainie, L. (2006). *Romance in America.* Per Research Center. Retrieved from http://www.pewinternet.org/2006/02/13/romance-in-america/#fn-860-1

Markman, H. J., Stanley, S. M., & Blumberg, S. L. (2010). *Fighting for your marriage.* San Francisco: Jossey-Bass.

Seligman, M. E. P. (2002). *Authentic happiness: Using the new positive psychology to realize your potential for lasting fulfillment.* New York: Simon and Schuster.

Shapiro, A. F., & Gottman, J. M. (2005). Effects on marriage of a psycho-communicative-educational intervention with couples undergoing the transition to parenthood, evaluation at 1-year post intervention. *The Journal of Family Communication, 5,* 1–24.

Stanley, S. M., Markman, H. J., & Whitton, S. W. (2002). Communication, conflict, and commitment: Insights on the foundations of relationship success from a national survey. *Family Process, 41*(4), 659–675.

Stanley, S. M., Whitton, S. W., Low, S. M., Clements, M. L., & Markman, H. J. (2006). Sacrifice as a predictor of marital outcomes. *Family Process, 45,* 289–303.

Chapter 10
Parent Coaching

> It is easier to build strong children than to repair broken men. (Frederick Douglass)

Rudolf Dreikurs, an Adlerian psychologist, wrote his book *Children the Challenge* (Dreikurs & Soltz, 1964), on the importance of parents helping their children to feel encouraged, supported, and guided. Parenting professionals across the globe began to help parents through this approach called parent guidance, considered a pre-cursor to family life coaching. This chapter provides a review of Adlerian parenting theory and strategies that are a must know for any parent coach.

Knowing parenting techniques is only part of what a family life coach needs to know to be effective at parent coaching. There are several theoretical foundations for parent coaching, and while the Adlerian parenting approach is the primary focus of this chapter, child development theories, parenting theories, and emotion coaching will also be covered.

Family life coaches must know how to translate knowledge about child development and parent child interactions in a way that is consistent with coaching. There is a delicate balance between the coaching process and relaying education, therefore a case study that highlights the importance of having both coaching skills and content knowledge for working with a family on a parenting issue is included. This chapter provides strategies and practices for how to translate knowledge about parent child interactions in a way that is consistent with coaching.

© Springer International Publishing Switzerland 2016
K. Allen, *Theory, Research, and Practical Guidelines for Family Life Coaching*,
DOI 10.1007/978-3-319-29331-8_10

Overview of Parent Coaching

If I had a quarter for every time I heard that children don't come with a parenting manual, I would have a lot of quarters. Although it is true that the majority of parents enter parenthood with limited coursework on parenting practices, there are a plethora of reading materials and programs geared for parents. When looking for parenting information, many parents seek information from their family, friends, and the internet (Baker, 2014). While parents, friends, and family have been the go-to for parenting advice for centuries, there is a science to parenting and parents are beginning to understand that professional help is available. In fact, coaching is considered a viable options to parents looking for help with parenting (Baker, 2014).

> I look forward to a time when coaching is part of what all parents do-it is just a part of life. I love my child and I have a parent coach helping me be the best I can be. **Sheryl Stoller, Parent Coach**

The field of parent education, in terms of both practice and research, has grown immensely in the past 30 years. Today, there are a multitude of programs available that target specific parenting populations such as Autism and ADHD, as well as programs that focus on generalized parent education content. Although there are variations among service offerings and styles of services, most have the primary foci on factors such as improving the relationship between parent and child in the specific context of the family, reduction in externalized child behaviors, and increasing the family's skills and resources (Gockel, Russell, & Harris, 2008). Parent education can take place across levels of intensity and settings, from basic workshops to more intensive interactions involving in-home services and coaching, such as Intensive Family Preservation (Duncan & Goddard, 2011).

New research suggests, in fact, that parent coaching is an option that parents see as an up and coming approach to receiving information (Baker, 2014). It is important to understand where coaching and parent education fall in the continuum of family science. Doherty (1995) proposes that there are indeed differences along a continuum of family practitioners, ranging from family educators to licensed therapist working with families. According to Doherty, parent education should contain components of imparting knowledge and skills while keeping a focus on the feelings, attitudes, and goals of the families served. Because of the personal and emotional focus in working with families, parent education involves a relationship, making it unique and separate from other academic subjects or courses one might study. While these one-on-one and group interactions may appear to resemble therapy and often contain elements of relational theory, Doherty stresses the importance of family educators to remain objective and refer the family, when necessary, for additional counseling and therapy.

Myers-Walls, Ballard, Darling, and Myer's Bowman (2011), attempted to reconceptualize Doherty's boundaries of Family Life Education by identifying domains of family practice. Myers-Walls et al. differentiated the domains of family life education, family therapy, and family case management, and encouraged appropriate collaboration among the fields of family science. Although coaching was not listed in Doherty's conception of boundaries or Myers-Walls et al.'s reconceptualization, Allen and Huff (2014) introduce Family Life Coaching as a separate and relevant extension of the domains of family practice (see Chaps. 1 and 3 for more information on the research of Allen & Huff, 2014).

> The crucial difference between a parent ed class and parent coaching is that in coaching you do not have to have the answer. In education, it usually is about an answer to something. The gift of being a coach is you discover together the answer that is right for the parent and child. **Adrian Kalikow, Parent Coach**

Theories of Child Development

Content knowledge is critical in parent coaching. Effective family life coaching involves a balance of utilizing the coaching process while helping parents better understand evidence-based practices that are effective at changing behaviors. In order for a parent coach to help the families being served, they must know child development and parenting theory and practice. This section provides a general overview of a few of the most common theories of child development.

Ethological Theories

Ethology is the study of animals in their natural habitat and for our purposes, it is the branch of knowledge dealing with human character and its formation and evolution. Ethologists tend to concentrate on innate behaviors (instincts). Theorists of human ethology include Lorenz and his work on imprinting, and the works of Bowlby and Ainsworth's attachment theory.

Attachment theory is a popular concept for parenting in the twenty-first century. Bowlby and Ainsworth's work on infant attachment has influenced a great deal of parent education programming and research (See Bowlby, 1988; Ainsworth & Bowlby, 1991). Bowlby and Ainsworth stressed the importance of responsive and sensitive parenting, citing the evolutionary design of childhood development and the biological and emotional needs of infants. Their work found that responsive parents generally had 1 year old children that were securely attached to one or both parents and were independent enough to play alone, but also enjoyed attention and time spent with their caregivers. Securely attached infants have been found to form more lasting and close relationships as adults than insecurely attached infants. Attachment Parenting consists of eight principles that appear to help parents form strong, healthy emotional bonds with their children.

- Prepare for pregnancy, birth, and parenting
- Feed with love and respect
- Respond with sensitivity
- Use nurturing touch
- Engage in nighttime parenting
- Provide consistent and loving care
- Practice positive discipline
- Strive for balance in your personal and family life

Cognitive Developmental Theory

The first name associated with cognitive development theory is that of Jean Piaget. Piaget's work on child development helped us understand qualitative changes in child thinking, and he felt strongly that development was more than nature and more than nurture. Piaget (1936) identified four stages of development:

1. Sensorimotor Intelligence (birth-2)
2. Preoperational Thought (2–7)
3. Concrete Operations (7–11)
4. Formal Operations (11-adulthood)

Piaget's Sensorimotor Intelligence Period details development from birth to age two. These processes build upon one another, creating a collective growth in cognition. Piaget used the term "*construction process*" to describe how infants coordinate movements and actions to develop more complex behaviors.

The Preoperational Thought stage is where a child begins to understand symbols. Children learn to think, but thinking remains illogical and they often have difficulty distinguishing imagination from reality. Language develops rapidly and socialization with peers becomes the norm.

In the Concrete Operations stage, children develop *scientific reasoning*: they gradually gain the cognition needed to understand the logical relationship between size, space, frequency, and group classification. They also develop *social thinking*: the ability to view the world from other's perspective. Rules and moral standards play an important role during this time.

For Piaget, the Formal Operation stage was the final stage, occurring in children around middle school age. At this time, children develop the ability to comprehend and create abstract thoughts and consider hypothetical concepts and they can use reasoning to mentally solve problems and consider alternatives. Piaget proposed an idea that adolescents pass through a third egocentric stage in which they dream of their futures and the impact they will have on changing the world. Piaget implied that the egocentric nature of development diminishes as the cognition of the child within a certain stage is more fully developed.

Moral Development

A moral principle is an obligatory or ideal rule of choice between legitimate alternatives, rather than a concrete prescription of action. – Lawrence Kohlberg.

Lawrence Kohlberg, a student of Piaget, expanded on Piaget's developmental stages with moral stages. Kohlberg (1981) hypothesized he would find trends that paired morality with human needs, but this was not the case. Kohlberg found that there are stages of moral development that are unique from cognitive development, however his morality levels follow developmental stages. Kohlberg studied morality by offering a scenario to boys ages 10, 13, and 14. Based on responses, Kohlberg identified three levels and six stages of moral development.

Level I: Preconventional Morality

- Stage 1: Obedience and Punishment Orientation: children in this stage follow rules stringently, fearing the consequence of punishment.
- Stage 2: Individualism & Exchange: People believe what is "right" is relative to what meets one's needs at the time. Punishment is only a risk if caught.
- People in these stages do not associate with values or doing what's best for the greater good.

Level II: Conventional Morality

- Stage 3: Good Interpersonal Relationships: People in this stage believe people should fulfill the expectations of family and their community and do "good."
- Stage 4: Maintaining the Social Order: People obey laws to keep social order.

Level III: Postconventional Morality

- Stage 5: Social Contract & Individual: People in this stage think of the world theoretically, as in how "it could be." They believe in working towards the betterment of society.
- Stage 6: Universal Principles: This stage, called the Theoretical Stage by Kohlberg, contains the principles by which justice is designed.

Gilligan (1982) voiced concern about Kohlberg's methodology of interviewing only males. She contended that Kohlberg's research, conducted only with male subjects, overlooked certain issues and was therefore not applicable to women. She pointed out that girls are socialized differently than boys and that men and women follow different voices. By using Kohlberg's masculine model to judge women, we reinforce the idea that women's attributes (nurturance, intimacy) are inferior to men's.

Gilligan was also concerned about the use of hypothetical dilemmas as moral reasoning may not actually translate into behavior. Gilligan went on to design a theory of her own, working on the belief that females had a "care" view in terms of moral development whereas males have a "justice" view. Moral research is still being conducted, and we are starting to see fewer differences in gender than in socio-economics, educational levels, and verbal skills.

Social Learning

Albert Bandura (1977) emphasized the role of thinking (cognition) and the role of environment (social learning). Whereas Piaget's work shows how children learn primarily on their own by engaging in tasks suitable to their developmental stage, Bandura disagrees that children learn independently and says children must be coaxed into learning, and says Piaget's stages limit children's development by placing arbitrary norms on development.

Bandura's theory leads us to understand that parents play a vital role in the positive development of children's self-efficacy. This theory can be connected to family science and family life coaching through the underlying theme of how parents act as major components of change in the family unit through their actions and the environment they create for their children.

- When Parents Believe, Children Believe
- When Parents Do, Children Do

Behaviorism and Learning Theory

J. B. Watson, and B. F. Skinner contented that behaviors and skills are the result of environmental stimulus. As a behaviorist, Watson saw no need to study thoughts, emotions or mental states. The only unlearned behaviors humans possess at birth are: love, fear, and rage. Watson worked with Mary Culver Jones on *behavior modification* and *systematic desensitization* to discourage and ultimately extinguish behaviors. His work with Little Albert showed that fear can be learned through conditioning. Watson also showed how fears can be "unlearned" through desensitization processes.

In the behavioral tradition, BF Skinner worked with rewards and punishments as ways of behavior modification.

- *Operant conditioning* refers to how a human responds to a reward (reinforcement) within its environment
- *Primary reinforcement*: directs action, for example food.

- *Conditioned reinforcement*: value is associated with a primary reinforcement, for example, when smiling while giving food, the smile is the conditioned reinforcement.
- *Shaping*: the steps by which conditioning occurs, starting gradually and increasing overtime.

Behaviorism is still highly popular for use with children in special needs and in classroom settings.

Parenting Theories

There are a plethora of theories that guide parenting education and parent coaching. Many of the theoretical underpinnings for parenting education are the same as family life education (see Chap. 3). The focus here is on parenting styles, models, and evidence-based strategies found in parenting literature.

Parenting Styles

Diana Baumrind (1966) identified three primary parenting types, permissive, authoritarian, and authoritative. In later work (see Baumrind, 1997), she went on to discuss the behavior patterns of both parents and their children. Based on her research, the field still points to these three primary parenting styles as essential learning for parent education. Family life coaches helping parents understand how their parenting style impacts their children's behavior and wellbeing can be both informative and difficult. Many parents continue the parenting style learned from their childhood.

According to Jane Nelson, author of the best-selling Positive Discipline book series (i.e., Nelson, 2006), the essential ingredients of positive parenting are to be KIND and FIRM. Research on children's development supports this notion. Barber, Stolz, and Olsen (2005) suggest there are two fundamental components of parenting that are related to positive child and youth outcomes: (1) supportive, nurturing parents (2) a stable environment that provides a good structure.

What does it mean to be kind and firm? It means helping our children by parenting them with love, warmth, respect, and kindness while also setting boundaries and giving them limits. Children that are disciplined with kindness are better able to connect with others, feel as if they have a place to belong, and behave better.

The three parenting styles can be conceptualized as according to the parenting strategies of *kind* and *firm*. Permissive: low firm/high kind; authoritarian low kind/high firm; and democratic, which is high kind and firm (see table below)

Allen, Jolly, Guin, &   NC STATE
Roper (2015)   UNIVERSITY

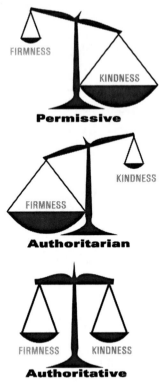

Authoritarian: Low in Kind, High in Firm Authoritarian parents value respectful children and traditional structures. This parenting style tends to be demanding, and regularly attempt to shape and control the behaviors and attitudes of their children. Authoritarian parenting style has strict standards, and religious or theological authorities often influence parenting decisions. Authoritarian parents value obedience and order, and often use punitive approaches including physical punishment, yelling, and threatening to influence behavior. They discourage independence and individuality. Children raised in authoritarian homes may lack spontaneity, curiosity and creativity and may have limited independence and assertiveness. These children struggle with making decisions for themselves, and are often unsure of how to behave. They may be anxious, withdrawn, and appear unhappy, but they typically do well in school and are less likely to engage in antisocial activities.

Permissive: High in Kind, Low in Firm Permissive parenting attempts to affirm and support the child's behavior, but is often done with little or no guidelines. In an effort to support the child, the parent offers little authority and allows the child enormous amounts of freedom to regulate his or her own activities. A permissive parent avoids control, and often gives too much control to the child. In return, a child that is raised with permissive parenting develops little self-control and is often immature and has poor emotional regulation. These children are likely to be aggressive at home, especially when challenged. These children often exhibit low self-esteem and antisocial behaviors due to delayed emotional development. Children of permissive parenting become frustrated easily and are likely to partake in high-risk behaviors.

Authoritative/Democratic: Balanced in Kind and Firm Authoritative parents strike a balance between firm and kind by providing rational and encouraging instructions. These parents tend to set reasonable standards and expectations, and they encourage independence and individuality. Authoritative parents enforce rules, while allowing for choices and respecting individual rights. Children raised by authoritative parents tend to be lively, happy, and responsible. They have higher levels of confidence and self-esteem, and develop positive social skills.

Gottman's Parenting Style and Emotion Coaching

John Gottman and his colleagues have gained an international reputation as the leading researchers of couples' relationships and on Emotion Coaching in parenting. The heart of great parenting, according to Gottman (1998), is through emotion coaching, or the process of helping children regulate their emotions and communicate their feelings. There are elements of the emotion coaching process that are helpful for family life coaches and parents to know. These include the importance of knowing and respecting your child, the ability to identify emotions, empathetic and supportive parenting, encouragement, and modeling desired behavior (Layton Blain, 2010). Like Baumrind, Gottman identifies styles of parenting as indicators of parenting practice.

Dismissive These parents tend to treat a child's feelings as trivial and pays little attention in communicating with the child. The children learn that feelings are inappropriate or wrong and thus have difficulty regulating emotions.

Disapproving These parents are similar to dismissing, but they are more negative. This parenting style believes emotions need to be controlled and they want conformity and obedience. These children also learn that feelings are wrong and have difficulty regulating emotion.

The Laissez-faire These parents accept emotions from their children and are kind and caring, but offer little structure or limits. The children often have social issues.

The Emotion Coach The parents are aware of the child's emotions and see the emotion as an opportunity for connection and teaching. These parents listen and take feelings seriously, helping the children label their emotions. The children trust their feelings, regulate emotions effectively, and problem solve.

Understanding parenting styles and appropriate approaches to child development can make the difference in the success of parent coaching. Parenting and discipline is such a personal element that coaches need to find the parents' strengths and build on those, rather than identify problems. There are assessments that exist for helping parents identify their parenting style (see Gottman, 1997 for example). However, parents can simply be informed of the benefits of good parenting practices and encouraged to make decisions that are best for their family. What parents and coaches focus on grows; so helping parents identify what works and moving forward is ideal. Still, some parents are at a loss of evidence-based practices. The following section identifies parenting practices that have been found to be effective.

Adlerian Parenting

When asked to identify what theories are most representative in the practice of parent coaching, Adlerian theory was the most prevalent theory listed either explicitly, or through implicit associations such as positive discipline, parenting strengths, and encouragement (Allen & Baker, 2016). This was of no surprise as Adlerian theory is the foundation used by the majority of parent education programs available to parents today, including Active Parenting, Systematic Training for Effective Parenting (STEP) series, Positive Discipline, just to name a few (Allen, El-Beshti, & Guin, 2014). Adlerian concepts are the crux of popular parenting programs such as Systematic Training for Effective Parenting (STEP) (Dinkmeyer et al., 1997), Active Parenting (Popkin, 1993), Positive Parenting Solutions (McCready, 2006), Very Important Parent Program (Allen, El-Beshti, & Guin, 2014), among others.

Alfred Adler, and his predecessor, Rufolf Dreikurs, were among the first to advance the field of parent education by identifying tenets of good parenting. Based on the work of Adler and Dreikurs, Adlerian family practitioners' focus on how parents can help encourage their child and meet the needs of their child to help them grow and develop through cooperation and personal responsibility for learning (Carmack & Carmack, 1994). Adlerian theory emphasizes parent education as the most efficient method for parents to help their children succeed by focusing on the family system (Croake, 1983).

Similarly, Family and Parent Coaching is most effective when it's made accessible through a system's perspective. Urie Bronfenbrenner (1979), father of the ecological system of child development, helped the field of family science understand that in order for the child to be successful, practitioners need to account for all systems influencing the child's life.

While the system is critical, the most prominent system in a child's life is the parental system. As parent educators, and as parent coaches, we must work with parents through the lens of family systems. This is why it is crucial to consider not only the child's behavior, but also the parents' behaviors, and the system in which the children live. For example, it would be unfruitful to coach a child to achieve goals of order and organization if they come from a home full of chaos and live in a community filled with unrest.

Adlerian Parenting Concepts Critical for Parent Coaching

While the jury is still out on which Adlerian parenting concepts are critical for inclusion of parenting help, there are few noted as quintessential for helping parents. Those concepts include:

- Encouragement
- Positive Discipline
- Family Meetings
- Goals of Misbehavior
- Natural and Logical Consequence

Encouragement

Dreikurs once said "A Misbehaving Child is a Discouraged Child" (p. 36). This is the very essence of Adlerian parenting theory and practice, and the concept that is most critical for coaching parents. Not only is it important for coaches to encourage the parent clients, but also training the parents to encourage their children. The healthiest power one has is influence (Adler, 1956). Parenting is a quintessential influence and it is through influence and relationship building that parents guide, model, and shape their children and their children's behaviors. Encouragement, as described by Dreikurs and Soltz (1964), "is more important than any other aspect of child-raising. It is so important that the lack of it can be considered the basic cause for misbehavior" (p. 36).

Think about your own influence, or even those of the parent clients you serve. It is human nature to be influenced positively by those that are supportive, kind, and encouraging. Could you imagine your clients remaining with you if your approach is discouraging, hurtful, or negative? Children are unable to grow, develop, and gain a sense of belonging without parental encouragement. It is the responsibility of a parent to foster their child's healthy development and that is done best through the use of positive approaches to parenting.

Positive Discipline

Positive discipline and encouragement are key elements parents may use to foster children's self-confidence, but many parents are unaware of the practice of positive discipline. It is easy to find parents that give encouragement. It is likely that parents come to parent coaching with many great skills and a history of encouraging their children for positive behavior. The goal is to help parents understand the use of positive discipline as a primary method of discipline.

While most parents agree that children need warmth, love, and affection, parents often do not have the skills to discipline, or teach their children with positive discipline. Many children are punished when they do something wrong. Most of us, in fact, grew up with a reward and punishment system that was so popular in the 1950s, during the height of Skinner's learning theory popularity. While we still see evidence of rewards and punishments as a popular parenting strategy, the flaw comes when children are not taught the correct behavior, but rather are punished for the misbehavior.

Positive Discipline strategies are implemented to help children learn positive behaviors and learn from misbehaviors. In essence, Positive Discipline strategies focus on the desired behaviors while ignoring the negative ones. For example, when little Jordan is picking up the toys, we encourage the parents to say "great job; thank you for working hard to clean up!" Conversely, when the child is misbehaving, the idea is to ignore the negative by redirecting the child, or simply showing the child the alternative behavior. For example, if a child hits another child, we might say "gentle touches" rather than offering a punishment of time out or a swat.

Parents I have worked with are often happy with the idea of reinforcing desired behaviors, or catching a child "being good". It is easy to train parents to watch for the child to make good choices and reinforce them. The difficulty comes in the notion of ignoring the bad behaviors. It simply goes against the very nature of parents to ignore the bad, and even worse, to not punish the bad behavior.

The goal of the parent coach, then, is to help parents understand alternatives to parenting when a child is exhibiting undesired behaviors. There is a whole science on misbehavior, and understanding the goals of misbehavior is yet another important step in helping parents. Jane Nelson, author of the best-selling Positive Discipline book series (i.e., Nelson, 2006), provides additional insights and suggestions for parents in her books and training materials. While it might not be easy, it is important to help parents get into the habit of practicing positive discipline.

Goals of Misbehavior

Dreikurs (1958) believed that all children's behaviors were for a purpose. He classified children's misbehavior as "goals" that are unique for each individual child and draw upon personal experiences, biology, and the child's environment (Adler, 1956). Although the child would not be aware of the purpose, Dreikurs suggested that the goals are designed to move the child from a feeling of inadequacy to perfection (Dreikurs & Soltz, 1964). Behavior is broken into four goals;

- attention
- power
- revenge
- inadequacy

Attention Have you ever been on the phone when a child begins to get louder, and louder, and louder, causing you to pause your phone conversation and address the annoying behavior? That is attention seeking behavior. Attention-seeking behaviors begin mildly and increase in nature as the child's need for attention continues to go unmet. Adlerian perspective explains how children seeking attention are in search for a sense of belonging.

As a parent coach, we can help parents understand the goal behind the behavior, so they can respond appropriately. If a child is seeking attention, it is from an unmet need for attention. Ideally, the parent will help meet the child's need by giving them attention at a time that is appropriate and determined by the parent. As in positive discipline, parents can ignore inappropriate behaviors, giving positive attention to desired behaviors.

Power Power is about control. Children who feel they have a lack of control might throw temper tantrums, become stubborn, and fight with the parent. They work to gain greater power over their situation, often making parents feel angry or challenged. Again, parent coaches can help parents learn to respond to these behaviors by offering the child choices, setting firm but kind boundaries, and encouraging activities that allow the child more control in their lives.

Revenge Revenge makes parents and caregivers feel hurt, disappointed, and sometimes even disgusted. A child that is truly hurting will seek revenge by acting out with behaviors such as damaging property, retaliating, and even physically hurting others. Because children feel hurt themselves, they find a way to belong by hurting others. These children are in dire need of healing and as parent coaches we must help parents address these behaviors through positive communication and active listening. Although it often goes against what the parents want to do or feel is appropriate, parents should avoid harsh punishment or criticism and work hard to build trust with the child (Dreikurs & Soltz, 1964). Dealing with the hurt feelings will help the child feel included and relieved.

Inadequacy Dreikurs stated that children internalizing feelings of inadequacy are the ones most discouraged. These children have come to believe they are inadequate, helpless, and they simply give up. These are the children that are passive, and often have no response to adult interactions. Parent coaches must help parents learn ways to encourage these children by noting any positive attempts, no matter how small. Actions need to be taken so that adults will remove expectations of performance, criticism, and pity (Dreikurs & Soltz, 1964). By focusing on the child's strengths, rather than their weaknesses, parents can help the child feel more encouraged.

The goals of misbehavior were reframed as the Crucial C's, Connect, Capable, Count, and Courage (Bettner & Lew, 1989). The graph below (Allen, 2016 based on Better & Lew, 1989 and Dreikurs & Soltz, 1964) shows how when children have the crucial c's, they have fewer unmet needs. This is a positive spin presented here to help parents understand how to help meet children's needs.

Crucial C's and Goals of Misbehavior

Crucial C's	Unmet needs: How discouraged children think and believe	Parent feels:	Encouraging Responses	When need is met, child believes
CONNECT	ATTENTION I only count when I'm noticed. I act out for attention.	Irritated Annoyed	Replace negative attention with positive attention. Plan activities together. Don't ignore child; Ignore unwanted behavior.	I belong.
CAPABLE	POWER My strength is in showing you that you can't make me.	Angry Challenged	Give choices so child can display power constructively. Maintain a friendly attitude.	I can do it.
COUNT	REVENGE I knew you were against me. I'll show you how it feels.	Hurt Wants to punish	Maintain appreciation in the relationship. Offer chances to help. Seek support and help in identifying positives. Don't give up.	I matter. I can make a difference.
COURAGE	GIVING UP I can't do anything right, so I won't try.	Despair Hopelessness	Notice strengths and ignore the negative. Set up steady exposure to manageable tasks that have a likelihood of success. Avoid criticism.	I can handle what comes.

Copyright NCSU. Crucial C's Adapted from Lew & Bettner, 1989. Goals of Misbehavior Adapted from Dreikurs & Soltz, 1964

Natural and Logical Consequence

While Adlerian parenting practices tend to focus primarily on identifying strengths and using positive discipline, they also identify a need to help children learn from their mistakes. This can be achieved through the use of natural and logical consequences. Dreikurs and Soltz (1964) distinguish natural and logical consequences through the presence or absence of parental intervention during a child's misbehavior. Natural consequences happen on their own; parents play no part in natural consequences. Logical consequences requires parents input.

A natural consequence occurs naturally through environmental or societal backlash sometimes beyond the control of the parent. For example, when a child goes outside to play in the cold and chooses not to wear a jacket, they get cold. When a child doesn't pick up a toy, it might get broken or lost. Natural consequences are most effective when parents help the child understand the consequence through communication and discussion for how to prevent the consequences in the future.

A logical consequence requires intervention from parents, but unlike a punishment, a logical consequence must fit the misbehavior. For example, if a child does not pick up toys, parents may take them away. If a child does not listen to the parent's request for them to wear shoes outside, they might have to play inside instead. It is important for the child to understand they can make better choices in the future. A logical consequence is an opportunity for a child to learn, and do better next time. After the time period lapses, the child will have another opportunity to play with and pick up their toys or wear shoes outside. The key to logical consequences is that they fit the behavior and reinforce appropriate behavior.

Family Meetings

While the statement, "Time for a family meeting" might draw groans and complaints from children, family meetings are critical component of Adlerian parenting. Dreikurs and Soltz (1964) identify the Family Council, as one of the most important activities or tools parents can implement to improve problematic behavior. Family meetings are simple because the basic principle is that the meeting is a place for each family member to respectfully discuss family happenings. Together the family works to find solutions to problems, and the process is centered in equality.

Applying Theory and Practice to Coaching Parents

Parents can't fix what they don't know is broken. While education and coaching has mixed reviews, there is general consensus among parent coaches that education is a critical component of parent coaching. Helping parents understand developmentally appropriate behaviors, appropriate and effective behavior change strategies, and evidence-based approaches to discipline is key to their success. At the same time, coaches have to balance educating parents with the coaching process. To help with the coaching process, parent coaches should consider the following:

The Changing of the Hats The coaching process is a partnership guided by the coach towards a goal set by the client. Education, particularly in parent coaching, is a critical part of coaching success. How to balance the two is the art of being a parent coach. With practice, most coaches are able to toggle back and forth between the world of coaching and education. While coaching should be the focus of the process, there will be times to interject educational tidbits. I recommend openly communicating with the client about the nature of parent coaching and education. During an intake, I will tell parents about coaching process, but that I am also aware of evidence based practices that many parents find helpful. I will be upfront and let them know I might switch roles as needed. How to know when it is needed?

- When the parent asks, or seems unsure. I've had parents say "I just don't know what to do." That is a clue to say "I'd be happy to put on my educator hat and share some information, if that is alright with you."
- When the parent is explaining a situation that is ineffective, or when they are stuck. If a client says, for example, "I've tried everything—spanking, sending to their room, taking away their toys, and nothing is working." I might respond "It does sound as if you have tried many tactics. Do you mind if I share a piece of education?" (They usually say yes). "The tactics you are describing are called punishments, which is different than discipline, and punishment has been found to be less effective than discipline" and then I go on to ask about times that have worked for her in the past, or share resources and information about positive parenting.

The 4-Ds of Appreciative Inquiry Discovery, Dream, Design, and Destiny— whether or not you use AI as your primary coaching model, this model can help parents identify strengths from their past, what they envision for the future, how to design action steps to get there, and then how to maintain the goal. This strengths-based process is used by many parent coaches and has been proven an effective process. See Chap. 4 for more information.

What You Focus on Grows Intuitively, this makes sense; in parenting, it is a hard concept to practice! Coaches can help parents understand this concept first by modeling, and then by concretely explaining the concept. If we want loving, kind children, we must focus on the moments when our children are being loving and kind, and we must model those behaviors as well. This is such a powerful tool, and one that parents can concretely identify ways to focus on the goals of coaching.

Case Study

A divorced mother, Lindsey, with one son, 6, is concerned that her ex-husband's remarriage is distressing to the child. She has noticed he has been withdrawn and moody since the news broke. Lindsey has had a steady boyfriend for the past year, to which the son has not shown any negative reaction. Lindsey wants to use coaching to determine a co-parenting structure that is best for the child's well-being. The father and his fiancé are open and enthusiastic about being a part of the coaching sessions as well, especially since the fiancé also has a young child from a previous relationship.

Note: this is starting after the introductions of first session

Coach: "So tell me about your son and the situation, and what would you like the focus to be of our time together today?"

Lindsey: "Well, in a nutshell, Dillan. I would like to focus on how to get Dillan to talk to me about his Dad's upcoming marriage. He just has not been himself ever since the news broke that they are getting married. I'm concerned because Dillan is so withdrawn, like he is depressed or sad and I want to help him with his feelings, but every time I try to engage him in conversation about it, he just shrugs his shoulders and walks away, or changes the subject. I think my ex-husband could be very helpful to Dillan with this transition and I would like to come up with a way to co-parent Dillan so that he feels secure and loved."

Note: the client has provided a great deal of developmental and parenting information. A coach might make mental notes of developmental milestones of a 6 year old, and notes of family structures and processes.

Coach: "Okay, so you'd ultimately like to help Dillon with the transition of his Dad getting remarried. What do you think is up with Dillan?"

Lindsey: "Well, I think he is unsure of his feelings and doesn't know how to explain things to me or what he is feeling. Maybe he's worried about hurting my feelings."

Coach: "I see. He is still little, he's only 6, and understanding his feelings is kind of hard for young children. This is still very new to him. Can you tell me a bit about the conversations you have had with Dillan's father about his reaction to this change?"

Note: reinforcing developmental concepts to parent.

Lindsey: "Yes, I have discussed it with him and he has agreed that Dillan seems withdrawn, in fact it was my ex-husband's fiancé that first mentioned it to me."

Coach: "Okay, so tell me, how is the relationship between Dillan and his Dad's fiancé?"

Lindsey: "Well, honestly I thought he liked her just fine. There were a couple times when they got together with her son that Dillan seemed kind of "off" but nothing serious."

Coach: "What does "off" look like?"

Lindsey: "Well, I guess you can say he was irritated. Or bummed. I just thought he was tired from playing so hard. I didn't think much more about it. They are both the same age."

Coach: "Okay, so your ex-husband's fiancé has a son. I noticed you said it was during times when your ex-husband's fiancé's son was around that he felt 'off' Can you tell me more?"

Lindsey: "Hmm. . . I don't see them together, but now that you ask, he does seem cautious or a bit weary after their get-togethers. (pauses to think a moment). . . are you saying you think Dillan is upset with Margo's son?"

Coach: "Well, I'm trying to understand the situation—you are the expert about Dillon, so I'm leaning on you for help in understanding. I do think it is worth exploring because you mentioned the times Dillan seems "off" are when he has been with Margo's son." [Lindsey seems to have an a-ha moment] "Your body language just changed. Can you tell me what you are thinking?"

Lindsey: "Yes, it never occurred to me before right now. Maybe Dillan feels competition with Margo's son, because Dillan will be living with me most of the time and he will be living with Dillan's father. Oh, no! This is awful. (Starts crying) Why does this have to be so hard? And how could I not see this. A son needs his father. I feel just awful for Dillan, this is so unfair for him."

Coach: "I can see that you are feeling quite sad. This is a real loss for Dillon. Here, would you like a tissue?" [Gives a moment for her to process feelings]

Lindsey: (crying and nods head) "Yes. It is a loss for us all. This just isn't what I thought would happen. It is just not what I wanted for my son."

Coach: "Divorce can be hard; in fact, transitions are hard for most people. There are so many different feelings for each member involved."

Note: coach has understanding of family transitions, and brings that to the table in an effort to offer support.

Lindsey: "Yes, but you know what? It is our reality. And so I have to try even harder to find a way to co-parent with my ex. I don't ever want him to feel he isn't loved or that either of us don't want him."

Coach: "I can see your passion Lindsey, and I think Dillon is lucky to have such supportive parents. I must agree that in order for Dillan to feel safe, he first needs to feel he belongs. All kids need to feel as if they belong. And, I think you are right in finding a co-parenting solution that will meet his needs to help him adjust to this transition. Let's look at some options. What do you see as a win-win situation here, for you, your ex, and most of all Dillan?"

Lindsey: "Well, right now we alternate weekends and Wednesday's."

Coach: "So it is important for your ex to be a part of weekday activities and weekend activities for Dillan, is that correct?"

Lindsey: "Yes, I have a couple friends who are divorced and the one that shares everything with her ex has much happier kids. They seem more well-rounded and content. I think it is imperative to have my ex be that much a part of Dillan's life, after all a boy needs his father."

Coach: "So what about the schedule for Dillon is working?"

Lindsey: "I am not clear on her custody arrangement, but I like the idea of knowing more about when her son will be there. That would help to schedule this better. I guess I need to meet with them. What should I tell them about this?"

Coach: "Well that depends. I believe there are just as many ways to co-parent as there are families, so there's a lot. It is going to depend on your values and Dillan's Dad's and his fiancé's. Let me ask you a question; can you tell me about a time or a situation in the recent past where you feel you and your son's father have successfully co-parented?

Note: looking for past successes to build on.

Lindsey: "Oh gosh. That's a mixed bag. Mostly, it is just about scheduling, so we are pretty relaxed about that. I guess I'd say we've successfully co-parented the schedule. Does that count?"

Coach: "If you think it counts, then I believe you! That is actually a major accomplishment. Parents that can work together around transitions really do help the child be successful. So what would you like to focus on when we all meet together? "

Lindsey: "So I don't want my ex to be a weekend dad. I want to share weekends with Dillan too. And it makes sense that my ex has him for weekdays too, so that is definitely important to me. What if we focus on the schedule, and then talk about how the schedule impacts Dillan, specifically around the issue of Margo's son and his schedule?"

Coach: "Good, well it sounds like you already know what your values are for co-parenting Dillan."

Lindsey: "Oh yes, I hadn't thought of it that way. I'm just thinking of other changes, like what about having a friend spend the night, or birthday parties. I am writing this down so I am sure to tell my ex about it. This is helpful."

Coach: "So what steps will you take to begin this conversation with your son's other parent?"

Lindsey: "Well, I think I need to talk with them about Dillon's feelings and about the schedule. I don't think it will be a problem, so I'll just call see where it goes. Do you have suggestions for me, or something I can tell them to help?"

Coach: "Okay, so you have a plan. I know that transitions are hard, and there is a lot of information about how to help kids in transition. I will get two fact sheets about co-parenting and a list of some web sites you may want to look up for different schedules that have worked for some families, as well as some general information about how to help children in transitions. Let's take a moment and review today's session. You came to explore Dillan's withdrawal regarding your ex-husband's upcoming wedding and explore some co-parenting options for Dillan. How do you feel the session has gone?"

Lindsey: "Oh I feel much better. I feel I understand Dillan's withdrawal better and I feel more equipped to talk with his Dad about co-parenting."

Coach: "Great. And then next time we can continue to discuss how to help Dillan transition.

Lindsey: "Yes, totally okay. Thank you very much. This has been very helpful."

Coach: "I am glad to hear that. So what day will be best for our next meeting, does the morning or afternoon work?"

Note: Family transitions and co-parenting is complex, and often needs small steps, support, and information. The coach followed the cues of the clients, but offered support and education as well.

Chapter Summary

Parenting is a difficult job, and parents are eager to find help with solutions to their parenting difficulties. Family life coaching and more specifically, parent coaching, is a field for helping families. Effective family coaches must know effective parenting practices, child development, and a variety of parenting theories. Chapter 9 provides information on translation of parenting concepts into practice for family life coaches. Parents can't do better if they don't know better, therefore knowing how to balance the coaching process with providing information is a key competency for family life coaching. Helping parents employ evidence-based practices and finding their own and their children's strengths are key.

Further Reading

Dinkmeyer, D., McKay, G., & Dinkmeyer, D. (1997). *The parent's handbook: Systematic Training for Effective Parenting.* Circle Pines, MN: American Guidance Service.

Dreikurs, R. (1958). *The challenge of parenthood.* New York: Hawthorne Press.

Gottman, J. (1998). *Raising an emotional intelligent child: The heart of positive parenting.* New York: Simon & Shuster.

Nelson, J. N. (2006). *Positive discipline.* New York: Random House.

References

Adler, A. (1956). *The individual psychology of Alfred Adler: A systematic presentation in selections from his writings.* New York: Basic Books.

Ainsworth, M. D. S., & Bowlby, J. (1991). An ethological approach to personality development. *American Psychologist, 46,* 33–341.

Allen, K., & Baker, T. (2016). *Family life coaching: A grounded theory.* Manuscript in preparation.

Allen, K., El-Beshti, R., & Guin, A. (2014). An Adlerian integrative approach to creating a teen parenting program. *Journal of Individual Psychology, 70*(1), 7–20.

Allen, K., & Huff, N. (2014). Family coaching: An emerging family science field. *Family Relations, 63*(5), 569–582. doi:10.1111/fare.12087.

Allen, K., Jolly, C., Guin, A., & Roper, R. (2015). *Very important parents curriculum workbook: 82 individual activities for parents.* Raleigh, NC: North Carolina State University.

Baker, T. (2014). *Family coaching: An exploratory study of parental perceptions.* Master's thesis. Retrieved from: http://repository.lib.ncsu.edu/ir/handle/1840.16/1/simple-search?query=family+coaching

Bandura, A. (1977). *Social learning theory.* Englewood Cliffs, NJ: Prentice-Hall.

Barber, B. K., Stolz, H. E., & Olsen, J. A. (2005). Parental support, psychological control, and behavioral control: Assessing relevance across time, method, and culture. *Monographs of the Society for Research in Child Development, 70*(4), 1–147.

Baumrind, D. (1966). Effects of authoritative parental control on child behavior. *Child Development, 37*(4), 887–907.

Baumrind, D. (1997). Necessary distinctions. *Psychological Inquiry, 8,* 176–182.

Bettner, B. L., & Lew, L. (1989). *Raising kids who can.* Newton Centre, MA: Connexions Press.

Bowlby, J. (1988). *A secure base.* New York: Basic Books.

Bronfenbrenner, U. (1979). *The ecology of human development.* Cambridge, MA: Harvard University Press.

Carmack, C., & Carmack, E. (1994). Children the change: The challenge of parent education in the new Russian Federation. *Journal of Individual Psychology, 50*(3), 322–328.

Croake, J. W. (1983). Adlerian parent education. *The Counseling Psychologist, 11*(3), 65–71.

Dinkmeyer, D., McKay, G., & Dinkmeyer, D. (1997). *The parent's handbook: Systematic Training for effective parenting.* Circle Pines, MN: American Guidance Service.

Doherty, W. J. (1995). Boundaries between parent and family education and family therapy. *Family Relations, 44,* 353–358.

Dreikurs, R. (1958). *The challenge of parenthood.* New York: Hawthorne Press.

Dreikurs, R., & Soltz, V. (1964). *Children: The challenge.* New York: Hawthorne Books.

Duncan, S. F., & Goddard, H. W. (2011). *Family life education principles and practices for effective outreach.* Los Angeles: Sage.

Gilligan, C. (1982). *In a different voice.* Cambridge, MA: Harvard University Press.

Gockel, A., Russell, M., & Harris, B. (2008). Recreating family: Parents identify worker-client relationships as paramount in family preservation programs. *Child Welfare Journal, 87*(6), 91–113.

Gottman, J. (1998). *Raising an emotional intelligent child: The heart of positive parenting.* New York: Simon & Shuster.

Kohlberg, L. (1981). *Essays on moral development* (Vol. 1). New York: Harper & Row.

Layton Blain, K. (2010). *The go-to mom's parent's guide to emotion coaching young children.* San Francisco: Jossey-Bass.

McCready, A. (2006). *Positive parenting solutions.* Retrieved from http://www.positiveparentingsolutions.com

Myers-Walls, J. A., Ballard, S. M., Darling, C. A., & Myers-Bowman, K. S. (2011). Reconceptualizing the domain and boundaries of family life education. *Family Relations, 60*(4), 357–372. doi:10.1111/j.1741-3729.2011.00659.x.

Nelson, J. N. (2006). *Positive discipline.* New York: Random House.

Piaget, J. (1936). *The origins of intelligence in children.* New York: International Universities Press.

Popkin, M. (1993). *Active parenting today.* Marietta, GA: Active Parenting.

Chapter 11
Coaching for ADHD and Special Needs

> Living with ADHD is **like walking up a down escalator.** You can get there eventually but the journey is exhausting. (Kathleen Ely, Helena)

For parents with children of special needs, the task of parenting can be overwhelming. Children and youth with neurodevelopmental disorders (NDD) such as Autism Spectrum Disorder (ASD), Learning Disabilities (LD), and Attention Deficit Disorder (ADHD), have a unique set of obstacles to overcome. It is estimated that roughly one in ten youth in the U.S. will be diagnosed with a NDD (Hysing, Elgen, Gillberg, & Lundervold, 2009) and the rate is rising. Even more startling is that 55 % of these children were found to exhibit behavioral problems (Lach et al., 2009).

Parent and family coaches are a support that many families of children with special needs are turning to for assistance. Family life coaches working with NDD diagnosed families need to be informed and well equipped with specific knowledge of the challenges and norms of these families. This chapter offers research and background information and tips for coaching families that have children with disabilities with emphasis on Attention Deficit/Hyperactivity Disorder (ADHD) and Emotional/Behavioral/Physical Difficulties.

Children, Parents, and Families with Special Needs

It is no surprise that the parents of special need children have unique circumstances and often seek the expertise of family life professionals. Research is clear that parenting practices are associated with social, behavioral, and cognitive developmental outcomes (Masten & Shaffer, 2006). Positive, warm, and consistent

© Springer International Publishing Switzerland 2016   205
K. Allen, *Theory, Research, and Practical Guidelines for Family Life Coaching*,
DOI 10.1007/978-3-319-29331-8_11

parenting is associated with pro-social behaviors (Hasting, Utendale, & Sullivan, 2007) while harsh parenting is associated with psychosocial and behavioral issues (Miller, Jenkins, & Keating, 2002).

Parenting children with disabilities is particularly challenging, and elicits exceptional barriers to overcome. There are increased stressors due to the costs of health care, logistics, and maintenance of familial relationships. Parents of children with special needs are more likely to report stress and score lower on psychosocial well-being indicators (Olsen & Hwang, 2001). Parents of children with special needs are less likely to provide positive and consistent parenting, and often practice ineffective parenting strategies (Arim et al., 2012). These parents often feel overwhelmed, judged, and lonely. Support for parents of special needs children is needed and has shown to increase positive parenting behaviors (Bailey, Nelson, Hebbeler, & Spiker, 2007).

Today, there are a multitude of programs available for youth with Autism and ADHD, behavioral difficulties, and children that have difficulty learning. While many of the general parenting concepts and strategies outlined in Chap. 10 work very well with these populations, there are differences that merit exploration.

Coaching Families and Special Needs

Services for families of children with special needs have been well researched, and come with specific evidence-based approaches to growth and well-being (Reiff, 2011), yet there is no one-size-fits-all approach to any disability. Though there are variations among service offerings and styles of services, most services for special needs families have the primary foci on factors such as improving the relationship between parent and child in the specific context of the family, reduction in externalized child behaviors, and increasing the family's skills and resources (Gockel, Russel, & Harris, 2008).

Skills and resource development play a particularly important role in the work of coaching. Often, parents need specific information about their child's specific issue, and valid, reliable information is not necessarily easy to acquire. While many people have strong opinions of what might work, what works for one family may not work for another and more so, what works for a family at one time might only work temporarily.

Specific to families, coaching provides a process in which knowledge can be shared, skills can be developed, and support is offered in a reciprocal process. In addition, nurturing feedback can be given to the key people in a child's life, their caregivers and/or parents (Rush, Shelden, & Hanft, 2003). This is where a parent or family life coach can be beneficial. Coaching can be used to teach parents new parenting techniques while supporting them in their process. Moreover, an overarching goal in most family life coaching efforts is to foster a sense of competence and mastery in the client—which in turn enables clients to implement strategies with their children, alter them when needed, and generalize those strategies across situations over time (Raj & Kumar, 2009; Rush et al., 2003).

It is imperative that family coaching promotes a reciprocal relationship between coach and client while also allowing the opportunity to practice new parenting techniques; intuitively, a coaching component is well suited as an adjunct service or even a replacement to most any parenting education class/forum. While research supports parent training (Reiff, 2011), parents report it difficult to apply new or unfamiliar skills learned in a classroom at home—there is a disconnect from the information on parenting and children in the classroom setting versus the real life situations at home (Beyer, 2008). Prochaska asserts that insight alone will not necessarily bring about behavioral change, and behavioral change will not matter if one lacks insight (Norcross & Prochaska, 2002).

Both insight and education are needed to bring about lasting and meaningful change. In support of this, we look towards two recent meta-analyses to provide insight into the components of services most closely associated with significantly improved interactions between caregivers and children, and significantly reduced externalized child behavior. These included directly teaching positive methods of interacting with and disciplining children, emotion coaching and communication skills, and in-vivo practice of new and existing skills, as opposed to classroom-only work, role-play, or and/or homework (Centers for Disease Control and Prevention [CDC], 2009; Kaminski, Valle, Filene, & Boyle, 2008).

Children with NDD often have additional behavioral issues, making the role of parenting these children even more complex. Sixty-Eight percent of children with NDD have behavioral problems such as emotional symptoms, conduct issues, or peer problems (Hysing et al., 2009). These children and youth face a great deal of stressors, as do their parents. This makes the need for information so important that combined with the need for support creates an important opportunity for parent coaching. Reiff (2011), editor in chief of the American Academy of Pediatrics, highlights key parenting components found as evidence of behavioral changes in youth with NDD include:

- Active listening
- Emotion coaching
- Increase positive interactions (affection, quality time together)
- Decrease negative interactions (sarcasm and criticism)
- Positive discipline (focus on what child does well or right)
- Ignoring rather than responding to negative behaviors
- Consistent parenting behaviors
- Consequences (time out, loss of related privilege)

Many of these concepts are covered in detail in Chap. 10, and remain equally, if not more important to families with children that have disabilities. Children with special needs are more likely to be victims of abuse and violence, and as such, it is imperative to help educate parents and caregivers on the importance of positive parenting practices. When enough is enough, the use of consequences should be provided with a calm and consistent manner (Reiff, 2011).

While it is every parent's decision to decide if or when to use punishment, spanking should be noted as one of the most ineffective forms of punishment and it models aggressive behaviors. Spanking can lead to a host of negative outcomes, such as increased aggressive behaviors, injury, and can negatively impact the quality of the parent–child relationship. Spanking and corporal punished are discouraged as forms of behavior modification.

Rules to parent by:

1. What you focus on grows: if you want to see more of a desired behavior, give that behavior the attention.
2. What you ignore goes away: if you find behavior that is not appealing, ignore it.
3. When enough is enough deal with it: if the behavior is dangerous (hitting, for example), use consequences.

While this book is not a training on all things special education, it needs to be stated that one of the things most parents struggle with is school success. There are federal laws that protect students with disabilities, and professionals serving these families will benefit from further research on special education services. A few of the laws and resources that can help special needs youth gain the services they need are IDEA, IEP and 504.

The Individuals with Disabilities Education Act (IDEA) is a federal law that ensures children with disabilities have access to free and appropriate education. Individual Education Programs (IEP) are plans created by the parents and the schools for children needing special education. An IEP is a legal document that outlines accommodations designed to help a child be successful in the school setting. Not all children qualify for an IEP as a child needs to perform below grade level to qualify. Section 504 of the Rehabilitation Act and the American's with Disabilities Act is a plan designed to provide accommodations for students with disables that are performing nearer to grade level, but that could use additional educational supports.

Families are often so overwhelmed that the support of a coach can help not only with parenting, but with a whole host of services. Family life coaches can work with parents to help them understand their child's abilities, identify the key players, review rights and responsibilities, and help families become organized.

Model of Coaching in Early Childhood for Children with Disabilities

One of the earliest, if not the earliest, groups to focus on coaching families and professionals serving young children is the work of Hanft, Rush, and Sheldon (2004). These practitioners developed a model of coaching for parents and practitioners serving children with developmental disabilities. Their work focuses on training early childhood practitioners' in the use of coaching with families. The model emphasizes where early intervention teams include roles such as speech, occupational, and behavior therapists, case managers, and others become trained to work with the family in a coaching approach. This came from a need for parents to learn the skills necessary to support their children in educational settings, but then had difficulty or simply did not implement the evidence-based practices in their home (Rush et al., 2003).

Rush, Shelden, & Hanft (2003) defines coaching as "an adult learning strategy in which the coach promotes the learner's ability to reflect on his or her actions as a means to determine the effectiveness of an action or practice and develop a plan for refinement and use of the action in immediate and future situations." Based on their years of experiences, the authors felt the focus should be on what families are able to do, built on parent knowledge and skill, and they wanted to help parents identify resources and become self-reliant. The team also recognized the importance of family strengths and the importance of family priorities and interests (Shelden & Rush, 2005). Based on their experiences, the coaching model of Hanft, Rush, and Sheldon's work includes five essentials of coaching families:

(1) Collaborative relationship between coach and learner;
(2) Reflection and use of questioning;
(3) Reciprocal observations and actions;
(4) Focus on performance; and
(5) Context-driven process determined by learner

Hanft et al.'s process of coaching, like most coaching models, focuses on four areas: initiation, observation and action, reflection, and evaluation. The process is not linear; the client and family can come in and out of the various areas. While this model is widely used by professionals in the early childhood developmental disability world, there is no literature on using this model in parent or family life coaching separate from the use with intervention teams.

Clearly, there are approaches to coaching with special needs families that have been found highly effective. Although there is no one size fits all approach to coaching, it is evident that including evidence-based family life content, and specifically parenting education content, is an important component of coaching parents of children with special needs.

A Parent's ADHD Perspective: The Invisible Illness

I sit on the Special Education Advisory Council for our school district. My role there, similar to all other non-school personnel roles, is that of parent advocate as I'm the parent of a child with ADHD, Anxiety, and Depression. At a recent meeting, it came up that children with ADHD, or other "invisible disabilities" have a difficult time getting services at school. The school administrators and parents of children with physical disabilities and "visible" disabilities had a difficult time understanding what this meant, or what it looked like. At that time, I could have shared a hundred stories of teachers telling my daughter that she is using her ADHD as an excuse to be lazy and that if she would only apply herself, she could do so much better. Instead I shared the story of a recent IEP meeting where I mentioned how my child's anxiety was making sleeping more difficult than usual, a teacher responded by informing me I should move my child's bedtime to an earlier time and then told my child that she needs to go to sleep earlier. (My sarcastic response in my head...OHHHH! If only I had thought of that! Or the sleep specialist, or the psychologist, or the pediatrician, or any of the moms of my ADHD support group...)

Families with children that have ADHD are chronically fighting to have their child's disability recognized and supported. After the SEAC meeting, we posted on our local CHADD discussion board to see if other families had experienced anything similar. The response was overwhelming. Unlike parents who have children with visible disabilities, the parents of children with ADHD overwhelmingly felt judged, ignored, and unsupported not only by the schools, but often by friends and family members.

ADHD and Children

Defined by the American Psychiatric Association as "developmentally inappropriate attention and or hyperactivity and impulsivity so pervasive and persistent as to significantly interfere with a child's daily life (Reiff, 2011), ADHD is one of the most prevalent chronic childhood disorders, topped only by asthma. While statistics vary, it is estimated that 11 % of children ages 4–17 have been diagnosed with ADHD and that number is on the rise (CDC, 2014). ADHD accounts for 30–50 % of all referrals to mental health providers (Reiff, 2011). ADHD is characterized by difficulty paying attention, impulsive behaviors, and high levels of activity. Children with ADHD tend to have short attention spans, are forgetful, and they often act before thinking. These children often have high energy and their behaviors interfere significantly with typical day-to-day tasks. The research on causes of ADHD is inconclusive, but there are a number of risk factors that have been noted as possible influencers. Genetics, temperament, environmental, and medical causes have been associated with ADHD. A combination of medication and behavior therapy tend to offer the most successful treatment plans (Reiff, 2011).

Research suggests that marginalized youth, such as youth with special needs (i.e., ADHD, ASD) are at a higher risk for mental health issues than their peers (Georgetown University Center for Child and Human Development (GUCCHD), 2014). ADHD has a high rate of comorbidity of other conditions including anxiety, depression, learning disabilities, and mood disorders. According to the American Academy of Pediatrics (AAP, 2013), there is also a reciprocal association between anxiety disorders and ADHD. Approximately one fourth of children with ADHD also have an anxiety disorder. Likewise, about one fourth of children with anxiety disorders have ADHD. This includes all types of anxiety disorders—generalized anxiety disorder, obsessive-compulsive disorder, separation anxiety, and phobia (including social anxiety). Younger children with overanxious disorder or separation anxiety are especially likely to also have ADHD (AAP, 2013).

While the rates of ADHD in children are growing, so is the field on how to best help families dealing with ADHD. The benefits of evidence-based parenting practices such as kind and firm nurturing, warm parenting and positive discipline are true for all children, and especially true for children with ADHD (Reiff, 2011). There are additional steps parents and caregivers can take to help structure an environment that will help children with ADHD thrive.

- *Consistency*. Consistency in parenting and in daily routines is important. Keeping children and youth on a daily schedule and helping them to prepare for changes or shifts in the routine can help them adjust and be successful.
- *Reminders*. Also called warnings, giving children small reminders in 5 or 10 min increments via verbal, written formats can help them prepare for changes.
- *Organized Environment*. Finding stuff is one of the biggest issues for parents and children with ADHD, so being sure everything has a place can help with success.
- *Planning*. Whether it is for homework or outings, and behavior at dinner, communicating a plan with children can help them understand and meet expectations.
- *Minimize distractions*. The world can be over stimulating for children with ADHD, so minimizing distractions fosters success.

ADHD and Adults

It is not just children that have ADHD and need support. Studies indicate that more than half of all youth that are diagnosed with ADHD meet the criteria in adulthood (Knouse, Bagwell, Barkley, & Murphy, 2005). As with children, the recommended treatment for ADHD is a combination of behavioral support and medication. Medication alone has proven to be ineffective in adulthood (Wilens, Spencer, & Biederman, 2000), so a combination of behavior support, education, and medication is the recommended approach.

Symptoms of ADHD in adults mirror those in children, with the exception that many adults have had an opportunity to learn and grow coping skills. These adults often have difficulties with organization and focus, and may have had trouble in school as a youth. As such, many adults with ADHD often have stressors in their lives. Activities that seems like simple day-to-day tasks to typical adults are extraordinarily difficult for adults with ADHD (NIH, ND). Tasks such as organizing and cleaning the house, getting to work on time, and maintaining relationships can be a real challenge. These adults are often in need to education and support to learn the skills needed to be successful.

ADHD Coaching

The field of ADHD coaching for both children and adults is rapidly growing (Murphy, Ratey, Maynard, Sussman, & Wright, 2010) and there is limited research on the efficacy of coaching clients with ADHD. What limited evidence there is has yet to link ADHD coaching as an evidence-based approach (Kubik, 2010). According to Kubik, however, the most effective approaches have included a partnership with therapists and the use of medications. The role of the ADHD coach is to educate adults on the outcomes of ADHD over the life course and helping clients make a logical connections to cognitive, emotional, and behavioral responses. Again, education is an important component of the ADHD coaching experience.

Clients that see an ADHD coach need to be mentally healthy. At this time, there is no evidence that family life coaching should be a primary mode of service for anyone with mood disorders, such as depression, anxiety, or major mental illness (Murphy et al., 2010). Since the field is highly unregulated and many ADHD coaches have no specific training in mental health, clients presenting these issues should be referred to a mental health professional.

Adult clients do best when they recognize that they have ADHD, and they need help managing the side affects of the disease. In other words, an acceptance of what is and readiness for change will dramatically increase outcome results. Commitment to the process is also a major contributor to success. As people with ADHD tend to be disorganized and distracted, the commitment to the process is needed for accountability. If an ADHD client is not ready or committed, the chances of success are limited, and the chances for frustration are increased.

Family Coaching for Youth with ADHD and Their Families

Many coaches will work directly with the adult around the issue of a child with ADHD, rather than working with the ADHD child. Like the recommendations for coaching parents, coaching parents with ADHD children includes a combination of education and coaching. Helping parents understand the evidence-based parenting practices such as authoritative parenting styles, positive discipline, and logical consequences is one facet of coaching. The other is to help families identify goals and strategies to reach those goals. In order to coach families of children with ADHD, having content specific training is advisable.

An even newer trend of ADHD coaching is coaching youth and young adults with ADHD. Coaching young people is not necessarily new; success or academic coaches are now a part of the educational experience and sports coaching for youth is a major part of the standard childhood experience in the US. Youth coaching for ADHD is based very much on the same concepts of coaching adults. The process of helping the clients identify, and reach goals, and working in partnership with the client is certainly part of the coaching experience with youth. Being an effective youth ADHD coach requires in-depth knowledge of ADHD (Sleeper-Triplett, 2010) and human growth and development. Understanding normal development, behaviors, and experiences specific to youth with ADHD will help the client navigate the process of coaching.

Sleeper-Triplett (2010) states that empowerment is a key component of ADHD coaching. May times, youth with ADHD are discouraged, and are not familiar with their skills, talents, and abilities. Coaching can help these young clients better understand and apply their strengths to achieve their goals. Empowering youth helps them reach their goals while increasing feelings of self-efficacy and esteem.

One question not addressed in the research is, if and how to include parents when coaching youth directly. There are two schools of thought on this. The first, which is identified as the process used by Sleeper-Triplett (2010), is the frame that the primary alliance is between the coach and the client. In this approach, the expectation is that the parent and child will have communication about the coaching process, but the coach will not have conversations with the parent about the coaching process. As such, the recommendation is to refrain from having direct communication with the young client's parent, but rather empower the youth to be the one communicating with the parents. The approach works better for older youth and young adults.

The other school of thought, and one used more often in the realms of psychology and therapy, is that the role of the practitioner is to inform the child's system and as such, coaches have direct communication with both the parent and the youth. In this approach, the coach connects and communicates with the parents to inform and gather more information. So the coach works directly with the youth client, but might spend a few minutes at the beginning or end of the session to connect with the parent.

Working Within a System

For anyone coaching a family with a child with special needs is going to be coaching within a system. The ecological framework (Bronfenbrenner, 1979) describes the importance of understanding and working within the various systems of a child's life as the most the most effective approach to serving families. This is of utmost importance when working families that have a child with a disability. Parents and caregivers often work with school systems, private therapists, tutors, psychologists, pediatricians. . .the list goes on and on. The shear coordination of this coordination process can be overwhelming for parents. The role of the coach is to support and help families reach their goals. It is of an advantage to also have an understanding the various systems at play.

In addition to systems theory, it is useful for family life coaches to have a framework for understanding parenting practices that yielded positive outcomes for children. In addition to the parenting practices highlighted in Chap. 10, the

National Extension Parent Education Framework and Model are good resources for understanding parenting practices and competencies for good parent educators. While parent coaches are not parent educators, many of the practices and standards are congruent.

National Extension Parent Education Model

A group of Cooperative Extension Human Development Specialists worked to create a parenting education model using synthesized literature on parenting practices that yielded positive outcomes for children (Smith, Cudaback, Goddard, & Myers-Wall, 1994). The National Extension Parent Education Model (NEPEM) included six content areas for inclusion in parenting education, and these six content areas are highly relevant to parents of children with special needs:

- *Care for self.* Importance of managing stress, identifying person strengths, and gaining support from others.
- *Understand.* Observing children, understanding child development, recognizing how to engage in surroundings.
- *Guide.* Modeling of appropriate and supportive behaviors. Kind and firm parenting.
- *Nurture.* Parenting with warmth, affection, and compassion.
- *Motivate.* Teach children about the world around them to stimulate growth.
- *Advocate.* Identify and utilize community resources that benefit the child. Building community relationships.

Each of these practices are relevant to all families, but *Advocate*, *Care for Self*, and *Understand* are uniquely important to parents with children that have special needs.

As a follow up to the model, an expanded group of Extension Specialists worked to identify through the literature and other assessments, a framework for parenting educator competencies. The literature of educational leadership, adult education, family life education, and parenting education were used to identify six categories and 42 professional practices within those areas. The content areas are highly relevant for family life educators that work specifically with parents. The categories include:

- *Grow*. Importance of professional development.
- *Frame*. Importance of solid theoretical underpinnings.
- *Develop.* Skills for creating effective programs.
- *Educate.* Develop strategies for effective teaching.
- *Embrace.* Develop competencies for serving diverse clientele.
- *Build.* Professional networking.

The image below shows the interconnectedness of the skills parents need with the competencies parenting professionals need when serving families. As with the model, the framework is true for professionals serving families with special needs. It is critical to gain specific training and knowledge about the families unique needs and circumstances, as well as embrace competencies for serving diverse families. Professional associations can be helpful in further development of the field of family life coaching for special needs.

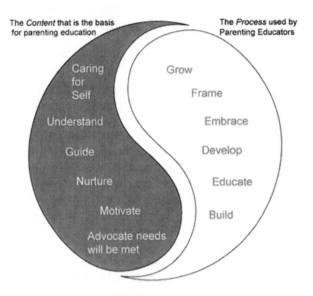

Although the field of ADHD is new, it is rapidly growing. As such, credentialing is now a part of the coaching process (Murphy et al., 2010). ADHD Coaches Organization (ACO), is a professional association for ADHD coaches. Although ACO does not credential ADHD coaches, there are credentials specific to ADHD. According to the Professional Association of ADHD coaches (ND), to become a Certified ADHD coach, a coach must have a combination of ADHD and coach-specific training and practice, references, and an applicant must pass a competency exam. It is important to note that a background in family life, therapy, or other parenting-specific is not required.

Interview with ADHD Coach Elaine Taylor-Klaus

Because ADHD coaching is a growing field with limited literature and reference materials, I wanted to share an interview with a current ADHD coach. Elaine Taylor-Klaus, CPCC, ACC is an ADHD coach in Atlanta, GA. Elaine has spent her life as an educator, advocate, and community entrepreneur, and now as a professional coach. She spoke to me about her experiences as an ADHD coach, and I have included an excerpt of our conversation.

KA: What made you interested in becoming a coach?

ETK: It started with me raising complex kids. The first 10 years of parenting were rough and it was tough. So I found a coach to help me through that time. When I started getting coaching, I saw a light at the end of the tunnel for the first time. The experience was so helpful that I thought, no parent should go through what I went through alone! I wanted to be a coach so that I could share that process with my clients.

KA: How did you get into coaching?

ETK: I set up a speakers series and ran a series for parents and professionals to raise awareness of specials needs and education. At the time, I was on my way to a PhD. I could not find a program to fit my schedule. I had read the Teaching the Tiger book (Dornbush & Pruitt, 1995) and decided to go to get a coaching credential as temporary measure to getting PhD. In the coach training program, I found what I'm supposed to do in the world.

KA: Sounds like it was a great fit for you from the start!

ETK: Yes, I went headfirst and got my training, certification and went through a leadership program. I take the professionalism very seriously. I really believe in certification and training. While I was on that journey, I discover that as I became a coach, I became a better parent. These skills where helping me more than anything as a parent.

KA: So what then what happened?

ETK: After my training, I started a business called touchstone parents. I worked with community partners from CHADD (Children and Adults with ADHD) and Impact ADHD was created. We wanted to teach parents how to take coach approach to parenting.

KA: So you coach parents with children with ADHD?

ETK: Yes, we talk about natural curiosity, using open-ended questions and 100 coaching skills that benefit parents. We teach parents how to use coaching stills with kids. We do a hybrid of coaching/training combo.

KA: What are your thoughts about the field of ADHD coaching?

ETK: There is a group of folks in the profession that take professionalism very seriously. Our field is young, so we will see changes and move towards more rigor and expertise. I do have concerns about anyone calling himself or herself a coach. So I do believe the field is in need credentials and rigor.

KA: What kinds of certification?

ETK: There needs to be training specific to ADHD content and coaching content. Early on, I was concerned about people taking a few coaching courses and then call themselves a coach.

Content and skill based coaching training is important. If you want to coach kids with special needs, you need to understand the medical state. You need to know the content. But that doesn't replace the need for coaching skills. ADCA is trying to do both. We have a policy that any coach also has to have ICF certification.

KA: It sounds like the ADHD component is very specific training. Can you talk more about that?

ETK: Sure. We have created a model and approach, we have two coaching schools and the training is based on 100 coaching skills. We use a parenting action model, but it also works in business, parenting, and relationships. Coaching is a masterful style of communication. The model is simple; it allows you to tackle a challenging situation on macro and micro levels. We focus on the 4–6 key areas that families struggle with complex needs.

KA: May I ask, what are the key areas?

ETK: The six key areas are:

- Emotional intensity
- Logistics
- Relationships
- Organization
- Education
- Impact on parent and caregiver.

We start with that, and encourage parents to look at the big picture. They choose the area where they want to work. It can be overwhelming to do too much at one time, so this helps them to choose. We are specific and challenge the parents to identify the change they want to see. So, saying mornings are challenging isn't specific. If I were coaching, I would take aim and be specific on the behavior they want to see changed. There are five steps:

1. Taking aim of what they want to change.
2. Collect information. This is more than just behavior; but to understand the circumstance contributing to the issue. Here parents get informed and understand the situation.
3. Plan. Here we focus on the 4 critical responses: activate brain, positive parenting, shifting expectations/realistic, and systems and structures. Most people want to dive to 4: systems and structures. However, structure only works if you do the first 3.
4. Action
5. Rinse and repeat. We evaluate the action plan, recognize that change is a process that requires modifications.

We use a value and energy based approach to the work. We looked at our own experiences, and saw what was really working and what created lasting change.

KA: Anything else you want to say or tell budding family life coaches?

ETK: The other piece that is so important when working with families with special needs is self-care. A big part of working with parents is helping them learn to care for themselves. We only work with parents right now. Our vision is to change the way parents approach medical issues. In every other field we expect training and continuing education. That's not true for parenting, but should be.

Chapter Summary

Coaching families with children with ADHD can be such a valuable, wonder resource. These parents have much stress and many decisions to make, and having the support and encouragement of a family life coach can make such a difference in their lives. Each family is different, and each need is special. However, there are resources, books, and websites that can aid in the development of competencies for coaches serving these families. Life experiences and professional training can help a family life coach have success, as can becoming a part of the community of your target audience.

Further Reading

Nadeau, K. G., Littman, E. B., & Quinn, P. O. (2011). *Understanding girls with ADHD*. Washington, DC: Advantage Books.

Reiff, M. I. (2011). *ADHD: What every parent needs to know*. Elk Grove Village, IL: American Academy of Pediatrics.

Sleeper-Triplett, J. (2010). *Empowering youth with ADHD: Your guide to coaching adolescents and young adults for coaches, parents and professionals*. Plantation, FL: Specialty Press.

References

American Academy of Pediatrics (AAP). (2013). *Anxiety disorders and ADHD*. Retrieved from http://www.healthychildren.org/English/health-issues/conditions/emotional-problems/Pages/Anxiety-Disorders-and-ADHD.aspx

Arim, R. G., Garner, R. E., Brehaut, J. C., Lach, L. M., MacKenzi, M. J., Rosenbaum, P. L., et al. (2012). Contextual influences of parenting behaviors for children with neurodevelopmental disorders: Results from a Canadian national survey. *Disability & Rehabilitation, 34*(26), 2222–2233.

Bailey, D. J., Nelson, L., Hebbeler, K., & Spiker, D. (2007). Modeling the impact of formal and informal supports for young children with disabilities and their families. *Pediatrics, 120*(4), 992–1001.

Beyer, M. (2008). Visit coaching: Building on family strengths to meet children's needs. *Juvenile & Family Court Journal, 59*(1), 47–60. doi:10.1111/j.1755-6988.2007.00004.x.

Bronfenbrenner, U. (1979). *The ecology of human development*. Cambridge, MA: Harvard University Press.

Center for Disease Control. (2014). *Attention-Deficit/Hyperactivity Disorder (ADHD) data & statistics*. Retrieved from http://www.cdc.gov/ncbddd/adhd/data.html

Dornbush, M. P., & Pruitt, S. K. (1995). *Teaching the tiger: A handbook for individual involved in the education of students with attention deficit disorders, Tourette syndrome, or obsessive-compulsive disorder*. Carol Stream, IL: Hope Publishing.

Georgetown University Center for Child and Human Development (GUCCHD). (2014). *Effective strategies checklist children and youth with developmental disorders and challenging behavior*. Retrieved from http://gucchdtacenter.georgetown.edu/publications

Gockel, A., Russel, M., & Harris, B. (2008). Recreating family: Parents identify worker-client relationships as paramount in family preservation programs. *Child Welfare, 87*(6), 91–113.

Hanft, B. E., Rush, D. D., & Shelden, M. L. (2004). *Coaching families and colleagues in early childhood*. Baltimore: Brooks Publishing.

Hasting, P. D., Utendale, W., & Sullivan, C. (2007). The socialization of prosocial development. In J. E. Grusec & P. D. Hastings (Eds.), *Handbook of socialization: Theory and practice* (pp. 638–664). New York: The Guilford Press.

Hysing, M., Elgen, I., Gillberg, C., & Lundervold, A. J. (2009). Emotional and behavioral problems in subgroups of children with chronic illness: Results from a large-scale populations study. *Child Care Health Development, 35*, 527–533.

Kaminski, J. W., Valle, L. A., Filene, J. H., & Boyle, C. L. (2008). A meta-analytic review of components associated with parent training program effectiveness. *Journal of Abnormal Child Psychology, 36*(4), 567–589. doi:10.1007/s10802-007-9201-9.

Knouse, L. E., Bagwell, C. L., Barkley, R. A., & Murphy, K. R. (2005). Accuracy of self-evaluation in adults with ADHD. *Journal of Attention Disorders, 2*, 221–234.

Kubik, J. A. (2010). Efficacy of ADHD coaching for adults with ADHD. *Journal of Attention Disorders, 13*(5), 442–453.

Lach, L. M., Kohen, D. E., Garner, R. E., Brehaut, J. C., Miller, A. R., Klassen, A. F., et al. (2009). The health and psychosocial functioning of caregivers of children with neurodevelopmental disorders. *Disabilitiy Rehabilitations, 31*, 607–618.

Masten, A., & Shaffer, A. (2006). How families matter in child development: Reflections from research on risk and resilience. In A. Clarke-Steward & J. Dunn (Eds.), *Families count: Effects on child and adolescent development* (pp. 5–25). New York: Cambridge University Press.

Miller, F., Jenkins, J., & Keating, D. (2002). Parenting and children's behavioral problems. In J. D. Willms (Ed.), *Vulnerable children: Findings from canada's national longitudinal survey of children and youth* (pp. 167–182). Edmonton, Canada: The University of Alberta Press.

Murphy, K., Ratey, N., Maynard, S., Sussman, S., & Wright, S. D. (2010). Coaching for ADHD. *Journal of Attention Disorders, 13*(5), 546–552.

Norcross, J., & Prochaska, J. (2002). Using the stages of change. *Harvard Mental Health Letter, 18* (11), 5–7. Retrieved from EBSCO*host*.

Olsen, M. B., & Hwang, C. P. (2001). Depression in mothers and fathers of children with intellectual disability. *Journal of Intellect Disability Res, 45*, 535–543.

Raj, A., & Kumar, K. (2009). Optimizing parent coaches' ability to facilitate mastery experiences of parents of children with autism. *International Journal of Psychosocial Rehabilitation, 14*(2), 25–36. Retrieved June 15, 2011, from http://www.psychosocial.com/IJPR_14/Optimizing_Parent_Coaches_Raj.html

Reiff, M. I. (2011). *ADHD: What every parent needs to know*. Elk Grove Village, IL: American Academy of Pediatrics.

Rush, D., Shelden, M., & Hanft, B. (2003). Coaching families and colleagues: A process for collaboration in natural settings. *Infants & Young Children: An Interdisciplinary Journal of Special Care Practices, 16*(1), 33–47.

Shelden, M., & Rush, D. (2005). Practitioner as coach: Our role in early intervention. *American Association for Home-Based Early Interventionists, 9*(3), 7–9, 11.

Sleeper-Triplett, J. (2010). *Empowering youth with ADHD: Your guide to coaching adolescents and young adults for coaches, parents and professionals*. Plantation, FL: Specialty Press.

Smith, C., Cudaback, D., Goddard, W., & Myers-Wall, J. (1994). *National extension parent education model of critical parenting practices*. Manhattan, Kansas: Kansas Cooperative Extension. Retrieved from: http://www.k-state.edu/wwparent/nepem/nepem.pdf

Wilens, T. E., Spencer, T. J., & Biederman, J. (2000). *Pharmacotherapy of attention-deficit/ hyperactivity disorders and comorbidities in children, adolescents and adults*. Washington, DC: American Psychiatric Press.

Chapter 12
Family Life Coaching: Where Do You Belong?

> Family is not an important thing. It's everything. (Michael J. Fox)

While new, the field of family life coaching is growing. Family life coaches today tend to be found primarily in the areas of relationship, parenting, and specials needs coaching. This chapter showcases how coaching is found in many areas of family life, family and consumer sciences, and the fields of social science, health, and education. Coaches are finding niches in a variety of family life content areas, including health and nutrition, which is a high growing field closely related to family life. A recent Google search on each of the topics covered in this chapter showed a variety of coaches that are specific to each topic. The work is not only applied; this chapter showcases research that has been conducted on effective approaches to coaching across the family life spectrum. This chapter provides a short overview of current or recent research studies in the following coaching areas:

- Youth
- ADHD
- Academic success
- Relationship
- Sexuality
- Parenting
- Divorce
- Special Needs
- Older Adults
- Health
- Nutrition
- Family Financial Planning

© Springer International Publishing Switzerland 2016   221
K. Allen, *Theory, Research, and Practical Guidelines for Family Life Coaching*,
DOI 10.1007/978-3-319-29331-8_12

Youth Coaching

Coaching youth. . .the images conjured from this term most likely include children on a field with a ball and an adult serving as a coach. While athletic coaching is certainly a part of the coaching experience, the field of coaching youth is expanding. While there is limited research specifically on the use of coaching methodologies in youth services, there is a suggestion in the literature of a natural fit of coaching and positive psychology in youth development realms (Leach, Green, & Grant, 2011). Leach et al. suggest youth programs could benefit from using coaching strategies such as positive psychology. Youth would also benefit from specific coaching tools such as the Values in Action Signature Strength Survey (Peterson & Seligman, 2004). Leach et al. further suggested that training for youth development professionals and volunteers serving youth should include coaching and positive psychology strategies to role model the services with the youth they serve.

ADHD Coaching

One area of youth coaching that has seen growth in the past decade is ADHD coaching. Similar to other family life coaching populations, the goal of ADHD coaching with youth and young adults is helping them identify their dreams and visions for the future, create goals, and implement a plan to help them reach their goals. Young people spend much of their lives being told what to do by adults, and the transition into independence can be particularly difficult for youth with ADHD (Reiff, 2011). As such, an ADHD coach that works with youth is a resource that helps provide structure, competencies, and strategies for success. Coaches also help these youth see and utilize their strengths, which is especially important with youth with ADHD as they often struggle socially and academically.

Jodi Sleeper-Triplett (2010) has spent years as an ADHD coach for youth and she trains other adults to coach youth and young adults. She suggests several reasons for working directly with youth through coaching and identifies a process for successful coaching. ADHD coaches, according to Sleeper-Triplett, ideally focus on the whole child, meaning academics, social issues, familial issues, health and well-being, decision-making—ADHD coaching is about helping youth in all areas of their life. Sleeper-Triplett also refers to the importance of empowering youth, helping them learn how to help and advocate for themselves.

The research on ADHD coaching shows that it is effective. Field, Parker, Sawilowky, & Rolands (2010) conducted a study looking at college students with ADHD that received coaching services. The students in the treatment group significantly improved in self-regulation, study skills, and will while the coaching process also improved their levels of confidence, organizational, and time management skills. The study also suggested coaching contributed to participant's increased positive emotional states. More information on ADHD coaching can be found in Chap. 11.

Academic Success Coaching

Academic success coaching is stemming from the growing acceptance that educational reform is needed to help youth meet the challenges of the twenty-first century. Schools are mandated to provide students with skills and resources necessary to succeed in an ever-changing world. Coaching is one strategy being tested and showed evidence of efficacy as an approach to help students gain the competencies needed for academic success.

Madden, Green, & Grant (2011) conducted a study evaluating a strengths-based coaching program for primary school students. Based on Seligman's Positive Education field (2009), a pilot program that sought to bring positive education to all aspects of a learners life, focused on the impact of evidence-based strength coaching program in primary schools. The aim of the study was to investigate the impact of the strengths-based coaching approach with youth in an all-male primary school. The youth (N = 38) were prescreened using the Beck Youth Inventory and then a coaching program consisting of eight group sessions was implemented. The students were coached to utilize personal resources to use while working towards a (Specific, Measurable, Attractive, Realistic, and Time Frame (SMART) goal. The findings in this study showed an increase in hope and want for engagement. Although this is a pilot study, it showed a great deal of potential for academic success coaching.

Directly coaching youth is one effective approach, but there is also an increase in coaching for school leaders and teachers. Professional development through coaching is a promising approach because good teaching is an indicator of student achievement (Knight, 2009). Joyce & Shower (1987) found peer coaching strategies effective toward improving student success through coaching teachers. Some school districts, such as the Oakland School district in California, created a leadership coaching department and team consisting of trained coaches with teaching experience to support school personnel. The results of this study showed the academic performance index rose dramatically, over three times that of schools without similar coaching programs (Aguilar, Goldwasser, & Tank-Crestetto, 2011).

Relationship & Sexuality Coaching

A comprehensive overview of relationship coaching is covered in Chap. 9. Relationship coaching is a process that can be valuable for helping couples and partners improve their relationship and can be a useful tool for couples preparing for a long-term commitment. Ives (2012) developed a model of coaching where the focus is on relationship attitudes, skills, and goals. He suggested that coaches work with individuals to explore their attitudes and perceptions of relationships. As with all forms of coaching, the process of relationship coaching includes the formation of goals and effective action plans. His GREAT model of relationship coaching includes:

Goal. Setting a goal.
Reality. Understanding the current situation
Exploration. Gaining of experiences, perspectives, and attitudes
Action Plan. Identify strategies to reach goal.
Take Action. Implement the action plan.

While Ives' model is one of the first models of relationship coaching, the field is growing. While considered a unique field in its own right, sexuality coaching fits nicely with relationship coaching. For coaches to be successful in this arena, they need a solid training in interpersonal communication and couple functioning as well as information human sexual development. That education coupled with coaching process training can create a valuable commodity for couples in need of help or those hoping to improve an already stable couplehood.

Parent Coaching

There is growing literature on using coaching as an approach to parent education. While much of this was discussed in Chap. 10, this chapter will highlight a few specific studies of parent coaching. It appears coaching strategies are already being used by some parenting practitioners. A specific example of using coaching in the familial setting is illustrated in a study by Salisbury, Cambray-Engstrom, and Woods (2010). Using home visits, researchers observed providers to see if various aspects of coaching were being used, such as discussing progress with the child's caregiver, demonstrating strategies for the caregiver, and problem solving, among others. After evaluating six home-visit providers, it was found that five out of the six providers used coaching strategies often with the families (Salisbury et al., 2010).

Maternity coaching is another area that is growing. Many parents, particularly mothers, struggle with the decision of returning to work after the birth of a child. Filsinger (2012) studied whether or not providing a coach during pregnancy is helpful for women to balance work-life issues. The women received coaching from their peers, or other women who were also mothers. The coaching process assisted with providing information, support, and resources. Results showed that maternity coaching was influential in the woman's future career decisions.

Sometimes parents are faced challenging their own biases when it comes to having children who are different than they expected. For example, in some cases, parents may have children who are gay, bisexual, or transgender and a few parents may find it especially difficult to be supportive and thus may reach out for professional help. Coaching is used here as a way of teaching parents how to be supportive and accepting of a child who is different than the parental expectations (Malpas, 2010).

Divorce Coaching

Although divorce education for parents is in the family court system, a new approach to family success is the use of divorce coaches. Portnoy (2006) explained how lawyers have begun using divorce coaches as a way to help their clients and case. The divorce coaches have been able to keep the clients more focused, goal-oriented and calm during the psychological stress of divorce. The function of the divorce coach includes reducing emotions, make the legal process smoother, teaching communication skills, creating solutions, manage conflicts, and educate.

Divorce coaches focus on a collaborative and problem-solving process during their meetings (Portnoy, 2006). Coaching versus therapy is explained that coaching is focused on managing situations where therapy is geared more towards finding a cure. Overall coaching can be used to ease the process of divorce by keeping clients focused on the goals identified from the divorce, thereby lessoning the emotional stress during the divorce process.

Special and Special Needs

The Department of Health and Human Services (2007) define special needs as:

> those who have or are at an increased risk for a chronic physical, developmental, behavioral, or emotional condition and who also require health and related services of a type or amount beyond that required by children generally (2007, p. 5)

According to DHHS, the prevalence of children with special needs is high; approximately fourteen percent of youth have a special health need while over one in five families live with a child with a special need. Parenting children with special needs brings a host of complications and stressors (Olsson & Hwang, 2001), and these parents are likely to seek out support.

Family life coaching for families with a child that have a disability has been practiced for decades. Sometimes called family-centered care, the coaching process of working with families to help them identify and reach goals is utilized. Gallagher (1996) developed an early intervention coaching model and found success in that the process helped families practice unfamiliar skills and try new skills, reduced isolation in families, increased idea exchange, and promoted effective communication between practitioners and the families they served. Coaching with youth and families with specific disabilities has also shown positive results (for examples see Bennet, Ramasamy, & Honsberger, 2013; Fiels, Parket, Sawilowsky, & Rolands, 2010; Meadan, Meyer, Snodgrass, & James, 2013).

Coaching and Aging

With the population of older adults growing rapidly and the complexity of aging and intergenerational issues becoming more prevalent, coaching older adults is gaining in popularity. Chronic illness, for example, is one area of aging that impacts many older adults (U.S. Department of Health and Human Services, 2000). Many illnesses associated with aging, however, are related to lifestyle factors such a nutrition and inactivity (Booth, Gordon, Carlson, & Hamilton, 2000), and changing such behaviors can delay or prevent chronic illness (Dunn, Deroo, & Rivara, 2001). Life coaching is one strategy identified as a promising approach towards helping older adults change lifestyle behaviors.

In a study by Bennett et al. (2005), 75 adults over the age of 60 that had been diagnosed with at least one chronic disease (diabetes, lung disease, heart disease, arthritis, or neuromuscular disease) began working with nurses trained in motivational interviewing as an approach to life coaching. The coaches and participants worked together in the first session to identify goals, follow up sessions were then determined based on the interest of the client, but there was a minimum requirement of one additional coaching session each month for 6 months. Both the control and intervention groups received educational information, such as newsletters, social events with guest speakers, and informational documents during the 6-month period. Results showed the group that received coaching had less illness and health distress (Bennett et al., 2005).

Health Coaching

Although not labeled so, Family Life Coaching can be used and is being used in a variety of ways, including health coaching and nutrition. Health coaching has seen a growth in practice and in the literature (Kreitzer, Sierpina, & Lawson, 2008). Olsen (2013) explains the concept of health coaching as a new phenomenon varying from athletics, weight loss, nutrition, and more. According to Olsen, health coaching has a variety of meanings and has become applicable in different roles. Palmer, Tibbs, and Whybrow (2003), define health coaching as "the practice of health education and health promotion within a coaching context, to enhance the wellbeing of individuals and to facilitate the achievement of their health-related goals" (p. 92). Olsen's systematic review showed the common attributes of health coaching include the partnership between coach and client, client and goal-centered approaches, process oriented approach that fosters empowerment, and enlightenment. Olsen's review suggested that coaching has been successful at improved health, increased healthy behavioral changes, and goal attainment.

Seghers, Van Hoecke, Schotte, Opdenacker, and Boen (2014) conducted a health coaching study that focused on physical activity. In this experiment, participants signed up for a 12-week physical activity program and were randomly assigned to one of two groups: standard intervention and intervention with coaching. The coaching intervention included a short coaching session at the beginning of the program where participants received coaching, targeting self-efficacy, action planning, and relapse prevention techniques. Participants were asked to answer six questions detailing a plan for success. Results showed the coaching intervention group increased in their feelings of self-efficacy and adherence to the program. The intervention was considered successful.

Nutrition

Health and nutrition often go together. One example of a study on health and nutrition coaching comes from Heimendinger et al. (2007). With the high obesity rate in the United States, and subsequent health problems such as diabetes and hypertension, there is a need for professional help when it comes to healthy eating habits for families. A program was implemented in order to help reduce the obesity rate among the rural population of Colorado. In addition to a school based and community-based program, a home-visit coaching program was put in place. Advisors visited families in order to help them understand their current eating and exercise habits and how they can be improved and help families set and achieve goals. Advisors were able to coach families by helping them set goals that were achievable and relevant to the family. A positive correlation between home visits and achievement of health goals was found.

Financial Coaching

Perhaps one of the family life areas to first offer coaching, the financial coach is highly relevant in family life coaching and there is research showing financial coaching as an effective strategy to help families. Dubofsky and Sussman (2008), for example, studied the efficacy of financial coaching to see if financial planners are turning towards coaching strategies in order to better serve their clients. Nearly 2000 (1726) financial planners responded to a survey asking questions about whether or not coaching techniques were used when helping their clients plan their finances. Most of financial planners (89 %) reported that they did a lot of coaching when working with their clients. Many financial planners said their clients felt close to them and would ask for advice about things other than finances, such as familial and marital issues. Financial planners are coaching their clients on issues of divorce, mediating problems with children, and helping with family planning for end of life issues.

Coaching and Social Work, Family Case Management, Nursing, and Education

Many of the studies cited in this chapter come not from the fields of coaching psychology or family science, but rather from a variety of fields including social work, nursing, education, and health science. It is clear that family practitioners are represented in a variety of fields, which lends strength the idea that family life coaching is a growing field.

Social work is a great example of a field utilizing coaching. There are several studies showing evidence-based coaching practices in the social work field (for example, see Beyer, 2008; De Jong & Berg, 2001; LePage & Garcia-Rea, 2012). Another recent study showed that while social workers do not necessarily consider themselves coaches, the work they do aligns well with coaching practices (Burroughs, Allen, & Huff, in press). Many of these social work studies are family case management studies, meaning that the coaching work is administered by case management professionals with coach training.

Similar studies are true of home visitation and health programs that utilize nurses and medical therapists as trained professional coaches. Timmer, Zebell, Culver, and Urquiza (2010) conducted a study to determine if coaching practices of in-home parent-child interaction therapy interventionists would improve parent outcomes. The parents received coaching via home visits. The coaches offered support and instruction after observations of 5-min cycles of parents playing with their children. The parents practiced skills in the session with the coaches. Results show that participation in the coaching home-visits lead to significant increases of parent functioning.

Finally, while I will not go into detail about the use of coaching in the realm of education, there is a growing science that shows the efficacy of coaching for academic success (Webberman, 2011). When coaching is offered as part of a holistic approach to learning and change, it makes a tremendous contribution in the educational setting (Devine, Meyers, & Houssemand, 2013). The field of academic success coaching is growing as a profession as well. Most colleges and many K-12 institutions, and even afterschool programs are hiring coaches because the process of supporting students to reach self-identified goals is effective. This is especially true of youth identified as at-risk (Webberman, 2011). This field is only growing, as is the use of coaching in a variety of fields that focus on improving the lives of youth and families.

Implications for Family Practice

Utilizing coaching in family work is a current trend, and family practitioners sit in a unique position to incorporate coaching in their work with families. Specifically, coaching provides a structured means by which knowledge can be imparted, skills can be shared in a reciprocal process and further honed, and nurturing feedback can be given to family members (Rush, Shelden, & Hanft, 2003). This is where family life practitioners can improve their results with coaching--coaching can be used to teach parents new parenting techniques, show partners how to budget, or help youth make healthy food and activity decisions.

Many practitioners already do much of what coaching is all about, work to foster positive change and familial wellbeing. The difference is in the approach of creating that change. In the coaching process, the client is responsible for defining success and is viewed as an expert on their life. It is the role of the coach to listen, converse, observe, and ask powerful questions to help the family or client achieve their goals.

Although some coaches are professionals that work directly with clients in a formal coaching session, another option of coaching includes using the tenets of coaching in an educational approach to serving families. Many family life professionals work in agencies already providing a variety of services, and coaching could become one of the services provided. Of course training is essential to be able to learn how to implement coaching, and there are steps practitioners or students can take to include coaching training in their existing programs.

As we have seen, coaching can be used in the familial setting to help fix a variety of issues ranging from nutrition (Heimendinger et al., 2007) to dealing with emotions (Lunkenheimer, Shield, & Cortina, 2007). Spreading knowledge about the use of coaching and its benefits can help bring coaching to more families. Coaching could have a positive impact on families that have children with behavioral problems, mental and or physical disabilities, and/or in general, parenting skills.

Interview with Dathan Rush

Dathan Rush is the Associate Director of the Family, Infant, and Preschool Program in Morganton, NC. He is a researcher and practitioner that is a pioneer of using coaching in work with families. I had the opportunity to interview him for this book, and here is an expert of that interview:

KA: Hi Dathan. Thanks for chatting with me.

DR: You are welcome.

KA: How did you get into the field of coaching?

DR: I've had a long career and spent the first few years doing traditional speech-language therapy. When Part H of the Individuals with Disabilities

Education Act came into law in the late 1980's the movement was for early intervention to be provided in the natural environment of infants and toddlers with disabilities and their families. The nature of that change made it clear that families had to be involved. The work we were doing in early 90s was family-centered care; we were figuring out how to support families with a child with disabilities. There was not a lot of information for how to do services in the in the home. We could see first hand that the process had to be functional and relevant. At first, families preferred for us to just work with the child rather than for the therapist and parent work together. It was clear, and research supported, that the child doesn't just learn from the therapist; it is the child's participation in the everyday life events that help a child learn.

So in the mid 90s, we went to the literature on how to work with families in home settings. Physical therapy, for example, that literature talked about the role of therapists as "coach" or "consultant". The same was true with occupational literature-they were doing work similar to coaching. Less of only the therapists working with child, more work with parents and child-care providers. The speech literature called it collaborative consultation.

We needed more information, however, so that drove us to the research. The word "coach" was being used more, but there was no process or common definition. Versions of coaching were based on individual author's views, so we needed a standard definition.

KA: So you began your research to try to better understand how to use coaching for families in home settings?

DR: Yes, and we wanted to operationalize what we were doing and observing. We wanted to be clear what each part of the coaching process looked like. We looked at evidence-based practices, and identified needs to determine the characteristics of the practice. We identified five characteristics of coaching from the research.

1. Observation
2. Action/practice of coach and client
3. Reflection (prompted by coach)
4. Feedback (coach lead)
5. Joint planning

KA: So that is the process you use with families?

DR: Yes. This is what we use and teach others to do. It is interesting. The medical model is something that some families are most familiar with. Families that begin with coaching, however, have an appreciation for it. They appreciate the acknowledgement that they have competence related to parenting. It really builds their confidence. We have had reports of parents saying that no one had ever asked what they thought before. Families who are under-resourced often come to us having had negative experiences with systems. Sometimes we are the first service that asked what they think and we are the first that highlight competence on their part. Other approaches tend to be more deficit based. We are strengths-based. We identify what the family is already doing well, and ask them what they think is going well. It all starts with strengths; finding out what is they know and are already doing.

KA: Sounds like a great response. Where is this coaching happening?

DR: We have worked to train coaches with Head Start across the county. Our work is mainly in early intervention, early childhood and other children with disabilities, but it is all over the US and abroad. Home visitors using coaching work directly with families. It has become a broad based approach to serving families in early childhood.

KA: That is very encouraging. Do you have any tips for family life coaches in training?

DR: Learn all you can about families. Especially about families that are different than your own family. Learn about what is effective, what encourages growth, and what is helpful. Some help is not helpful at all, so using evidence-based approaches is very important. Reflection is also key, learn how to support families through reflection. First, find out what the families know and what they are doing well; then use reflective questions.

Chapter Summary

While this book focuses on the theoretical underpinnings and practical how-two of family coaching, This chapter was designed to showcase a few sub-fields of family life coaching. Because the field of FLC is so new, research is sparse. However, the trends are clearly pointing towards growth in a variety of family life arenas.

References

Aguilar, E., Goldwasser, D., & Tank-Crestetto, K. (2011). Support principals: Transform schools. *Educational Leadership, 69*, 70–73.

Bennet, K. D., Ramasamy, R., & Honsberger, T. (2013). Further examination of covert audio coaching on improving employment skills among secondary students with Autism. *Journal of Behavioral Education, 22*, 103–119.

Bennett, J. A., Perrin, N. A., Hanson, G., Bennett, D., Gaynor, W., Flaherty-Robb, M., et al. (2005). Healthy aging demonstration project: Nurse coaching for behavior change in older adults. *Research in Nursing & Health, 28*, 187–197.

Beyer, M. (2008). Visit coaching: Building on family strengths to meet children's needs. *Juvenile and Family Court Journal, 59*(1), 47–60.

Booth, F. W., Gordon, S. E., Carlson, C. J., & Hamilton, M. T. (2000). Waging war on modern chronic diseases: Primary prevention through exercise biology. *Journal of Applied Physiology, 68*(2), 114–787.

Burroughs, M., Allen, K., & Huff, N. (in press). The use of coaching strategies within the field of social work. *Coaching: An International Journal of Theory, Research, & Practice.*

De Jong, P., & Berg, I. K. (2001). Co-constructing cooperation with mandated clients. *National Association of Social Workers, Inc, 46*(4), 361–374.

Devine, M., Meyers, R., & Houssemand, C. (2013). How can coaching make a positive impact within educational settings. *Procedia-Social and Behavioral Sciences, 93,* 1382–1389.

Dubofsky, D., & Sussman, L. (2008). The changing role of the financial planner. *Journal of Financial Planning, 21*(12), 8–9.

Dunn, C., Deroo, L., & Rivara, F. P. (2001). The use of brief interventions adapted from motivational interviewing across behavioral domains: A systematic review. *Addiction, 96,* 1725–1742.

Fiels, S., Parket, D., Sawilowsky, S., & Rolands, L. (2010). *Quantifying the effectiveness of coaching for college students with attention deficit/hyperactivity disorder: Final report to the edge foundation.* Detroit, ME: College of Education, Wayne State University. Retrieved from https://edgefoundation.org/wp-content/uploads/2011/01/Edge-Foundation-ADHD-Coaching-Research-Report.pdf

Filsinger, C. (2012). How can maternity coaching influence women's re-engagement with their career development: A case study of maternity coaching programme in UK-based private law firms. *International Journal of Evidence Based Coaching and Mentoring, 6,* 46–56.

Gallagher, J. J. (1996). A critique of gifted education. *Journal for the Education of the Gifted, 19*(2), 12–19.

Heimendinger, J., Uyeki, T., Andhara, A., Marshall, J., Scarbro, S., Belansky, E., et al. (2007). Coaching process outcomes of a family visit nutrition and physical activity intervention. *Health Education & Behavior, 34*(1), 71–89. doi:10.1177/1090198105285620.

Ives, Y. (2012). What is relationship coaching? *International Journal of Evidence Based Coaching and Mentoring, 10*(2), 88–99.

Joyce, B., & Showers, B. (1987). Low cost arrangements for peer-coaching. *Journal of Staff Development, 8,* 22–24.

Knight, J. (2009). The big four: A simple and powerful framework to dramatically improve instruction. *Strategram, 21*(4), 1–7.

Kreitzer, M., Sierpina, V., & Lawson, K. (2008). Health coaching: Innovative education and clinical programs emerging. *Explore: The Journal of Science and Healing, 4*(2), 154–155.

Leach, C. J., Green, L. S., & Grant, A. M. (2011). Flourishing youth provision: The potential role of positive psychology and coaching in enhancing youth services. *International Journal of Evidence Based Coaching and Mentoring, 9*(1), 44–58.

LePage, J. P., & Garcia-Rea, E. A. (2012). Lifestyle coaching's effect on 6-month follow-up in recently homeless substance dependent veterans: A randomized study. *Psychiatric Rehabilitation Journal, 35*(5), 396–402. doi:10.1037/h0094500.

Lunkenheimer, E., Shield, A., & Cortina, K. (2007). Parental emotion coaching and dismissing in family interaction. *Social Development, 16*(2), 232–248. doi:10.1111/j.1467-9507.2007.00382.x.

Madden, W., Green, S., & Grant, A. (2011). A pilot study evaluating strengths-based coaching for primary school students: Enhancing engagement and hope. *International Coaching Psychology Review, 6*(1), 71–83.

Malpas, J. (2010). Between pink and blue: A multi-dimensional family approach to gender nonconforming children and their families. *Family Process, 50*(4), 453–470. doi:10.1111/j.1545-5300.2011.01371.x.

Meadan, H., Meyer, L. E., Snodgrass, M. R., & James, H. W. (2013). Coaching parents of young children with autism in rural areas using internet-based technologies: A pilot program. *Rural Special Education Quarterly, 31*(3), 3–10.

Olsen, J. M. (2013). Health coaching: A concept analysis. *Nursing Forum, 49*(1), 18–29.

Olsson, M. B., & Hwang, C. P. (2001). Depression in mothers and fathers of children with intellectual disability. *Journal of Intellectual Disability Research, 45*, 535–543.

Palmer, S., Tibbs, I., & Whybrow, A. (2003). Health coaching to facilitate the promotion of healthy behavior and achievement of health-related goals. *International Journal of Health Promotion and Education, 41*, 91–93.

Peterson, C., & Seligman, M. (2004). *Character strengths & virtues: A handbook and classification.* New York: Oxford University Press.

Portnoy, S. M. (2006). Divorce coaches: A new resource for matrimonial lawyers. *American Journal of Family Law, 19*(4), 231–235.

Reiff, M. I. (2011). *ADHD: What every parent needs to know.* Elk Grove Village, IL: American Academy of Pediatrics.

Rush, D., Shelden, M., & Hanft, B. (2003). Coaching families and colleagues: A process for collaboration in natural settings. *Infants & Young Children: An Interdisciplinary Journal of Special Care Practices, 16*(1), 33–47.

Salisbury, C., Cambray-Engstrom, E., & Woods, J. (2010). Providers reported and actual use of coaching strategies in natural environments. *Topics in Early Childhood Special Education, 32* (2), 88–98. doi: 10.1177/0271121410392802.

Seghers, J., Van Hoecke, A. S., Schotte, A., Opdenacker, J., & Boen, F. (2014). The added value of a brief self-efficacy coaching on the effectiveness of a 12-week physical activity program. *Journal of Physical Activity and Health, 11*, 18–29.

Seligman, M. E. P., Ernst, R. E., Gillham, J., Reivich, K., & Linkins, M. (2009). Positive education: Positive psychology and classroom interventions. *Oxford Review of Education, 35*, 293–311.

Sleeper-Triplett, J. (2010). *Empowering youth with ADHD: Your guide to coaching adolescents and youth adults for coaches, parents, and professionals.* Plantation, FL: Specialty Press.

Timmer, S. G., Zebell, M. N., Culver, M. A., & Urquiza, A. J. (2010). Efficacy of adjunct in-home coaching to improve outcomes in parent-child interaction therapy. *Research on Social Work Practices, 20*(1), 36–45.

U.S. Department of Health and Human Services. (2000). *Healthy people 2000: National health promotion and disease prevention objectives.* Hyattsville, Maryland: Public Health Services.

U.S. Department of Health and Human Services. (2007). *The national survey of children with special health care needs chartbook 2005–2006.* Rockville, MD: U.S. Department of Health and Human Services.

Webberman, A. L. (2011). Academic coaching to promote student success: An interview with Carol Carter. *Journal of Developmental Education, 35*(2), 18–20.

Chapter 13
Family Life Coaching: Building a Business, Building a Profession

Kimberly I. Allen, Ph.D., B.C.C. and Debra Kruenegel-Farr, Ph.D.

> A pessimist sees the difficulty in every opportunity; an optimist sees the opportunity in every difficulty. (Winston Churchhill)

A common from prospective students is what, exactly, do family life coaches do? This question inevitably leads to a further discussion on where do family life coaches work, what are the credentials needed, and if I do decide to get my training in FLC, how do I start a coaching business? Chap. thirteen focuses on what happens after training to become a family life coach.

The chapter covers professionalism in family life coaching, highlighting the various credentialing options, training requirements, and professional associations related to family life coaching. Additionally, this chapter provides an overview on the business of family life coaching. While much of what is covered in this chapter is relevant regardless of location, the resources identified are primarily located in North America. Readers will learn about and begin the process of building their business plan, identifying their target audience, marketing themselves, and covering their liabilities.

Credentials

Family Life Coaching stems from two distinct yet related fields; family life education and coaching psychology (Allen, 2013). Both of these fields have existing protocols for credentialing, standards of training, and expectations for professional development. While family life coaching is a new field, professionalism of this field is an important consideration (Allen & Huff, 2014) and efforts are underway to move the field in a professional direction (Kruenegel-Farr, Allen, &

© Springer International Publishing Switzerland 2016
K. Allen, *Theory, Research, and Practical Guidelines for Family Life Coaching*,
DOI 10.1007/978-3-319-29331-8_13

Machara, in press). Both fields also have private practice options for the practitioners, creating a need for information about starting and maintaining a business.

Coaching is being used in a number of fields, careers, and situations as we saw in Chap. 12. High usage does not guarantee quality, however. At this time, a dramatic gap exists in the field of family life coaching with the lack of standardized credentialing and education. Like the broader field of coaching, there is no overseeing organization or association catering specifically to family life coaches. Individuals who are coaching families are congregating towards each other to some degree, either for family life-specific training or through professional associations with specific foci. Ad-hoc groups tend to be formed by a group of individuals who have a common interest and shared goals, rather than under a larger, governing body of professionals or are formed by a few individuals for the purposes of training other coaches in a particular niche. For example, there are groups primarily associated with specific training programs for ADD/ADHD coaches (ADHD Coaches Organization, ADD Coach Academy, JST Coaching), relationship coaches (Relationship Coaching Institute), and parenting coaches (Parent Coach Institute, Academy for Coaching Parents International, Academy for Family Coach Training).

A number of professionals who work with individuals and families are incorporating some level of coaching into their work (Allen & Huff, 2014; Burroughs, Allen, & Huff, in press). However, at this time, those skills or activities are not standardized and may or may not be of high quality, especially if the coaching exists as an addendum or addition to the services being provided. Delivery of any sort of coaching strategies for those in family life jobs is purely due to personal interest, prior coaching training, prior training in a different field, or through natural styles of the individual.

Currently, family practitioners who want to be certified as a family life coach have limited options. They have the option of getting a credential from family-specific training programs, but those certifications are specific to the training program and content area. For family life coaches that want more of a global credential, there are options, but few focus on family science content. The International Society for Coaching Psychology is an organization that is working on credentialing of psychologists who work as coaches. This is the closest to a professional organization in the field for behavioral scientists working with families. The group is specific to psychology and does not yet have a coaching credential to offer. The Center for Credentialing & Education has recently begun offering the Board Certified Coach (BCC) credential. To become a BCC, a person must demonstrate they have met educational requirements, passed an examination, obtained experience, have peer references, and pledge to adhere to a code of ethics. Most areas of study for the BCC credential include helping professions such as professional counseling, social work, health, and behavioral science.

The International Coach Federation (ICF) is one of the world's largest coaching organizations with over 10,000 credential holders. ICF certifies coaches based on specific coach training and hours, but is not specific to behavioral sciences and does not include any specific training for working with families. The Association for

Coaching (AC) is another global coaching organization that emphasizes the field of coaching and the need for evidence-based research on coaching, but again, does not have a sub-section that is specific to family life coaching. In fact, the majority of coaches do not have any training in psychological or behavioral sciences (Grant & Cavanaugh, 2007).

"I would love to see parent coaching as a component of graduate programs and I'd love to see people getting degrees, even a Ph.D. in coaching. I think the way society is going, parents are isolated and separate from extended family. It would be a dream to have every parent have a parent coach. If our field had a standard credential or licensure, we could be seen as a profession; one that everyone knows about and families seek us out. Without the support of credentials, people still ask "what is parent coaching" and if you don't know it exists, you don't get the help. I'd love a professional organization and more networking, conferences, and grass roots support. **Adrian Kalikow, Parent Coach**

At this time, some individuals working as a family life coach have other certifications that can offer credibility, even though they are non-coaching titles. Myers-Walls, Ballard, Darling, and Myers-Bowman (2011) identify three domains of family practice: family life education (CFLE), marriage and family therapy (MFT), and family case management (FCM). Family life coaching is relevant to those three domains as well as Licensed Practicing Counselors (LPC), and Certified Parent Educator (CPE). Both the MFT and LPC come from a psychological perspective, grounded in psychological and family systems theories. The CFLE and CPE come from an educational perspective, with human development and family science theory as foundations. Family case management comes from a social work perspective and is inclusive of psychological and educational perspectives. Anyone working as a family life coach who has also obtained one of these credentials certainly has not only applicable core knowledge, but an understanding of ethical standards as well. For example, one can assume that an MFT who also works as a family life coach will have an understanding of necessary family theory as well as ethical standards of how to work with families. Yet an MFT will not necessarily have critical foundational coaching knowledge.

Next steps for certification credentials for family life coaching are varied. Currently the National Council on Family Relations (NCFR) and the National Parenting Education Network (NPEN) are two well-recognized national programs in which a number of current family life coaches belong. NCFR is responsible for the Certified Family Life Educator (CFLE) program which has ten content areas that mesh well with requirements of a potential certification for family life coaches. Through research, NCFR has determined those who work with families need to have an understanding of ten different content areas. Successfully demonstrating knowledge in the content areas gleans the title of Certified Family Life Educator – a title that parents and families can recognize as indicating core knowledge and a level of quality that can be expected from that knowledge. The ten content areas for the CFLE are (1) families and individuals in societal contexts, (2) internal dynamics of families, (3) human growth and development across the lifespan, (4) human sexuality, (5) interpersonal relationships, (6) family resource management, (7) parent education and guidance, (8) family law and public policy, (9) professional ethics and practice, and (10) family life education methodology (NCFR, 2014). Knowledge in most, if not all, of these content areas would be applicable to a potential certification for family life coaches.

At the time of this writing, the National Parenting Education Network (NPEN) does not have any sort of certification process for parenting educators. It does, however, have a set of core principles. They state parenting educators have a background in human development, relationships, parenting education, and group facilitation. But they also stress a parenting educator continually expands his or her knowledge, has familiarity of various theories, provides services with respect, and provides "education and support parents need to make and implement effective decisions for their families" (NPEN, 2015a). This last core principle is a direct connection to the potential services offered through family life coaching and could be included at some level for certification.

Another next step, however, might be to utilize one of the existing internationally known coaching organizations such as ICF or BCC. Certainly many coaching strategies can be applicable to a variety of situations. In fact, the core competencies of the ICF dovetail well with the NCFR and NPEN ethical considerations when working with families. ICF has identified 11 core competencies that are grouped into four groups, namely (1) setting the foundation, (2) co-creating the relationship, (3) communicating effectively, and (4) facilitating learning and results (ICF, 2015). Is it possible that a combination of these three programs (as an example) may create the foundation for a credentialing process for family life coaches? Indeed, next steps for certification credentials for family life coaches are varied and open for further exploration.

Regardless of what program or programs are used as foundations for credentialing in family life coaching, it is clear they must stress the importance of quality education and training in family science, coaching psychology, and family life coaching. Currently family life coaches come from all walks of life and all levels of education. Yet rigor in training and consistency in practice will be the ideal way to ensure when parents and families seek a family life coach they are getting a well-trained, credentialed individual. It is exciting to be at the forefront of such a movement.

Professional Organizations

Since there is no professional association specifically for family life coaches and since there is no national or state-wide credential, it is currently an open playing field for those who call themselves professional family life coaches A number of professional organizations do exist, however, that offer family life coaches a wealth of knowledge in family theory, family process and dynamics, and family psychology. The National Council on Family Relations (NCFR) is one of those organizations. It holds an annual conference, drawing thousands of attendees and hundreds of workshops and poster presentations. Although family life coaching, per se, has not been a focus of this organization, they have become aware of this newly developing field and are considering including it in their mission. NCFR offers online workshops, online resources, and three peer-reviewed journals (Family Relations, Journal of Family Theory & Review, and Journal of Marriage and Family). A number of states also have their own NCFR affiliate, enabling personal connection on a more regular basis. Many of these state affiliates offer their own conferences as well. Finally, NCFR offers the Certified Family Life Educator (CFLE) certification mentioned previously. A number of universities offer courses that are accredited through NCFR for the CFLE. All of these services can provide useful information and support for family life coaches.

The American Association for Marriage and Family Therapy (AAMFT) offers professional, research-based support for those working in the field of family therapy. Although family life coaches should not be providing counseling or therapy to clients, membership in this association would provide additional information regarding family issues. Some family life coaches may hold licensure through AAMFT and still operate as a coach. For those family life coaches who are not a licensed MFT, an affiliate membership is available. The AAMFT publishes the peer-reviewed Journal of Marriage and Family Therapy and offers division and national conferences as well as webinars, online trainings, and symposia.

The National Parenting Education Network (NPEN) offers a wealth of information for those working as parent educators, but also for anyone working with parents and/or families. This professional organization is volunteer-run and operates a website with resources, contact information for university programs offering certification in parenting education, and blogs on various topics. It also posts current research related to parenting education. An active listserv provides family life coaches an instant network.

The International Society of Coaching Psychology (ISCP) is a professional membership body that was formed specifically for the discipline of coaching psychology. ISCP is truly an international organization where participation from over eighteen counties have united in hopes of facilitating and encouraging the development and professionalization of coaching psychology. To join, a person must have a graduate degree in psychology and have post-graduate qualifications, such as licensure as a psychologist. The ISCP has a formal partnership with the Division 13 of the American Psychological Association. The ISCP offers a coaching psychology specific credential to those with existing psychological credentials from their home counties.

The American Psychological Association (APA) is the largest scientific organization representing psychology in the US with over 130,000 members. APA's focus is on the development and application of psychology through the promotion and application of research. It is a professional resource that includes 56 specific divisions, including Division 13, The Society of Consulting Psychology. Division 13 holds the formal partnership with ISCP, and is the home to most coaching psychologists in the US. Other divisions of APA that can be helpful for family life coaches include Division 37, Society for Child and Family Policy and Practice as well as Division 43, Society for Family Psychology. APA does not offer a credential specific to family life or family life coaching.

One of the key professional organizations for those in the coaching industry is the International Coaching Federation (ICF). ICF is professional organization for coaching professionals, but it is not-specific to family science. In fact, the majority of focus of the ICF is for coaching professionals, most of whom work in the fields of executive, business and life coaching. The ICF offers both individual credentials as well as program accreditation for coach training organizations.

Because some family life coaches may come from a social work background, the National Association of Social Workers (NASW) may be a helpful professional organization. The NASW states the "practice of social work requires knowledge of human development and behavior" (NASW, 2015, p. 1) thus a family life coach could find resources within this organization. They offer various trainings and conferences as well as continuing education and advocacy opportunities. Social Work is NASW's journal offered free to members, although other related journals are available for a fee.

While the professional organizations mentioned in this section are the ones most related to family life coaching, there is a growing practice of coaching families in other fields such as counseling, nursing, and family and consumer sciences just to name a few. As such, additional professional associations to consider includes:

ACA: American Counseling Association
AAFCS: American Association of Family and Consumer Sciences
ANA: American Nurses Association

The Training of Family Life Coaches

Simply put, until 2015, there was no overarching professional association specialty specific to those who operate solely as family life coaches. However, the newly development Family Life Coaching Association (FLCA) is working to fill this gap. There is a concern among FLCs because the field of family life coaching is on the radar of many family practitioners (Allen & Huff, 2014), and growing every day. Family professionals are interested in education and credentialing as a way of validating the quality of the services they provide. Without evidence-based research and training grounding the field of family life coaching, the probability of highly effective coach training programs is unknown. There are plenty of coaching training opportunities that focus on specific family life issues (ADHD, parenting, etc.), but it is not clear which, if any, are effective. Universities have historically been the place where research is conducted to test the theories of helping professions, yet there is a deficit of university-based coaching programs.

The Family Life Coaching Association is a group of over 40 self-identified parent and family coaches that have developed a professional association. The group, representing various professionals from over 20 states as well as Canada, meets monthly via phone to discuss the need for professionalism of family life coaching. While the group is concerned with credentialing, professional associations, and expanding research, the group's primary interest is establishing training standards and credentialing.

In response to the need for more information about training options, FLCA members recently completed a study looking at training organizations in the US that offer family or parent coach trainings (Kruenegel-Farr et al., 2015). At the time of the study, there were 12 training organizations identified through internet searches and group conversations; two from accredited universities, one loosely identified with a university, and nine stand-alone training organizations. Of the 12 identified, seven agreed to participant in the study. Results showed five of the programs focus on parent coach training while two are family coach focused.

Of the seven training programs, standards and requirements ranged considerably. Two of the training programs required a bachelor's degree, one program required a master's degree, and one program required a certificate in coaching. The number of training hours ranged from 8 h of self study to a full master's degree of 30 graduate credit hours. All training programs had a distance education component, most had an experiential component, but only two offered a face-to-face component. Program length ranged from 2 weeks to over a year.

If those inconsistencies were not enough, each training program awarded a different credential, as well as different theoretical underpinnings. Although all programs claimed to train people to become family or parent coaches, the researchers noted the lack of consistency would make it difficult for any parent to know the level of quality and knowledge of a family or parent coach unless they understood the program that had been completed. While Grant (2011) cited Cognitive Behavioral Therapy as being the most common theoretical underpinning for coaching psychology, only one training program identified CBT in this study. Other theories mentioned included Adler, Dreikurs, family systems, transactional analysis, Payne & Cowan, Gordan, and Ginott as well as some self-developed theories.

Although this is the first study of its kind to look at the training requirements for family life coaching, there is a growing rigor in the field of coaching psychology on the teaching of coaching. As Grant (2011) stated, "if coaching psychology is to continue to grow and develop, then some kind of educational and teaching framework will eventually need to be established." He went on to explain there is a deficit of literature on the topic and that while the market is flooded with books on the industry of coaching, there is still a deficit of texts that would be appropriate for coaching psychology course work. Stober and Grant (2006) and Palmer & Whybrow (2008) are the books most commonly used as a textbook for coaching psychology coursework.

For the field of family life coaching to move forward as a professional field, much work is required, particularly in the realm of education for family life coaches. Clearly, this is a new, yet growing field that is in need of rigorous research and theoretical framing that will help to establish training and credentials. Although some stand-alone programs offer certification for coaches, the certifications are not universally recognized. Without evidence-based research grounding the field of family life coaching, the probability of highly effective coach training programs is unknown. Universities have historically been the place where research is conducted to test the theories of helping professions, yet there is a deficit of university-based coaching programs.

Allen and Huff (2014) identified coach training programs of accredited universities in the United States (see Table 13.1). Of those, only three are identified specifically as family or parenting specific –North Carolina State University, Concordia University, and San Diego University. Although there are training programs that are not affiliated with a university, rigor in training is more commonly found within university programs. This does not mean that organizations and/or for-profit programs would not provide quality training. But other family science credentials such as Marriage Family Therapist (MFT), Licensed Professional Counselor (LPC), and Certified Family Life Educator (CFLE) are all grounded in research and academic requirements. Nevertheless, established core principals, specific requirements, and specific content required by a credentialing organization would help ensure any family life coaching program to be of high quality.

Using the programs at, North Carolina State University, Concordia University and San Diego University as a template may be helpful. North Carolina State University offers both a certificate in family life education and coaching, which includes 4 graduate level courses in family science and coaching psychology as well as a master's degree with a family life coaching concentration. Concordia University offers a Parent Coaching Certificate, which includes courses in theory, skills, attitudes, and coaching techniques, culminating in a supervised field experience. Students "need a background in Family Life Education (FLE), parent education, social work, education, psychology and related field" (Concordia University, 2015, p. 1). Finally, San Diego University offers a Certificate in Family Leadership Coaching designed for family practitioners and educators. Students are required to complete 7 courses in family science, contemporary issues, and coaching.

The families served by Family Life Coaches would benefit from a more unified approach to credentials, training, and professional development. Most educational opportunities for family-specific coaching training are with small, private, coaching-specific training organizations that were created to meet the need of an influx of family coaching professionals looking for some sort of credentialing. Research and rigor, however, is not at the forefront of these training programs as evidenced in the fact that they have never been published in peer-reviewed literature. So, while these programs may or may not be grounded in rigorous research, more information would be needed on the specifics of their programs. Likewise with credentials; while a certificate from a family or parent specific training

Table 13.1 University-based coaching programs

College or university	Name of coaching program(s) offered
Adler Graduate School	Professional Life Coaching Certificate
Bellevue University	Master of Science in Leadership & Coaching
Capella University	Leadership Coaching Psychology Specialization
Columbia University	Coaching Certificate
[a]Concordia University	Parent Coaching Certificate
Duquesne University	Professional Coach Certification
Erickson International	International Coach Federation Certificate
Fielding Graduate University	Evidence Based Coaching Certificate
George Mason University	Leadership Coaching for Organizational Performance Certificate
Georgetown University	Certificate in Leadership Coaching
Liberty Online University	Specialization in Life Coaching
Massachusetts School of Professional Psychology	Graduate Certificate in Executive Coaching
New York University	Certificate in Organization and Executive Coaching
[a]North Carolina State University	Graduate Certificate or Concentration in Family Coaching
Northwestern University	Graduate Certificate in Coaching for Learning and Performance
Pennsylvania State University	Graduate Certificate in Mentorship and Coaching
Queens University of Charlotte	Executive Coaching Certificate
Royal Roads University	Graduate Certificate in Executive Coaching
[a]San Diego University	Certificate in Family Leadership Coaching
Simon Fraser University	Certificate in Professional Coaching
Southwestern Christian University	Master's degree in Life Coaching
	Growth Coach Certificate
	Professional Coach Certificate
	Coach Trainer Certificate
University of Calgary	Coach Training Certificate
University of CA at Berkeley	Certificate in Executive Coaching
University of Cambridge	Certificate in Coaching
University of Delaware	Health Coaching Graduate Certificate
University of Georgia	Certificate in Executive Coaching
University of Illinois	Certificate in Leadership Coaching
University of Miami	Certificate in Professional Coaching
University of Reading	Master's degree in Coaching and Behavioral Change
University of Sydney	Graduate Certificate in Coaching Psychology
University of the Rockies	Executive Coaching Specialization
University of WI at Madison	Professional Life Coaching Certificate

[a]Family-related coaching programs

program might very well be beneficial, until the profession has a unified credential, the chances of families knowing where to seek quality help is limited.

Building a Business

Many current family life coaches arrive at their position via varied paths, processes, and programs. Many family life professionals begin in a community based setting, such as a non-profit or educational organization that serves families (Darling, Fleming, & Cassidy, 2009). However, those entry-level positions often lead to more professional positions and leadership opportunities, and many family life professionals eventually start their own businesses. Although family life coaches may be employed by state agencies, non-profit organizations, or local programs as coaches, educators or consultants, it is not uncommon for a family life coach to branch out on his or her own. Some have professional credentials from other organizations (as mentioned above) but found a need for more of a coaching model, rather than a strictly educational or therapeutic model. Some started coaching because they saw a need for individual assistance when working with parents in group settings. Still others arrived at family life coaching because they personally experienced positive growth from life coaching or business coaching.

Because family life coaching is still coming into its own, many of these individuals are starting their own businesses with minimal direction and/or support. Without a standardized credentialing process, there is not only no template for a base of knowledge, but there is no template for starting a family life coaching business either. There are some basics, however, that offer prospective family life coaches some first steps in the process of starting their own business. Not accomplished in any particular order, the steps covered in this section include

1. establishing a clear purpose and goals,
2. creating a name and a tagline,
3. creating a business plan,
4. seeking financial, legal, and start-up assistance,
5. creating initial documents,
6. networking and collaboration,
7. marketing,
8. insurance.

When I decided I wanted to start my own business, I really had no clue what to do first. As I went through the process I found some things couldn't be done until other decisions had been made, but those decisions couldn't be made without other information! For example, I needed to have a business name before I made a business plan, but I couldn't use the business name until I had

(continued)

checked through my state's business name database. Therefore, the smartest thing I did was connect with the local SBDC and meet with them. They connected me with others including marketing people, legal counsel, and local support organizations. **Debbie Farr, Flourishing Families**

Purpose and Goals

Before a business plan can be put in place or business cards made, a business owner will want to decide whether he or she wants to solely operate as a family life coach or whether it will be combined with other services. For example, some individuals offer more than one service, such as coaching and consulting. Some may offer coaching in tandem with health services while others want to work within niche areas such as coaching of parents of teens or parents of children with special needs. Likewise, some family life coaches are interested in working with parents only while others want to work with both parents and children. Being clear on what the target audience is as well as the specific role the coach will play is key to starting the business.

Once roles and target audience(s) have been established, clarifying a purpose and goals will help solidify plans. It is possible the purpose and/or goals will change, but this is to be expected, especially if one wants to be responsive to the market. However, an overarching purpose can help a new family life coach stay focused and motivated. If this task is difficult, seeking advice from others may be helpful, including seeking advice from business coaches!

20 Questions Before Starting:

1. Why am I starting a business?
2. What kind of business do I want?
3. Who is my ideal customer?
4. What products or services will my business provide?
5. Am I prepared to spend the time and money needed to get my business started?
6. What differentiates my business idea and the products or services I will provide from others in the market?
7. Where will my business be located?
8. How many employees will I need?
9. What types of suppliers do I need?
10. How much money do I need to get started?

(continued)

11. Will I need to get a loan?
12. How soon will it take before my products or services are available?
13. How long do I have until I start making a profit?
14. Who is my competition?
15. How will I price my product compared to my competition?
16. How will I set up the legal structure of my business?
17. What taxes do I need to pay?
18. What kind of insurance do I need?
19. How will I manage my business?
20. How will I advertise my business?
    (SBA, 2015d, p. 1)

Name and Tagline

Once the purpose/goals, audience, and coach role have been established, a business name and tagline (if desired) can be determined. To find what will work best, one should look at other business names – what catches your attention? What taglines or slogans are simple and clear? What catches your eye when someone hands you a business card? Certainly, if one will be working within a non-profit or for-profit organization or company, these details may be moot. But because many do start their own business, the business name needs to be memorable, applicable to the role, and meaningful for families. Likewise, a tagline needs to be a slogan that is descriptive, yet succinct. Seeking assistance from a consulting company may be worthwhile as this can be an important step in branding. The U.S. Small Business Administration (SBA) has some helpful information that can be accessed at their website (SBA, 2015c).

Once a name has been chosen, it needs to be verified through the appropriate state name database to ensure the name is not already being used. This may be done by accessing the state database to do an initial search, or it may be done by completing a required form and submitting for approval. Each state's requirements will be different, but ultimately the family life coach's business name will need approval at the state (not federal) level. Again, helpful information can be found at the SBA website (2015c).

Creating a Business Plan

A business plan will be an important tool to help establish the operational details of a new business. In fact, if financial loans will be applied for, a business plan will be essential. According to the U.S. Small Business Administration (SBA), topics such as an executive summary, a company description, market analysis, organization and management structure, and so on should be included (SBA, 2015a). However, many family life coaches start their own business and are the only employee of that business. Additionally, a market analysis can be difficult due to the niche market of family coaching. Therefore, a business plan, although helpful, will need to be tailored to the individual's specific business structure.

A goal of a business plan is to put into place parameters and operational procedures for the new business. However, there is some literature indicating business plans are evolving, especially for small businesses. Blank (2013) stated one reason to move away from a standard business plan is because "business plans rarely survive first contact with customers" (p. 5). He stated the newer methodology for small start-up businesses is the *lean start-up*. This method centers around three key principles, namely

a) creating a business model canvas utilizing nine building blocks (see text box),
b) customer development (test the market and react), and
c) agile development (make changes quickly).

For those wishing to start a family life coaching business, this model may be more applicable, especially since the field is not yet well known, nor is a large amount of capital typically needed (one of the key reasons why business plans are created).

The Business Model Canvas – a summary of business hypotheses in 9 building blocks:

1. Key partners – who are they
2. Key activities – what are they
3. Value propositions – what are we doing to help the client
4. Customer relations – how to get & keep clients
5. Customer segments – what kind of clients are we looking for
6. Key resources – what are they
7. Channels – how will we reach clients and which channels work best and are cost-efficient
8. Cost structure – what are our costs and for what
9. Revenue streams – pricing strategies
   (Blank, 2013)

Seeking Start-Up, Financial, and Legal Assistance

There are a number of organizations and government entities that exist to assist those starting a small business. The Small Business Administration (SBA) has already been mentioned as being helpful in the planning stages, but they can be utilized for a wide variety of issues. The SBA is sponsored through the federal government and offers easy links to a variety of programs, forms, state information, and so on.

Another example of start-up assistance is SCORE. Their mission is to "foster vibrant small business communities through mentoring and education" (2015b, p. 1). They offer various webinars, workshops and one-on-one counseling on a variety of topics and for all aspects of starting and running a business. Local branches are available and can be found by going to the SCORE website (2015a). There are over 11,000 volunteers that work with SCORE, in over 320 locations.

A third organization that may be helpful is the Small Business Development Center (SBDC). These are typically unique to each state and not all states have them, but doing a general search should pull up your state's location. The Small Business Administration is a partner organization but for some people, working with the SBCD in their area may be advantageous for specific local and/or state information.

One other organization deserves mention. The American Association for Retired People (AARP) offers help as well. This organization is particularly helpful for those who are starting a family life coaching business as a second career or a part-time venture after retiring. Some local AARP chapters may also provide workshops that can be helpful. For more information, check their website (AARP, 2014).

Financial and legal assistance can be found through the groups mentioned above, but some coaches may wish to consult with legal counsel for specific advice. For example, many current family life coaches struggle with the decision of whether to be a sole proprietor or an LLC. This decision should be made with assistance from professionals, whether it be a lawyer who specializes in starting a business or from one of the above organization's staff or volunteers. Each person's situation will be unique and therefore specific advice is not included here.

Financial advice and assistance should also be sought from professionals as well. They can help you establish what will be needed to record income, expenses, taxes, and so on. They can also offer advice as to whether you will need to get an employee identification number (EIN) and how a business bank account should be set up. Most businesses do apply for an EIN as that will most likely be used to set up bank accounts and file taxes. The application process is very straight-forward and can be done easily on the IRS website. Issues regarding collecting taxes will need to be addressed through your state government as each state is different as to what services require taxation. If you do business in multiple states, you will need to research tax implications for each of those states.

One other possible source of revenue for family life coaching is grants and contracts. Many family-serving organizations and non-profits receive grants as a way to fund important work with families that might not otherwise be able to afford family services. Writing a grant requires specific information and resources, but many foundations and some governmental grants are available to individuals that provide unmet services. Grants.gov and foundationcenter.org are two websites that provide information on possible grant funding. Additionally, community organizations that receive grant funds can often contract out services needed. Networking and collaboration with community partners is a great way to identify possible funding.

Creating Initial Documents

Throughout your planning, you will want to establish what kinds of documents will be needed. Most likely you will want to create some sort of contract that will be used with each client. This contract should explain what the client can expect from you and what you can expect from the client. The contract may also include a pricing structure of some sort, as well as basic personal information. It may be advantageous to have legal advice on specific contractual agreement wording. There is an example of a client contract in Chap. 6.

Be aware that HIPAA (Health Insurance Portability and Accountability Act) laws require personal health information be handled confidentially. Any personal information you collect needs to be handled securely and with confidentially. There are also specific requirements as to if and when information can be shared with others, even if they are professionals. Certain laws also pertain to the safety of personal information shared through email and the internet. The U.S. Department of Health & Human Services (2015) has a specific website for the privacy of health information and can be accessed at http://www.hhs.gov/ocr/privacy/hipaa/under standing/summary/index.html. To be sure you are following all laws, it is highly recommended you seek legal counsel for what information you can solicit, how it should be stored, who it can (or cannot) be shared with, and how long it must be kept. Lastly, as you are creating documents requesting personal information, ask yourself "do I really need this information?"

Other documents you may need might be invoices, a summary sheet of your services, helpful handouts, cancellation policy, code of ethics you adhere to, client log sheets, take-home note forms for the client, and so on. The exact forms may depend on whether you operate solely as a family life coach or whether you combine other services such as consulting, educating, counseling, or social work.

A final note on creating documents is warranted here. Similar to the information above regarding a lean start-up, you can assume that whatever you create initially will soon require changes and updates as you react to new situations and client feedback. Additionally, the chances are good that whatever form or document you need has already been created by another family life coach. Do not be afraid to reach out to others and request samples. You will need to be upfront about how you will use their forms, though, and you will also want to make sure you do not use someone else's form in entirety without their permission. Make changes to fit your specific needs, including adding some sort of logo and/or your business name at the top (or bottom) of all documents.

Networking and Collaboration

As previously discussed, some family life coaches may work within for-profit or non-profit settings, as a direct employee or on a contractual basis. To some extent, networking and collaboration may be built into the process, although this is not always the case. For those within an organization or those starting their own business, family life coaches will indeed need to ensure networking and collaboration is part of their weekly, if not daily, process.

One of the key networking opportunities for family life coaches is the Family Life Coaching Association. This is a new professional organization under development, so another option is the National Parenting Education Network (NPEN). NPEN has a listserv specifically for this purpose and focuses on "issues of substance related to the improvement of parent education" (NPEN, 2015b, p. 1). For example, one listserv member may email a question that he or she has received from a client (no names shared), soliciting input from others. Various listserv members will respond, according to their experience, training, or research. Because all listserv members can view the initial question as well as any responses, this serves to not only educate but to foster collaboration. NPEN listserv members come from all backgrounds and work in myriad settings thereby providing a rich foundation for collaboration on various issues. Additionally, the NPEN listserv enables users to share information on upcoming events, conferences, and applicable legislation. Any new or seasoned family professional has the opportunity for networking via NPEN's listserv.

Similarly, the National Council on Family Relations (NCFR) has various listservs, focused on particular areas of interest. For those new to the family life field, the *students and new professionals* listserv would be a great way to network (NCFR, 2015). Other listservs have been established for NCFR affiliates as well as various focus groups. All listservs require permission to join.

The NPEN and NCFR listservs offer an online way to network and are but two examples. Certainly other online opportunities exist within various other professional organizations, such as ISCP's LinkedIn page which has over 28,000 members. In fact, many small business owners feel social media such as LinkedIn, FaceBook, Twitter, Pinterest and so on are excellent ways of not only networking, but marketing (see below). Networking and collaboration *in person* is highly recommended, if not required, in order to be successful in a start-up business.

Networking is the quickest way to connect genuinely with others who may be able to recommend you or who may want to use your services. Think of networking in terms of what the actual word breaks down to – "net" and "working." So, think of this as a way for a group of people to work as your net. You can "catch" more clients with a wider net. But you are part of the net, which means you will also be helping them in return.

An example of networking might be that you attend a meeting at a local Chamber of Commerce. You meet someone who tutors students with special needs. During your conversation with that person, she explains she works with some families that might need some coaching on parenting skills. She offers to check with her families about using your services while you take her business card to have as a reference when working with your clients. In a few weeks, one of your clients mentions concern about his son's ADD getting in the way of homework. You now have a person he can contact should he choose to hire a tutor. Networking may not produce results instantly but is an essential conduit for building a successful business.

Check for various networking opportunities in your area or in the area where you hope to do business. For family life coaches that would include opportunities at local schools, libraries, civic organizations, places of worship, and businesses. Many communities also have collaborations through the local health department or county extension office that focus on health and wellbeing. There are also organizations specifically established for networking such as your local Chamber of Commerce or Business Networking International (BNI) group. Some have found networking opportunities through a local Toastmaster's group (Corbett, 2014) even though the organization's actual goal is to assist members in gaining confidence in public speaking (potentially a useful organization for those family life coaches who may also want to conduct workshops).

10 Tips for Successful Business Networking

- Keep in mind that networking is about being genuine
- Ask yourself what your goals are in participating in networking meetings
- Visit as many groups as possible that spark your interest
- Hold volunteer positions in organizations
- Ask open-ended questions in networking conversations
- Become known as a powerful resource for others
- Have a clear understanding of what you do and why, for whom, and what makes your doing it special
- Be able to articulate what you are looking for and how others may help you
- Follow through quickly and efficiently on referrals you are given
- Call those you meet who may benefit from what you do and vice versa.
(Speisman, 2015)

Collaboration is similar to networking although it typically refers more to connecting with those in similar lines of work. Collaboration is especially important for family life coaches because some clients may have multiple issues or be seeing several specialists. Collaborating with a nurse who is providing home visits to a new mother or collaborating with a local nursery school are two examples. Collaboration with local organizations, such as doctor's offices, therapists, or early childhood education centers can also be helpful. Think of collaboration as a win-win scenario. When you collaborate with someone on behalf of a client, you are not only helping the client but you are helping each other as well. Collaborations can become permanent ventures to the extent that some family life coaches may be able to secure contract work with a non-profit organization in helping them meet the needs of their clients. Certainly family life coaches will want to stay true to their business's purpose and goals but it is not uncommon to have collaborations help achieve those goals.

Marketing

Although written for parent educators, Bill Corbett's e-book entitled *Parenting Expert: How to Build a Business Speaking to Parents and Teachers* (2014) has some excellent suggestions on how to market a business. He discussed key areas such as building a quality website, utilizing LinkedIn and other social media sites, writing blogs, doing press releases, doing talk radio and TV spots, and building a marketing/press kit. All of these ideas give a family life coach the opportunity to be seen and heard.

Gone are the days when new business owners do a mass mailing to all the homes in a particular town, announcing their new business, and consider that their marketing. Certainly mailings can be helpful as can be ads in local newspapers or magazines or distributing brochures to local businesses. A personal website is a must. Social media has also become the pipeline for most contemporary marketing. The social media market is always changing. Currently, FaceBook, LinkedIn, Pinterest, Google+, Twitter, YouTube are great places to market, but that could change. Staying relevant and finding where your target audience goes is key. For many, technology and social media are familiar but for others, the learning curve can be steep, especially when trying to navigate all of them at the same time.

Checking the SBA or SCORE website, your state's SBDC website, or simply googling "social media courses" will give you a plethora of options for learning. Certainly you could take a webinar, workshop or online course that teaches you basic and intermediate skills. Or, you could attend a hands-on mini-series possibly offered by your local community college. That does not mean you need to become an expert in all avenues of social media. Rather, it will be important to hone in on two or three avenues you feel you have some level of confidence and begin with those. Some business owners choose to hire out social media activities so they can stay focused on meeting the needs of current clients. It is up to each individual as to how this piece of marketing is handled, but suffice it to say, marketing is important.

Marketing through social media is very important but creating a professional website will be of utmost importance at the very beginning stages of setting up your business. Your business card, often your first marketing tool, will need to not only have your name and contact information, but your website address as well. Once you've handed that business card to a prospective client, you want to make sure what they see when they go to your website is informative, professional, and inviting.

> Initially, I set up a website through GoDaddy.com. It was reasonably priced and fairly simple to figure out so I could do it on my own. But I had more than one person tell me it didn't look very professional no matter how hard I tried. I finally gave in and got a professional to help me set up a Word Press website, which gleaned me all sorts of kudos and attention. Starting a business meant I didn't have much money to spend, but spending the money on a quality website is definitely worth it and I feel so much better about referring potential clients to my website. **Debbie Farr, Flourishing Families**

Keep in mind there is an entire field for marketing: marketing degrees, market research, marketing gurus. Therefore this chapter cannot begin to cover all your options. Consider the act of marketing an important part of your business. Some people say they spend 1 day per week on marketing. Some say they spend another day on networking. Until you've built a business that can run solely on word-of-mouth (which may never happen), you will want to ensure you are spending sufficient time on both.

Insurance

With all the hard work that goes into starting a business, you will want to make sure you purchase appropriate insurance to cover any liability you may have. Your specific needs will depend on what you will be doing, how you plan to do it, and where you will be doing it. Many family professionals get group discount rates on liability insurance through professional associations, such as through APA or ISCP. The SBA website has some excellent information to help guide you in what is needed. They identify 5 types, namely general liability, product liability (although this may not be applicable unless you plan to sell actual products), professional liability, commercial property, and home-based business insurance (SBA, 2015b). Insurance products are available through any insurance company. As with any insurance, you will want to get several quotes from several different companies before making a decision. In order to receive an appropriate quote, make sure they understand your needs. Do not be afraid to ask clarifying questions to ensure you are not paying for something you don't need. Ultimately, obtaining the appropriate insurance will be one of the most important things you do for your business.

Steps Towards a Business Goal

A number of topics have been covered here as a precursory introduction to starting a family life coaching business. As you progress on your unique journey, you will learn of other requirements or hear helpful stories from others. You will find unique resources to your area and will discover short cuts or new ideas through your networking and research. You will want to also check with the town or city you will be doing business in for any specific requirements, approvals or taxes. The process can seem daunting at the outset but as you progress through your journey you will be surprised at how much you learn and how far you've come. Do not expect the process to move quickly, however. Local, state, and federal requirements will need to be followed completely regardless of the amount of time and process it might require. Additionally, do not expect to gain clients quickly. Depending on what your purpose and goals are, it can take a year or two before you and your business are well-known, respected, and sought-after.

While we attempted to provide guidance and resources, this is in no way an exhaustive summary of the gamut of resources available to anyone starting a family life coaching business nor is it a complete list of things to do. Because family life coaches are a part of a service industry rather than selling a product, the initial financial investment need not be large. The benefit of this lies in the fact that changes can be made fairly quickly in what you do and how you do it in order to meet the needs of each client in each community. Until family life coaching becomes more mainstream and recognizable within our communities, new family life coaches will need to be highly visible and willing to dig in to learn the ropes. But by utilizing some of the resources covered above, new family life coaches will not be traveling this path alone. Being willing to accept feedback from clients, suggestions from other coaches, and recommendations from one's network will help propel a new family life coach into a fulfilling job and a successful career.

> *Imagine a world where people are committed to truly listen, not only to the words but to everything behind the words. What if we held out the biggest picture possible of what we and our children could be instead of pointing out everybody's limitations? What if we came to expect greatness instead of failure or inadequacy, and treated failure, when it happens, not as a disgrace but as a form of fast learning? What if we acknowledged people's strengths instead of picking at their flaws? This would be a world of curiosity and wonder and listening in extraordinary ways. Imagine a world of compelling visions set loose to create and prosper, totally supported, totally encouraged, totally celebrated. This would be a transformative world indeed.* (Kimsey-House, Kimsey-House, Sandahl, & Whitworth, 2011)

Chapter Summary

It takes a village to raise a family, and to build a family life coaching business! This chapter covered a number of topics to help a budding coach build their own business. There are a number of things to consider when building a coaching practice, including training, credentials, and professionalism. The fields of family science and coaching psychology both have professional organizations to support practitioners, and the Family Life Coaching Association is a budding professional organization that aims to be a resource specifically for family life coaches. In addition to building oneself as a professional, a family life coach must also learn the business of family life coaching. This chapter provided a great deal of resources and suggestions for steps to building a successful practice.

Recommended Readings

Corbett, B. (2014). *Parenting Expert: How to build a business speaking to parents and teachers.* [Kindle edition]. Retrieved from http://cooperativekids.vpweb.com

Fairley, S. G., & Stout, C. E. (2004). *Getting started in personal and executive coaching.* Hoboken, NJ: Wiley & Sons.

Lobberecht, M. S., & Smith, M. H. (2008). *Bottom line quick start for emerging entrepreneurs.* Parker, CO: Outskirts Press.

NCFR. (2015). *Careers in family science.* National Council on Family Relations. Retrieved from https://www.ncfr.org/sites/default/files/downloads/news/careers_in_family_science_booklet_2014.pdf

References

AARP – American Association for Retired People. (2014). *Your guide to self-employment.* Retrieved from http://www.aarp.org/work/self-employment/?cmp=RDRCT-STABS_JULY27_012

Allen, K. (2013). A framework for family life coaching. *International Coaching Psychology Review, 8*(1), 72–79.

Allen, K., & Huff, N. (2014). Family coaching: An emerging family science field. *Family Relations, 63*(5), 569–582. doi:10.1111/fare.12087.

Blank, S. (2013). *The business model canvas-a summary of business hypotheses in 9 building blocks.* Retrieved from http://www.businessmodelgeneration.com/downloads/business_model_canvas_poster.pdf

Burroughs, M., Allen, K., & Huff, N. (in press). The use coaching strategies within the field of social work. *Coaching: An International Journal of Theory, Research, & Practice.*

Concordia University. (2015). *Parent coaching certificate.* Retrieved from http://www.csp.edu/admission/adult-undergraduate/certificate-offerings/parent-coaching-certificate/?source=search-result

Corbett, B. (2014). *Parenting expert: How to build a business speaking to parents and teachers.* Enfield, CT: CCK Publishing.

Darling, C. A., Fleming, W. M., & Cassidy, D. (2009). Professionalization of family life education: Defining the field. *Family Relations, 58*, 330–345.

Grant, A. (2011). Developing an agenda for teaching coaching psychology. *International Coaching Psychology Review, 6*(1), 84–99.

Grant, A. M., & Cavanaugh, M. J. (2007). Evidence-based coaching: Flourishing or languishing? *Australian Psychologist, 42*(4), 239–254.

International Coach Federation. (2015). *Core competencies.* Retrieved from http://www.coachfederation.org/credential/landing.cfm?ItemNumber=2206&navItemNumber=576

Kimsey-House, H., Kimsey-House, K., Sandahl, P., & Whitworth, L. (2011). *Co-active coaching.* Boston: Nicholas Brealey Publishing.

Kruenegel-Farr, D., Allen, K., & Machara, M. (in press). Family and parent coaching certification processes: What do current programs do? *Family Sciences Review.*

Myers-Walls, J. A., Ballard, S. M., Darling, C. A., & Myers Bowman, K. S. (2011). Reconceptualizing the domain and boundaries of family life education. *Family Relations, 60*(4), 357–372. doi:10.1111/j.1741-3729.2011.00659.x.

National Association of Social Workers – NASW. (2015). *Practice*. Retrieved from http://socialworkers.org/practice/default.asp

National Council on Family Relations. (2014). *Family life education content areas*. Retrieved from https://www.ncfr.org/sites/default/files/downloads/news/fle_content_areas_2014.pdf

National Council on Family Relations. (2015). *Listservs*. Retrieved from https://www.ncfr.org/listservs

National Parenting Education Network. (2015a). *Core principles*. Retrieved from http://npen.org/about-npen/core-principles/

National Parenting Education Network. (2015b). *Listserv*. Retrieved from http://npen.org/listserv/

Palmer, S., & Whybrow, A. (2008). *Handbook of coaching psychology: A guide for practitioners*. New York: Routledge.

SBA – U.S. Small Business Administration. (2015a). *Thinking about starting a business?* Retrieved from https://www.sba.gov

SBA – U.S. Small Business Administration. (2015b). *Types of business insurance*. Retrieved from https://www.sba.gov/content/types-business-insurance

SBA – U.S. Small Business Administration. (2015c). *Choose your business name*. Retrieved from https://www.sba.gov/content/how-name-business

SBA – U.S. Small Business Administration. (2015d). *20 questions before starting*. Retrieved from https://www.sba.gov/content/20-questions-before-starting-business

SCORE. (2015a). *Find a chapter*. Retrieved from https://www.score.org/chapters-map

SCORE. (2015b). *Mission, vision, and values*. Retrieved from https://www.score.org/node/4342854

Speisman, S. (2015). 10 tips for successful business networking. *Business Knowhow*. Retrieved from http://www.businessknowhow.com/tips/networking.htm

Stober, R. D., & Grant, A. M. (2006). *Evidence based coaching handbook: Putting best practices to work for your clients*. Hoboken, NJ: Wiley.

U.S. Department of Health & Humans Services. (2015). *Health information privacy*. Retrieved from http://www.hhs.gov/ocr/privacy/hipaa/understanding/summary/index.html

Index

A

Academic success coaching, 223, 228
Accountability, 5, 60, 82, 99, 115, 133, 180, 212
Accreditation, 14, 124, 240
Action steps, 5, 34, 55, 64, 65, 71, 73, 82, 85–87, 97, 99, 115, 132, 133, 137, 141, 157, 158, 180, 198
ADHD coaching, 7, 10, 184, 205–218, 221–223, 236, 240
Adlerian parenting, 40, 66, 183, 192, 193, 196, 197
Adult learning theory, 21, 29–30, 33–35, 48, 60, 66–67, 76
Ainsworth, M.D.S., 185
American Association for Marriage and Family Therapy (AAMFT), 40, 239
American Association of Family and Consumer Science (AAFCS), 40, 240
American Counseling Association (ACA), 240
American Nurses Association (ANA), 240
American Psychological Association (APA), 25, 28, 40, 123, 239, 253
American's with Disabilities Act, 208
Appreciative inquiry (AI), 16, 63–65, 112, 114–115, 121, 130, 132, 173, 198
Assessing Parenting, Keys to Interactive Parenting Scale, 123
Assessments, 10, 34, 63, 67, 69, 112, 121, 123–126, 128–138, 169, 171, 173, 180, 192, 214
Association for Coaching (AC), 82, 236, 237
Association for Couples in Marriage Enrichment (ACME), 162
Attachment Parenting, 186

Attachment theory, 185
Authoritative parenting, 130, 189–191, 212
Autism, 184, 205, 206

B

Bandura, A., 21, 60, 69–70, 76, 172, 188
Baumrind, D., 189, 191
Beersma, B., 25
Behaviorism, 47, 188, 189
Behavior modification, 188
Board Certified Coach (BCC), 236, 238
Bowlby, J., 47, 185
Brannick, J., 24
Bronfenbrenner, U., 48, 173, 192, 213
Business model canvas model, 247

C

Carter, B., 7, 14, 84, 87
Certified Marriage and Family Therapist (MFT), 36, 163, 237, 239, 242
Check in, 86, 98
Coach competencies, 24, 81–82, 99, 206, 222, 223
Coaching agreement, 82, 91, 103, 117, 121, 177
Coaching contract, 103, 248
Coaching early childhood for children with disabilities, 208–209
Coaching in early childhood, 71, 208–209
Coaching psychology (CP), 4, 5, 7–11, 13–18, 21–36, 39, 42, 43, 55, 56, 59, 60, 66, 73, 76, 81, 101, 161, 228, 235, 236, 238, 239, 241–243, 254

© Springer International Publishing Switzerland 2016
K. Allen, *Theory, Research, and Practical Guidelines for Family Life Coaching*,
DOI 10.1007/978-3-319-29331-8